Global Suburbs

D0148993

Global Suburbs: Urban Sprawl from the Rio Grande to Rio de Janeiro offers a critical new perspective on the emerging phenomenon of the global suburb in the western hemisphere. American suburban sprawl has created a giant human habitat stretching from Las Vegas to San Diego, and from Mexico to Brazil, presented here in a clear and comprehensive style with in depth descriptions and images. Challenging the ecological problems that stem from these flawed suburban developments, Herzog targets an often overlooked and potentially disastrous global shift in urban development. This book will give depth to courses on suburbs, development, urban studies, and the environment.

Lawrence A. Herzog is Professor of City Planning in the School of Public Affairs, San Diego State University, California. He has been a Fulbright Scholar twice (Peru, United Kingdom), a consultant to the U.S. Agency for International Development in Peru and Bolivia, and a Visiting Scholar or Visiting Professor in Italy, Spain, U.K., Netherlands, Mexico, Peru and Brazil. He is author/editor of ten books, including *Return to the Center* (2006) and *From Aztec to High Tech* (1999). Herzog has published over fifty academic journal articles or book chapters, as well as over fifty popular essays in newspapers and magazines, including the *Los Angeles Times, San Francisco Chronicle, New York Newsday, San Jose Mercury News* and *San Diego Union Tribune*.

Cultural Spaces Series

Series Editor: Sharon Zukin, *Brooklyn College and CUNY Graduate Center*

Cultural Spaces presents in-depth, sociological portraits and interpretations of geographical areas, social districts, and archaeological outcroppings that resonate with contemporary cultural innovations and conflicts.

Books Available

After the World Trade Center: Rethinking New York City edited by
   Michael Sorkin and Sharon Zukin
Silicon Alley: The Rise and Fall of a New Media District by
   Michael Indergaard
Buyways: Billboards, Automobiles, and the American Landscape by
   Catherine Gudis
Capitalism's Eye: Cultural Spaces of the Commodity by
   Kevin Heatherington
Branding New York: How a City in Crisis Was Sold to the World by
   Miriam Greenberg
The Global Architect: Firms, Fame, and Urban Form by
   Donald McNeill
The Diaspora Strike Back: Caribeño Tales of Learning and Turning by
   Juan Flores
Foodies: Democracy and Distinction in the Gourmet Foodscape by
   Josee Johnston and Shyon Baumann

Global Suburbs
Urban Sprawl from the Rio
Grande to Rio de Janeiro

Lawrence A. Herzog
San Diego State University, California

Routledge
Taylor & Francis Group

NEW YORK AND LONDON

First published 2015
by Routledge
711 Third Avenue, New York, NY 10017

and by Routledge
2 Park Square, Milton Park, Abingdon, Oxon, OX14 4RN

Routledge is an imprint of the Taylor & Francis Group, an informa business

© 2015 Taylor & Francis

The right of Lawrence A. Herzog to be identified as author of this work has been asserted by him in accordance with sections 77 and 78 of the Copyright, Designs and Patents Act 1988.

All rights reserved. No part of this book may be reprinted or reproduced or utilised in any form or by any electronic, mechanical, or other means, now known or hereafter invented, including photocopying and recording, or in any information storage or retrieval system, without permission in writing from the publishers.

Trademark notice: Product or corporate names may be trademarks or registered trademarks, and are used only for identification and explanation without intent to infringe.

Library of Congress Cataloging-in-Publication Data

Herzog, Lawrence A. (Lawrence Arthur)
  Global suburbs : urban sprawl from the Rio Grande to Rio de Janeiro / Lawrence A. Herzog. – 1 Edition.
    pages cm. — (Cultural spaces)
    Includes bibliographical references and index.
  1. Suburbs—North America. 2. Suburbs—South America. 3. Cities and towns—North America. 4. Cities and towns—South America. 5. Cities and towns—Growth—Environmental aspects—North America. 6. Cities and towns—Growth—Environmental aspects—South America. I. Title.
    HT352.N7H47 2014
    307.74—dc23
    2014002344

ISBN: 978-0-415-64472-3 (hbk)
ISBN: 978-0-415-64473-0 (pbk)
ISBN: 978-1-315-79463-1 (ebk)

Typeset in Caslon
by Apex CoVantage, LLC

DEDICATION

To Denise and Adin,
You remind me of what really matters.

Contents

SERIES FOREWORD

In *Global Surburbs: From the Rio Grande to Rio de Janeiro*, Lawrence Herzog exposes the dystopian underside of the suburban American dream. A house of one's own, on a little plot of land, is no longer a place of domestic comfort, spiritual renewal, and communion with the green space and clean air of nature. Instead, the mass suburban habitat that Americans pioneered features oversized McMansions stuffed with giant TVs and electronic gadgets, to which their owners commute in gas-guzzling SUVs, enduring stressful journeys on traffic-clogged roads, leaving neither space nor time for pleasure.

This human habitat, Herzog warns, is neither a happy nor a healthy place. It is, instead, a treadmill of over-consumption that burdens our bodies, our spirits, and the natural environment. Obesity, anxiety, toxic air: how can we think this is a good life?

Most important, the suburban dream that Herzog describes now spreads throughout North and South America. In a Manifest Destiny that goes beyond the nation-state, urban sprawl expands the reach of western metropolises like Phoenix, Las Vegas, and San Diego from their historic center to new settlements far out in the desert, and from the southwestern United States through the largest, richest Latin American countries, Mexico and Brazil. Every metropolitan area in the Western hemisphere bears a tragic cost: Overbuilding reduces the water supply, destroys the trees and insects on which all life depends, and creates an eco-disaster.

Is this habitat "urban" or "suburban"? Herzog calls it by both names: *urban* sprawl and global *suburb*. When he looks at the expansion outward from the city center, he sees urban sprawl. But when he thinks about the car-centric way of life, air conditioning, shopping malls, and individualized domestic sphere of millions of houses, he sees a suburban model that is reproduced around the world with hardly any cultural variation. Aside from differences of geography and climate, the borderland between San Diego and Tijuana looks and feels like the periphery of Rio de Janeiro. The megalopolis that in the twentieth century extended from Boston to Washington, D.C. along the eastern seaboard may be dwarfed, in time, by another megalopolis that stretches from Mexico City to São Paulo.

It's not just that we are consuming our cities. When we read *Global Suburbs*, we understand that our cities are consuming us.

Sharon Zukin
Cultural Spaces Series Editor

PREFACE

The inspiration for writing this book lies in a career divided between two cultures: teaching/working in my home university in southern California, and frequent sojourns to my "second home" in Latin America. Since my undergraduate semester abroad in Cuernavaca, Mexico, in the 1970s, through my graduate studies along the Mexican border, and a Fulbright professorship in Peru, consulting work in the Bolivian Andes, and across the more than three decades of my academic career, Latin America has been my home-away-from-home, both literally and spiritually.

When I first resided in Mexico in the 1970s as a young exchange student, the presence of the United States in the built landscape of our southern neighbor was far more subdued. I lived in the city of Cuernavaca, Mexico, and attended a school on a former estate just outside the city, a school run by writer/philosopher Ivan Illich. I walked everywhere, or rode buses. In those days, the outskirts of Cuernavaca and other Mexican cities had scattered homes for the upper classes, and pockets of poor *colonias*, but the city's main hub was its central core around the historic downtown. There were no mass suburbs in Mexico. Yet.

Fast-forward thirty years. While on sabbatical as a Visiting Scholar at the Tec de Monterrey, Querétaro campus, I lived on the northern outskirts of the booming urban region of Querétaro, along the "NAFTA highway" between Mexico City and the border cities of Texas. The love affair with American suburbs was in full bloom in the early 2000s, less than a decade after the signing of NAFTA. Many high-tech companies were relocating to the Querétaro region, creating a demand for housing among the growing middle and upper class migrants from Mexico City and beyond. The region was expanding outwards along highways, especially to the north and west. Traffic congestion was now a way of life in Querétaro. Freeways, shopping malls, and suburban subdivisions were sprouting in all directions. In one agglomeration of malls and shopping centers along the freeways north of town, Costco, Office Depot, and other signs of American consumerism prevail. A Mexican architect friend of mine jokingly refers to this section of the city as "McAllen," because it reminds him of the intense consumerism of the U.S. border city in Texas, where so many middle and working class Mexicans often go north to shop.

While writing about the movement to revitalize Querétaro's downtown among artists, architects, and local merchants in the historic center, I was struck by the countervailing growth of a "U.S. suburban culture" in the northern part of the city. Subdivisions were being built even before master plans established infrastructure or services. This same phenomenon, as it turns out, was being reproduced across Mexico, on the outskirts of Puebla, Guadalajara, Tijuana, and, of course, Mexico City, where the American suburb was embraced as early as the 1950s.

The export of the American suburb model was also spreading like wildfire across the Americas well beyond the Rio Grande. A few years after living in central Mexico, I traveled to the southern cone, and witnessed the mass suburbs being built outside Buenos Aires, Argentina, and Rio de Janeiro, Brazil. I was later fortunate to return and study the Rio de Janeiro region more closely, and never ceased to be surprised that residents who could afford to live in cosmopolitan, older neighborhoods in Rio's Zona Sul (south zone) would nevertheless trade their comfortable, walkable life for the car-oriented exurbs further out.

As a professor and practitioner of urban design and planning, I felt compelled to write about the emerging phenomenon of the global suburb in the western hemisphere. It is no simple task to write this book, since so much attention is usually devoted to the problems of the poor on the outskirts of Latin American cities, and, indeed, those problems have not gone away and deserve all the attention they receive. However, it seems equally problematic that, in the midst of the unresolved difficulties facing squatter neighborhoods across the Americas, the worst elements of American suburban sprawl have now spread to the periphery of cities south of our border, from Mexico to Brazil. In fact, in many places U.S.-style suburbs are displacing land that once housed the poor. We must, therefore, challenge the ecological problems inherent in these flawed suburban developments as passionately as we seek solutions to the dilemmas facing *favelas* and *colonias* outside these same cities. I trust this book will contribute to this effort.

ACKNOWLEDGMENTS

I am grateful to many friends, colleagues, and fellow "urbanists," both in the U.S. and Latin America, who contributed to the completion of this book. At my home university in San Diego, I am indebted to the staff in our School of Public Affairs, San Diego State University (SDSU), for their support and assistance during my travel and various absences from campus to complete research for this project. Thanks go out to the Director of our School, Dr. Stuart Henry, as well as our two invaluable staff members, Julie O'Connor and Nancy Flitcraft. Your contribution is never forgotten. I also appreciate collaboration with colleagues around town, including Ramona Perez, Director of our Center for Latin American Studies at SDSU, Keith Pezzoli and Steve Erie, from the University of California, San Diego (UCSD), Urban Studies and Planning (USP) program. I also benefited from my professional affiliation with the International Relations and Pacific Studies (IR/PS) graduate program at UCSD, where I have been a Visiting Professor in the Global Leadership Institute over the past decade and had the privilege of sharing some of the ideas in this book with scholars and public officials from around the world.

In Mexico, I've been fortunate to build a network of scholarly contacts in Mexico City and along the border. Many contributed either directly or indirectly to this book. They include: Daniel Hiernaux (formerly at the Autonomous University of Mexico, UAM, now at the Autonomous University of Querétaro), Boris Graizbord (Colegio de Mexico),

Benjamin Bross (Universidad IberoAmericana), Sergio Tamayo (UAM), Felipe Leal (Universidad Autonoma de Mexico, UNAM), Adrian Guillermo Aguilar (UNAM), and Rene Peralta (Woodbury University). I also want to thank journalist and writer David Lida for helpful exchanges of ideas about Mexico City.

My introduction to and understanding of Brazil is directly linked to two talented Brazilian urban design professionals. Vicente del Rio, Professor of City Planning at Cal Poly San Luis Obispo, is one of the leading urban design experts on his native Brazil. Vicente, originally from Rio de Janeiro, spent three days showing me around his native city in June, 2005. Our subsequent friendship has been profoundly rewarding both personally and professionally. Vicente also introduced me to his sage co-author of a major urban design study of downtown Rio, Dr. Denise de Alcantara Pereira, who is currently Professor in the School of Architecture and Urbanism at the Federal Rural University of Rio de Janeiro (UFRRJ). Denise has been the main catalyst and inspiration for my work in Brazil, a companion in my travels both in the Rio region as well as other cities in Brazil. Further, she introduced me to her colleagues at the Federal University of Rio de Janeiro (UFRJ), where she was previously a Visiting Scholar. I am grateful to many urbanists there who helped me with this project, including professors Paulo Afonso Rheingatz, Vera Tangari, Cristiane Rose Duarte, and Luciana da Silva Andrade. Also, I thank Geronimo Leitão, Professor of Architecture at the Federal Fluminense University (UFF) in nearby Niteroi for his helpful feedback.

I appreciate the help from other scholars, writers, and friends who either gave me direct feedback or otherwise inspired me or contributed to this effort in ways they might not realize. They include Ralph Sanders (formerly at State University of New York, College of Environmental Science and Forestry), Richard Rodriguez (writer), Mike Davis (University of California, Riverside), Leslie Sklair (London School of Economics, LSE), Gareth Jones (LSE), Peter Ward (University of Texas, Austin), and Daniel Arreola (Arizona State University).

I cannot say enough about my editors at Routledge, who provided support and wise counsel throughout this project. Stephen Rutter, Social

Science editor, was a superb voice of reason, wisdom, and occasional humor in the right moments, and helped keep me on target. Without Sharon Zukin, Series Editor, this book would be a shadow of what it became. Sharon not only possesses an expansive understanding in our field; she also has vision, wit, and a sharp editorial talent. Her interventions were stunning in their detail and insight. Thank you Sharon and Steve! I want to add a shout out to Editorial Assistant Margaret Moore for efficient communication throughout. And to the anonymous reviewers, kudos to you all for helping push the manuscript to a higher level.

Finally, and most importantly, I must thank my family, to whom I owe the biggest debt of all. To my wife, Denise, you have been a devoted companion who introduced me to all things Brazilian, and especially to *Carioca* (Rio) culture, in all its nuances, which I confess I am still learning. You are able to equal, if not surpass, my enthusiasm and energy for walking cities, from the hilly, lush, tropical neighborhoods in your native *Carioca* metropolis, to the streets of São Paulo, Brasília, Recife, Salvador, Ouro Preto, Manaus, and every other city we've visited together in Brazil, and discussed for hours over many *cafezinhos. Obrigado, Denise!* And a second *obrigado* (thanks) goes to my step-daughter, Manuela Alcantara de Mello Vianna, for tolerating my frequent intrusions into her household and teenage life in Rio. My son, Adin, now a freshman in college in the U.S., continues to inspire me every day with his intensity, focus, and zest for life. I introduced Adin to the joys of hiking the wilderness on the earth's surface, and now this already licensed nineteen-year-old pilot is taking me to the skies above. We've soared over oceans and mountains, across deserts and cities. I've witnessed urban sprawl from the heights of a very different vantage point, propelled by the skill and wisdom of a polished aviator. To share the heavens with my son is the highest form of spiritual connection . . . and love. It has made the journey of this book so much brighter.

Lawrence Herzog
San Diego, California
2014

1

THE GLOBALIZATION
OF URBAN SPRAWL

Urban sprawl has been the defining quality of American urbanism for more than a half century. And now sprawl is spreading across the planet. In 1950, about one-quarter of all Americans in cities resided in the sub-urbs; a decade later that proportion had increased to one-third. By 1990, half of all metropolitan-based Americans were living a suburban life.[1] Today, despite the crescendo of publicity about climate change, sustainable communities, and smart growth, the fact is that, for now and for the foreseeable future, most Americans still live in the suburbs, and still commute to work by car.

Roughly one hundred forty million people, or nearly two-thirds of all U.S. citizens who reside in metropolitan areas, live on the outskirts of cities. This represents almost half of the total population of the U.S.[2] After World War II, waves of urban dwellers moved from inner cities to the older first suburban ring. Others migrated to the newer outer tiers during the last quarter century. One report predicted that, of the one hundred million people in U.S. cities who will move by 2050, 25 percent will relocate into existing homes, while the other seventy million will install themselves into sprawling suburban developments. This will require some two hundred million miles of new roads, and add one hundred million more vehicles speeding along our highways.[3]

Much has already been written about the flawed ecology of American suburbs and urban sprawl. Yet, a new challenge is posed by the *globalization* of urban sprawl. Since the end of the last century, there has been a global diffusion of the American suburban model, or the idea of an American type suburb (rather than its actual physical form) along with its ecological challenges, across the border to other nations of the Americas.[4] These global suburbs repeat many of the errors of U.S. suburbs. They are creating isolated communities increasingly dependent on the automobile. This means that they too are developing the environmental problems that have been well documented in North America. Global suburbs south of the border are also falling under the influence of "fast urbanism," a dependency on electronics, technology, and consumerism that tends to disconnect citizens from their local ecosystems, while also compromising their sense of community. This, then, is the subject of this book.

I should clarify, at the outset, my use of the term "suburb." The etymology of the word comes from the Latin *suburbium*, which referred to Ancient Rome, where poor citizens lived at lower elevations, thus "sub" (under) and "urb" (city), while the rich lived higher up in the hills. In this book I am using "suburb" to refer to the original post-World War II American urban design prototype—single family, detached homes laid out on low density subdivisions, typically with curvilinear street patterns, surrounded by separate shopping centers, schools, offices and other amenities generally only reachable by car. This design model evolved in the United States in the 1950s and 1960s. The suburb was typically located in a peripheral district, away from the downtown, and deliberately divided into separate land use zones—residential, shopping, office—all designed principally around automobile travel.[5]

I consider "suburb" as an urban planning idea that came to represent certain cultural values—privacy, exclusivity, and security. We will see that as one moves south of the border, the word "suburb" itself takes on a different meaning. But the influence of America's suburban prototype is growing, and that is the point of my book. Whatever term may be used to describe those suburban enclaves emerging on the urban periphery of Mexico or Brazil, the fact is that these "global suburbs" are exploding across the Americas.

Today we see that the basic elements of America's suburbs—automobile dependency, faster living, consumerism, privatization, and the decline of civic life—are migrating to Latin America. Though the architectures of the emerging elite and middle class "global suburbs" south of the border may take on different densities and visual forms, the ecological problems of North American style sprawl are now materializing on the periphery across the Americas. This evolving pattern demands serious attention.[6]

For over a half century, the American suburb was viewed as one of the nation's supreme achievements in modernist twentieth century urban design. Indeed, the American suburban prototype was so admired that architects and planners copied it worldwide. Therefore, I begin by establishing a baseline critique of the contemporary ecologies and landscapes of urban sprawl in metropolitan regions across the Americas. Chapter 2 outlines the environmental and public health crisis that urban sprawl has generated in the U.S. Chapter 3 explores specific ecological problems facing the peripheries of three of the fastest growing cities in the U.S. southwest border region—San Diego, Las Vegas, and Phoenix. In Chapters 4 and 5, I explore the problems associated with the emergence of these suburban prototypes in Mexico and Brazil, the most populous and wealthiest of our Latin American neighbors. Chapter 6 presents some of the main policy directions for moving beyond urban sprawl in the Americas. The final chapter poses some important directions for urban and sustainable planning in the future.

Fast Cities/Fast Suburbs

"In America, we're all in such a rush. Here (in Paris) they have their lifestyle priorities . . . Here everyone takes their time." Thus spoke filmmaker Sofia Coppola in a *New York Times* interview, observing the differences between life in her native Los Angeles and Paris. Coppola explained that, during months of a 2006 Paris shoot for a movie, no matter what kind of deadlines they had on different scenes, her Parisian film crew refused to take a short lunch break. They would always pause to set up a table, pour wine, and "no matter what was happening you could not cut their lunch short."[7] At first Coppola, conditioned by the

Los Angeles "time is money" culture, found this frustrating. Eventually, she reported, she learned to enjoy slow eating and the daily respite from the fast lane of movie-making.

The observation that "everyone in America is in such a rush" hints at one critical dimension of twenty-first century urban life in the Americas. We are a nation that has become habituated to fast living on a variety of levels, all of which produce unhealthy outcomes—from the fast foods that harm our bodies to fast fashion and "throwaway chic" consumerism that is wasteful, to fast cities that are environmentally destructive. This ethos of fast living has both environmental and ethical costs that cut across every major layer of our lives—food, clothing, shelter, and ecology.

In modern American suburbia, we are accustomed to travelling fast, typically in our cars and often on our mammoth system of metropolitan region freeways. The average American travels 12,000 miles per year, almost double the distance travelled by citizens in most other industrialized nations.[8] We expect to travel fast even if the reality is often different; indeed, much of our travel in the U.S. occurs on increasingly congested freeways to get to distant suburbs. Traffic congestion, mainly along freeways in the urban periphery, has in fact been scientifically linked to higher rates of collisions. Americans also have among the highest traffic fatality rates for industrialized nations.[9] Studies show that the more than 40,000 deaths per year in U.S. auto collisions are occurring at higher rates in suburban sprawl counties than in inner city neighborhoods. These mortalities reportedly take place along freeways as well as on feeder roads that lead to freeways, where high speed access and high volume traffic exacerbate the chance of having an accident.[10]

Americans who commute from the suburbs spend a great deal of time in their automobiles stalled in traffic.[11] They also suffer from a "time crunch" by working longer hours than citizens in most other nations. Taken together, longer work hours and the absence of quality time contribute to what I am calling "fast urbanism"—city dwellers living their lives at an accelerated pace within a built environment (spread out suburbs, freeways) that exacerbates this pattern. We must now acknowledge the consequences, including traffic fatalities, higher levels of air pollution, and a variety of public health problems.[12] While critics have been pointing to the social and psychological impacts of this "cult of speed" in general,[13] I am interested in how it plays out in our contemporary built environment. Our car culture, freeway travel, and the "fast urbanism" lifestyle associated with it are deeply embedded in Western culture, to the point that speed is not merely accepted as normal but is even celebrated, whether it is people, objects, or data moving at high velocities. NASCAR auto racing is one of the two or three most popular sports in the United States. Driving at high speeds is part of the culture surrounding it. The Pocono Celebration of Speed and Design is a spinoff event, an annual east coast racecar festival. The Festivals of Speed are a series of Florida-based celebrations of various forms of fast transportation—racing cars, motorcycles, watercraft, and aircraft. A 2013 TV commercial by AT&T promotes the idea that "faster is better."[14]

Applied to living spaces, the above mindset has contributed to "fast urbanism."[15] Life in metropolitan areas is increasingly defined by speed, notably due to the influence of electronic, computer, and other technologies that seem to be accelerating the pace of life. Whether faster is better or not, many Americans like doing things more quickly to save time. But we also begin to detect a contradiction, between "doing more" and "doing faster." It may not be the case that Americans are hurrying only because they have "less" time, but because they have less *quality* time or less *productive* time, or simply less time to freely choose what they wish to do.[16]

Although central cities have traditionally been the locale for fast paced urban life, the new fast world has now also spread to peripheral, low density urban communities. The dispersed, auto-centric, and mall-oriented lifestyle of suburbia lends itself quite well to fast urbanism, a point I explore later in this chapter, and in the final policy chapter of this book. "Fast urbanism" is not the only behavioral feature defining America's (or Latin American) sprawling suburbs; yet, it is a surprising and increasingly important element that has not typically been thought of as a defining feature of the ecology of metropolitan regions.

One might argue that the cores of cities—downtowns like Manhattan, or Chicago's inner loop—are the places that epitomize fast urbanism: speed, hustle-bustle, noise, crowds, and movement. That was certainly the case in the 1920s and 1930s at the beginning of the modern age,

Figure 1.1 Fast Urbanism: City in a Rush
Source: Photo by Lawrence A. Herzog

when great cities like New York, Chicago, San Francisco, and Boston were booming, as they engaged in the project of modern city-building. In just a decade or two, skyscrapers, subways, bridges, viaducts, train stations, department stores, hotels, theaters, museums, and great squares and parks suddenly rose up, and collectively generated the energy and buzz of excitement that writer John Dos Passos epitomized in his book *Manhattan Transfer.* Dos Passos' novel was set in New York City in the 1920s, in all of its dazzling modernity, a mechanical world of machines and power, of fast moving subways and cars, but also a breeding ground of consumerism, restlessness, and greed.[17]

However, while central cities are places where things are more concentrated and thus sped up, does it logically follow that suburbs are slower and quieter? Are they idyllic retreats from the fast paced city? Are they still closer to nature, more spread out, and thus more buffered from the hyped-up ambience of downtown? Although the goal of being close to nature and more serene was part of the original reason for building suburbs, over the last three decades suburban sprawl has been systematically shedding many of the features that originally made it slower, and desirable. In cities like Phoenix, Las Vegas, and San Diego, natural settings have been gradually bulldozed away by more and more development. Some two million acres of farm land and open space are being lost every year across the United States, replaced by master planned suburban communities, which typically remove native vegetation and introduce non-native grass lawns and other less sustainable landscape features.[18] In post-1990 suburban growth, the density of homes in suburbia has been increasing, as well as the incidence of problems that formerly occurred in inner cities. In the words of one scholar, "drug addiction, racial tension and gang activity are among the urban social ills that plague suburbs."[19]

Meanwhile, as this horizontal urbanism spread further and further out, residents are increasingly forced to spend more and more time commuting to work. For example, recent research points to a new phenomenon of "super-commuting" that is on the rise. According to the American Community Survey, carried out by the U.S. Census, there is now a separate category of work trips called "mega-commuting," which is defined as travel of ninety minutes (and over fifty miles) or more one-way.[20] Stuck in their cars for larger chunks of their waking lives, suburban dwellers find themselves rushing from one destination to another. Suburbs are now defined by fast urbanism too, and it is that culture of speed, woven within the larger values of suburban life, that has become a critical component of the emerging ecologies of the American periphery, a model that is gradually spreading to other parts of the Americas.

The building blocks of "fast urbanism" include the cult of speed, the transformation of work, and a consumerist driven homogenization of urban space. I explore these features below.

Speed, Time and Western Culture

Speed is inherently interwoven with the changing built environment of metropolitan regions in the U.S. and, more recently, with the global suburbs evolving in other parts of the world. New forms of technology allowed nineteenth century American city dwellers access to residential space further from the city center. The development of "streetcar suburbs" meant that workers were now able to travel to work fast enough on trolleys or cable cars to live in new homes in the outskirts beyond the older downtowns. By the twentieth century, "freeway suburbs" duplicated this pattern, with yet another machine, the automobile, to speed up movement to even more far-flung locations. Speed, or the desire to move quickly between destinations, had now become part of the transformation of metropolitan space. Fast transport redefined the built environment of American cities. But travelling at higher speeds had a number of important side effects.

In the modern world, we now move faster and live at a faster pace. The socio-psychological and public health impacts of living with more technology in an accelerated world are not fully understood. Research on the health implications of "fast urbanism" is probing new and uncharted terrain. Speaking of the psychological impacts of fast paced lifestyles, one expert commented: "I find that, for most people, a sped-up life leads to feelings of guilt and anxiety, instead of productivity and relaxation."[21] The act of travelling fast (in automobiles) itself is distracting and can be argued to cause people to tune out the environment. Writer and philosopher Ivan Illich wrote that "the automobile has created more distances than it has bridged."[22] Ecologist Richard Register cites a long list of the ways in which the automobile lifestyle is ecologically destructive: a half million people and millions of animals killed annually in car accidents; a third of a million people who die from auto-induced air pollution each year; water polluted by oil and auto-generated waste on the surfaces of roads; car engine and other noises from autos; psychological frustration, hostility, and violence including "road rage"; and separating people behind walls of glass, steel, and speed that "breed isolation, alienation and loss of human contact in daily activity."[23] Our high tech culture of speed and machines may be creating new forms of anxiety and other stress-related illnesses, according to the latest research by psychologists. Smart phones and social media may induce what one study calls "a relentless need to immediately review and respond to each and every incoming message, alert or bing."[24] Responding to the growing number of children diagnosed with attention deficit disorder (ADD), a recent book on the subject demonstrated that when children are exposed to nature and slowing down, they suffer far fewer anxiety or attention deficit disorders.[25]

Speed was one of the pillars of modernity—it represented the human ability to conquer space by moving faster across or through it. The history of transport innovation in the industrial era shows that transit technology progressed rapidly—from bicycles in the 1880s, to slow automobiles in the early 1900s, to faster cars, trucks, and trains by the early 2000s. Some transport vehicles were constructed with the sole purpose of going faster. Auto racing began as a sport around the time gas-fueled cars were invented. The first car races probably occurred around 1894, in Paris. Air racing also began about the time man was learning to fly a plane. In fact, the first air race was held in Reims, France, in 1904, with an aviation exhibition and an air race that attracted some of the top aviators and aviation manufacturers in Europe.

Figure 1.2 Speed and Technology Are Hallmarks of Western Culture
Source: Photo by Lawrence A. Herzog

Racing is fundamental to human nature. Horse and chariot racing were passed along from the ancient Greeks to the Etruscans and eventually became a huge sport during the Roman Empire. In ancient Rome, the Circus Maximus was a giant racing hippodrome that could hold 250,000 spectators. Chariot racing endured through the era of the Byzantine empire as a way of reinforcing social class and the political power of rulers, but it gradually disappeared in the West after 600 and in the East after 1200.[26]

Notwithstanding horse or chariot racing in ancient cultures, one can argue that racing is most strongly linked to the modern age. The last century has seen a rising fixation with technology and movement at ever greater speeds—from motorcycling and sports car racing, to motorboat and speed-bike racing. Speed has always been both a hobby of certain personality types as well as a measuring stick for "progress" in Western culture. It was also a convenience that allowed people higher quality lives as they moved more rapidly from place to place. In the end, speed became a central feature of the modern economy. Production required efficiency and on-time delivery of products. As one observer notes: "Industrial capitalism fed on speed, and rewarded it as never before. The business that manufactured and shipped its products the fastest and undercut rivals came out on top."[27]

Cities, in particular, have become the primary human settlement spaces where speed is cultivated. Living in cities during the industrial revolution was to live in places that were defined by speed, energy, movement, and invention. An important goal was to produce and move things, ideas, and people more quickly within and between cities. The dazzling array of innovations in the nineteenth century that achieved this goal of facilitating "fastness" included: elevator (invented in 1853), escalator (1859), transatlantic cable (1860s), subway (1863), telephone (1876), electric streetcar (1881), and wireless radio (1891). This trend continued in the twentieth and early twenty-first centuries, with the automobile, television, computers, fax machines, the internet, and, most recently, portable devices (smart phones, iPods, PDAs, Blackberries, and iPads).

Speed is also underpinned by the concept of timekeeping and clocks, which made humans more conscious of time and speed. Louis Mumford, one of America's great urban historians and commentators, called the clock a key machine of the industrial revolution.[28] By 1884, twenty-seven nations agreed to recognize Greenwich as the prime meridian, thus creating a global standard for measuring time.[29] Punctuality and time were values solidly driven into the life of industrial workers, epitomized by what became known as the science of management efficiency or "Taylorism."

Taylorism is a theory of management that analyzes and synthesizes workflow processes, improving labor productivity. The core ideas of the theory were developed by Frederick Winslow Taylor in the 1880s and 1890s, and were first published in his monographs *Shop Management* (1905) and *The Principles of Scientific Management* (1911). Taylorism involved a division of labor and a task-oriented approach to production. It became the benchmark and is still used today in industry. It led to the creation of assembly lines and made factory work menial, repetitive, and tedious. Taylorism was based on the notion that productivity must be measured as a function of time and cost. The Taylorist notion of time and industrial organization became a uniquely Western phenomenon. In Western culture, time was considered linear, finite, and precious.[30] You only had so much time, in the day, or the week, or in your life. Therefore time must be conserved, and the faster you could do things, the more time you would theoretically have to do other things.

Yet, the linearity of time is not shared across the planet. In Eastern cultures, and Eastern spiritual practices such as Taoism or Buddhism, time is viewed as cyclical, not linear. Time and life continually renew themselves. Time is not viewed as finite and precious as in the West. Eastern philosophies are more relaxed about time. They see humans existing in time but not struggling against it, since it will inevitably flow in its cyclical fashion. Buddhists believe that by living in the moment we are able to avoid the "disease of uncontrolled thought."[31] Techniques such as deep breathing, yoga, and meditation offer tools for helping people become more "mindful," that is, more aware of each thing as its own sacred moment. These concepts are now being incorporated into the medical field. "Mindful practice" is seen as contributing to stress reduction, pain tolerance, and recovery from illness.[32]

One rationale for the linearity of time in Western culture is that a sequential time framework lends itself well to increasing consumerism. Global advertising seeks to convince consumers that they only have limited time on this planet, so they have to consume as much as possible. The well-known credo "time is money" captures this position well. Although it appears to be a phrase suited to the modern era, it's been shown that the idea can be traced back to the ancient Greek empire. Antiphon, an orator who wrote speeches for defendants in court cases, recorded the earliest known version of the saying: "The most costly outlay is time." Benjamin Franklin rendered the exact wording of the current version in "Advice to a Young Tradesman" (1748), and the saying afterward came into wide use.[33]

As Western concepts of time became a way of life during the industrial revolution, as mentioned above, they also had a huge impact on the physical form of the Western city. Each new invention facilitated new relationships between city dwellers and the spaces they occupied. At the beginning of the industrial revolution, as factories crowded in and around the downtown hubs of cities, which had been defined by how far one could walk, the invention of cable cars, electric trolleys, and subways shifted the geometry of city life by the late nineteenth century beyond the crowded center to new corridors of "streetcar suburbs." Only a few decades later, the next important invention—the internal combustion engine—then facilitated yet another shift from rail line suburbs to freeway suburbs. The city reinvented itself as a dispersed set of settlements sprinkled across a decentralized freeway network. These spread out suburbs then spawned more technologies to replace what had been lost from the streetcar era. Cell phones, text messaging, social media, and car radios, among other innovations, seek to facilitate human contact and even to rekindle the lost sense of community in increasingly placeless suburbs where we may be able to move faster but not necessarily to get somewhere that makes us feel better.

The entire planet is being swept up in a new era of instantaneity. Computers and digital technology have played a central role in redefining our sense of time, especially among younger generations, who thrive on instant access to information through social media and micro-blogging.

These trends have quickly spilled to the larger population. In most cities today, citizens have access to smart phones and mobile devices that facilitate fast communication and instantaneity. The expectation to do things quickly is accelerating, as mobile devices allow citizens to carry out everyday tasks from buying a plane ticket to purchasing groceries from virtually anywhere, and often very quickly. Young people now text each other more than they talk by phone. Twitter has become a global phenomenon of sharing "shoot-from-the-hip" commentary (called "tweets") limited to a brief 140 characters and shared among growing legions of digital "followers." Mobile and rapid exchange of information is exploding as innovators constantly invent new applications ("apps") to enhance rapid communication and information sharing at the fingertips of almost everyone. One example is the "Summly" app, which summarizes news articles for smart phone users. It was invented by a UK teenager and purchased by Yahoo in March, 2013 for thirty million dollars.[34] The world seems to be moving faster.[35]

The internet has evolved within this new era of spread out living and "fast urbanism." An array of online forms of rapid exchange have emerged, most notably through the world of social media, posting, and blogging. Facebook is the leading twenty-first century model for social interaction, especially as mobile devices have improved to the point of imitating laptop computers in more compact form (from smart phones to iPads). Blogging has also become the new fast mechanism for communicating, with dozens of major and minor blog communities emerging in a rapidly changing landscape. New websites epitomize the changing world. One very notable one is Reddit, a social news and entertainment site that is user controlled, with content supplied either through posts or links. Many key writers, thinkers, and entertainers have used this site to promote their work, though observers have also been critical of how Reddit users actually define "news," as opposed to editorials or other commentary.[36]

Meanwhile, entrepreneurs continue to employ the internet in new ways. "Fast Company" is a business website founded in 1995 by two former *Harvard Business Review* editors. It has advocated a number of platforms, including one it calls "Fast Cities," which it described as places that "are the cauldrons of creativity where the most important ideas and organizations of tomorrow are centered. They attract the best and brightest. They are great places to work and live."[37] The site celebrates large cities as collections of talent masses and innovation.[38] A related webzine from the site speaks of groups like the Institute for the Future (in Palo Alto, California) which defines the "Fast City" as having: opportunity, innovation (physical, cultural, intellectual), and energy, collections of people who feed off each other. The point is that speed, in the form of energy, innovation, and opportunity, translates to business success.[39]

Knowing that people believe they need to live at a faster pace, entrepreneurs have surfaced who market an array of new services that enable people to speed up everyday tasks. Some work and others fail. In 2007, a website called "Brijit" was launched; it offered such time-saving services as paragraph summaries of complex themes, or express versions of games like Monopoly and Scrabble, which get you through a whole game in twenty minutes.[40] Brijit folded, but there are many start-up companies emerging that offer internet shortcuts for banking, investment, travel, shopping, paying bills, and searching for jobs. Speed dating and online dating have become big businesses around the nation. Inventors and entrepreneurs are searching for new ways to cash in on the growing culture of speed. An exercise machine called "Range of Motion" was marketed using claims that it can create the equivalent of a full workout in only four minutes a day. It costs $14,615.[41] Back in the mid 1990s, when Steve Jobs was promoting the new iPod, he highlighted some of the same themes—the new iPod was thirty times faster in downloading music than any other MP3 player, it was "ultraportable," and it had a ten hour battery life that could be recharged in one hour.

Another example of the popular celebration of speed can be found in the cultural phenomenon of "multi-tasking." "Multi-tasking" is a term that is now embedded in our everyday language and argued to represent a form of innovation for a high tech society. In fact, it's been shown that multi-tasking is more wasteful than many people assume. Neuro-scientific research suggests that the human brain is actually not particularly good at multi-tasking. While some routine tasks can be carried out simultaneously, humans are far more efficient when they

Figure 1.3 iPod Ad, San Francisco
Source: Photo by Lawrence A. Herzog

engage in one activity at a time. As one commentator notes: "Much of what passes for multitasking is nothing of the sort: it is sequential toggling between activities. And the research suggests that this flitting back and forth is actually very unproductive: tasks can take more than twice as long to complete when performed in this way."[42] Even in the business world, companies are beginning to ask employees to focus on one activity at a time and wall themselves off from the barrage of electronic interruptions whenever possible.

The Transformation of Work

We must also recognize the huge impact of the transformation of work in the United States, which, over the last three to four decades, has dramatically reduced leisure time for the average American, and simultaneously increased stress levels. As mentioned above, since the 1970s Americans have been working longer hours and receiving significantly less paid vacation time than their contemporaries in any other industrialized nation in the world.[43] Americans are being squeezed from two directions—on the one hand, they are driving back and forth to work from increasingly distant suburbs with more congestion and delays; on the other hand, their workday is longer than ever, and they end up having either less quality time or just less time to freely choose activities. With an ever higher percentage of Americans now living in the suburbs, and with less quality time, more citizens understandably feel stressed. They rush from one task to the other and, on a very basic level, are unable to live a more "slow urbanist" life, engaging in activities like walking, riding bicycles, reading, or gardening.[44] Thus, the forces defining fast urbanism are not merely low density urban form and technological dependence on automobiles, but also the greater degree to which work has come to define the lives of so many suburban dwellers, rushing around to use the diminished time they do have, while enjoying less leisure time to pursue slower lifestyle activities.

The contemporary pattern of increasing the length of the workday in the United States goes against the grain of American labor history. Early in the nineteenth century, as the industrial revolution gained a foothold in the U.S., labor unions were fighting for shorter workweeks, since many factories had long been operating under twelve-hour workdays. This battle continued for a century. In 1914, industrial giant Henry Ford implemented a permanent decrease from nine-hour to eight-hour days, because he was convinced that satisfied workers were more productive. This philosophy caught on, and by 1937 President Franklin D. Roosevelt crafted the New Deal, which enshrined the forty-hour workweek, which became an iconic symbol of modern American culture. The forty-hour workweek was based on scientific evidence that showed that it maximized productivity and maintained high morale in the workforce.

But, beginning in the 1970s, a dramatic change unfolded—millions of Americans suddenly began putting in ten and twelve-hour workdays. Even though the U.S. Fair Labor Standards Act legally obligates employers to maintain a regular forty-hour workweek, some have argued there are too many exceptions to this law. For example, the generic category of "professionals" is being used for a wide array of workers to skirt the forty-hour workweek rule.[45] Explanations for the demise of the forty-hour workweek vary, but many social researchers agree that the trend started with the emergence of "knowledge workers," white collar jobs that were viewed by employers as potentially less physically demanding than factory work, and therefore it was open to interpretation as to whether the forty-hour workweek rule needed to be followed.[46]

Some trace the change more directly to the evolution of a new class of science/technology workers in California's Silicon Valley in the 1970s. These workers became legendary for their passion and quirky lifestyles, showing up to work in blue jeans and sneakers at noon, but working through to midnight on a daily basis. They developed a reputation for their total commitment and enjoyment of their work as a way of life. The lines between work and the rest of their lives blurred. These new talented programmers and engineering types were sometimes stereotyped as "geeks," but they made it clear that they considered the forty-hour workweek and other protocols (like dress codes) as old fashioned, dull, and out of touch with cutting edge changes in the emerging economy.[47] As a new cultural prototype began to form, it was celebrated in the media and by best-selling authors.[48]

During the 1980s the momentum continued to grow in favor of the new work ethic and against labor unions. That decade overlapped with the two-term presidency of Ronald Reagan (1981–9), an era in which the new conservative political power bloc celebrated what might be termed the "cult of the entrepreneur." Work culture was shifting: where in the past workers were unionized and usually loyal to one company for life, with pensions, vacations, and so forth, the new cultural model was that workers were being told to expect to change jobs every three to five years.[49] In the new fast world, nothing stayed the same. A contemporary corporate work ethic was taking hold, while the forty-hour workweek was disappearing. In its place was a mandatory, exhausting, and possibly illegal sixty-hour workweek. One observer said of this new development that "the only inducement employers currently offer in exchange for submitting yourself to this abuse is that you get to keep your job."[50]

Today, nearly 86 percent of male workers and 66 percent of females work more than forty hours per week in the United States. Every year now, on the average, Americans work 137 hours more than the Japanese,

260 hours more than the British, and an incredible 499 hours per year more than the French![51] America is the only industrialized nation on the planet that has no legally mandated annual leave. Most studies suggest the U.S. still lags behind most affluent nations on granting paid vacation leave. The United States averages a mere ten days of paid vacation annually, whereas the French get thirty days, Scandinavian countries receive an average of twenty-five days, and most other nations, e.g. the United Kingdom, Switzerland, the Netherlands, Australia and New Zealand, average twenty days, more than twice the U.S.[52]

The effects of this combination of too many weekly work hours and minimal vacations for Americans are quite clear. Americans simply have less free time to enjoy leisure activity. What time they do have is so precious that they end up rushing around to accomplish all their errands, and look for short cuts to speed up time to get to the cherished "leisure time" that other "slow urbanist" cultures take for granted—walking, engaging with neighbors, hiking, reading, and participating in local/community activities.[53] This development has been termed a "loss of social capital," because it signifies time lost that could be used to be part of one's community and contribute to it.

The changing nature of work in the U.S. is on a collision course with the urban built environment. On the one hand, there are documented increases in workdays and workweeks. On the other hand, traffic congestion for millions of commuters who travel back and forth to distant suburbs has intensified over the last few decades.[54] As a result, some writers predict that more Americans will either move back to the inner city or live in mixed use, pedestrian friendly new "smart growth" developments.[55] It's too early to know if this trend will permanently change the current suburban pattern, but for now American home sizes continue to grow, and recent studies show that four out of five prospective home buyers still want a single family house in the suburbs.[56]

Consumerism, Homogeneity and Urban Space

Fast urbanism is linked to the gradual homogenization of the urban built environment. While most people accept the existence of corporate name brands on individual consumer goods, it has perhaps been less obvious to many observers that, like the products on the shelves in big box stores, the landscapes of America's metropolitan regions have themselves become packaged and homogenized. From master planned lifestyle communities, condo complexes, and strip malls, to mega-shopping centers, or downtown festival marketplaces, we have become a nation of homogenized places. Most of these places are located in the suburbs, which are themselves homogeneous entities. Seen from the air, the cookie cutter suburbs of New Jersey look like those in Iowa, which in turn resemble those in southern California.

During the second half of the twentieth century, transnational companies like Coca Cola and McDonald's sought to homogenize consumer tastes, so they could then be controlled through advertising.[57] The ideal consumer was the consumer who learned to behave in ritual ways—eating, drinking, or staying in hotels, for example. This drive to create uniform consumer taste, over the last three decades, has now been transferred beyond consumer products to the larger built environment. The world is witnessing a gradual shift toward homogenization of built landscapes—housing developments, retail centers, malls, hotels, and streets.

Homogenized spaces often foster fast urbanism. Fast food (McDonald's), fast coffee (Starbucks) and fast purchasing (strip malls) are examples. The process of packaging spaces is built around efficiency—mass marketing of consumer spaces that can quickly absorb as many buyers as possible, and give them the same product and service each time. Further, many of these homogenized spaces are set up with the premise that people in the modern world are busy, so they need their consumer products quickly. Also, strip malls, shopping malls, drive-in establishments, big box stores, and super-centers are designed for that fast machine that moves people around cities—the automobile.

A guiding principle of global marketing has been termed the "culture-ideology of consumerism." "Consumerism" is roughly defined in this context as a set of ideas aimed at making people believe that human worth is best ensured and happiness best achieved through consumption and acquisition of material wealth.[58] Proponents of this point of view argue that global corporations use advertising and transnational media

Figure 1.4 Globalization and Homogeneity: McDonald's in Tijuana, Mexico
Source: Photo by Lawrence A. Herzog

not merely to sell their products across the globe, but also to promote a style of consumerism that becomes part of a standardized global culture.[59] Examples of globalized consumerism include soft drinks (such as Coca Cola, Pepsi, and Sprite), fast food (McDonald's, Burger King), coffee (Starbucks), and cellular telephones (iPhone, android phones). There are over seven thousand Starbucks stores outside the United States. Some of the success in marketing these kinds of commodities globally is traced to corporate strategies to homogenize consumer tastes. By engineering globally uniform consumer behavior (through advertising and the construction of recognizable images) multinational corporations can better control the marketing of their products.[60]

But the global homogenization of consumer taste has shifted beyond consumer products to the larger mainly suburban "built environment"— the malls and big box super-centers where we spend most of the time away from our homes. For example, by the 1990s it was reported that in the U.S. shopping had become the second most important leisure time activity after watching TV. Shopping was the new dominant mode of public life.[61] We have slowly shifted in our everyday lifestyles from being public citizens to private consumers. The design and organization of our city spaces reflect this transformation.

How did these packaged and highly controlled commercial land-scapes evolve? One answer lies with the evolution of the late nineteenth century time management theories mentioned earlier, including "Taylorism." Taylorism, a by-product of the modern industrial era, engineered the crisp, orderly assembly-line approach to manufacturing. But its principles were also to be applied to urban built environments. The idea of exerting rational and bureaucratic control to mass-produce products within a factory was directed toward the task of mass-producing houses after World War II. In the early 1950s, the company Levitt and Sons began building the first mass-produced single family residential subdivisions in the U.S. The first development was Levittown, built on former potato fields in the Long Island suburbs of New York City (later repeated in Pennsylvania). Levittown was notable for the standardized, assembly-line approach to house construction, lot layouts, streets, and communities.[62]

The Levitts built warehouses, woodworking shops, sand and gravel plants, and plumbing services on site to control every aspect of Levittown's construction. They created a template that would then be used across the United States in the mass-produced residential suburbs built over the next three decades. The Levittown model included systematic control of every phase of production, even marketing and advertising. Marketing professionals were trained to use a standardized sales pitch, which emphasized catchy strategies aimed at convincing skeptical buyers— they included emphasis on low down payments and low monthly costs (rather than the actual cost of the house, or the number of years it might take to pay it off).[63]

Levittown became the precursor for a massive wave of "cookie cutter" suburban development in the U.S. Even though later suburbs would become socially more diverse, the physical layouts and architectural features of American suburbs remained furiously static and predictable, some might even say monotonous, and certainly gave a feeling of being the quintessential packaged landscapes. One critic calls America's suburban residential developments "jive-plastic, commuter track home waste lands."[64] Others refer to "cookie cutter houses, wide, treeless sidewalk-free roadways, mindless, curving cul-de-sacs, a streetscape of garage doors, a beige vinyl parody of Leave it to Beaver . . . not that you would ever have reason to visit its monotonous moonscape."[65]

These large scale suburban communities began as a kind of experiment, a novel idea by Levitt and Company. But this approach to urban development soon took off and became the defining business and design approach to the development of urban land on America's periphery. Eventually, mass-produced and, later, master planned suburbs swept across the nation and would define American cities for more than a half century, and continue to do so today.[66] Some critics believe this Taylor model contributed to an emerging American indifference toward aesthetic and architectural beauty and uniqueness for individual houses, a kind of numbness that has been part of a changing culture that persists today. As one writer notes:

> Architectural structure, surface, detail, are no longer communicators of popular messages . . . our eyes are conditioned by film, video and computers to see objects in states of representation, dramatization, animation, and, of course, commodification. By comparison, most buildings appear lethargic, devoid of life.[67]

The standardization of housing production mainly in suburban locations was introduced at about the same time as a system of rational and uniform shopping mall development was being invented. Shopping malls as predictable, sanitized, enclosed spaces of consumption became another anchor of the new suburban model. Even before the shopping malls of American suburban development of the half century beginning around 1960, however, there were earlier attempts to create large scale, standardized spaces for consumption in cities. European cities began experimenting with the construction of grandiose spaces for consumption that would go beyond the individual shops that already existed on the streets or in interior markets. The new approach in the late nineteenth century was to create spaces for many stores inside one grand building, or what became known (in French) as *magasin des nouveautés.* These grand buildings had central halls, galleries, and a monumental staircase. They were the first great department stores of cities; one of the most famous in Paris was the Bon Marché, built 1869–72, an iron and glass structure that included cafes, bars, and a reading room, as well as the cutting edge interior elements of Art Nouveau—iron staircases, domes and balustrades.[68] Before the department stores, there had been an earlier attempt to collect stores in a single space—covered iron and glass arcades or "passages" in Paris and other European cities. Around this time in Italy and elsewhere in Europe, entrepreneurs actually created the first precursors to the modern shopping mall—palatial and elegant glass and steel interior spaces referred to as "galleria" (or galleries)—one in Milan and another in Naples.[69]

Importantly, the early department stores are the first example of modern city-builders and designers trying to invent predictable spaces for the consumer culture of booming industrial cities of the era. As industrial workers earned a good wage, more people had surplus income and leisure time, so shopping spaces were emerging as important elements in the design of modern cities. But unlike the shopping malls of the second half of the twentieth century, these earlier spaces were really designed more for the upper classes, and tended to be mainly used by them, although the working classes enjoyed visiting them and allowing them to embody their hopes. The celebrated French novelist of that era, Émile Zola, wrote an emblematic book in 1883 called *Au Bonheur des Dames* (The Ladies' Delight) which was set in one of the Parisian grand department stores of the era. It described the life of a twenty-year-old sales woman who had migrated to Paris to find work. The main character suffers thirteen-hour workdays, poor food and living conditions, and works in a place that Zola characterizes as being destructive of the neighborhood scale shops. Zola goes on to suggest that these grand department stores for the rich, like the famous Bon Marché, were symbols of capitalism, and the elevation of fashion and shopping to recreational pastimes for the upper classes. In fact, some would say that this first generation of mass stores created the women's modern equivalent of a downtown men's club.[70]

Department stores represented the first large scale generic spaces of consumerism in modern cities. Once the department store became successful, its prototype was recreated in most Western cultures. It became a sound investment for wealthy investors and property owners in the twentieth century. During the 1920s, a developer in Kansas City, Missouri, came up with the idea of building a "modern shopping center" away from downtown. In 1922, J.C. Nichols built the first one, named Country Club Plaza, as part of a larger plan for a mixed use/residential development. During the 1940s and 1950s, the first suburbs in the U.S. acquired large scale stores like Sears Roebuck and Montgomery Ward's.

But the real explosion in the scale of uniform consumer spaces came with the proliferation of regional shopping malls in the suburbs of cities across the United States. The first indoor shopping mall was built in Edina, Minnesota, in 1956, not coincidentally around the same time the McDonald's franchise was launched in California, and later in Arizona and Illinois.[71] Fast food and shopping malls were both symbols of a new age of car-oriented consumerism that would explode onto the scene in the post-1950 era. The first mall was designed by Austrian architect Victor Gruen, who would later go on to design fifty shopping malls in the U.S. over the next twenty years. The mall in Edina was the first fully enclosed, climate controlled shopping space.[72] It had a garden courtyard, theater, goldfish pond, aviary, hanging plants, and an orchestra. Shopping malls would soon become part of the daily culture of suburban communities. By the year 2000, there were more than 45,000 shopping malls in the U.S., occupying some 5.47 billion square feet of space.[73]

If shopping malls represented one important form of homogenized and mass-produced commercial space that dominated the urban periphery of

American cities, certainly the other important post-war prototype that came a bit later was the big box store, also known as the "mega-store" or superstore. The big box phenomenon is epitomized by Walmart. In 1962, Sam Walton and his brother opened the first Walmart in Rogers, Arkansas. Two other future superstores—Target and K-mart—opened their first stores around the same time. By the 1970s and 1980s, another type of mega-store, the retail warehouse, also was introduced; the two successful companies were Price Club (which later became Costco) and Sam's Club. These various enterprises spread across the U.S., and by the 1990s the big box era was at full tilt. By far the main geographic location for these mega-stores was in U.S. suburban regions, where land was available, and where economic expansion was ripe for these kinds of businesses. Indeed, the proliferation of superstores and big box projects was aided by the stock market and housing booms of the 1990s and 2000s, as well as by loose credit. As more Americans moved to suburbs, and into ever larger homes, there was a greater demand for more home consumer goods to fill their expanding residences, and thus a demand for big box retail outfits near where the expanding peripheral populations were moving.

In fact, research has shown that companies like Walmart and Target used an aggressive strategy to market the location of new stores: they would tell the town government that if it refused them a permit for construction, they would simply get one from a neighboring town—the traffic and other negative impacts would still be there, but now that town would lose the tax revenues that might help them mitigate those problems. This proved to be a winning strategy. By 1990, Walmart had 1,700 stores in the U.S. and was the largest retailer in the nation. It soon began to look to expand in others parts of the world, beginning in Latin America. A wave of stores opened in Mexico, Puerto Rico, Brazil, Argentina, and Canada, and later a second wave in China, South Korea, Germany, and the United Kingdom. By the year 2000, Walmart had nearly one million employees in the U.S., the second largest employer in the nation after the Federal government. By 2004, it had over 1.4 million employees worldwide, with 3,600 U.S. stores, 1,600 super-centers, and over 1,000 stores in Europe, Asia, and South America.[74] In 2012, Walmart had 4,200 stores in the U.S. and over 6,000 in other parts of the world.[75]

Big box, mega-stores, and super-centers have become the standard in US suburban design, and part of the everyday lives of suburban dwellers. These symbols of mass consumerism and super-sizing have also witnessed a counter-movement. Citizen groups have formed to fight back, books are being published and studies of the destructive impacts of big box developments on community life and traditional business districts are being carried out. The biggest environmental concerns are massive increases in traffic, air pollution, and noise around super-centers, and the loss of neighborhood scale shops and a sense of community when people only travel long distances to shop. One survey, for example, in the state of Iowa found that since 1983 the arrival of Walmarts has led to the shutting down of 50 percent of other clothing stores, 30 percent of hardware stores, 29 percent of shoe stores, and 26 percent of other department stores, as well as a decrease in tourism, less historic preservation, and a decline in the vitality of downtown business districts.[76]

Figure 1.5 Big Box Stores and the American Mania for "Stuff"
Source: Photo by Lawrence A. Herzog

Despite all the consumerism in the United States, one could ask the question: does more consumption indicate a better quality of life? While "quality of life" is a somewhat abstract construct, one can argue that whether people are consuming more household goods is not necessarily a measure of their well-being. Such critical matters as health care, education, and psychological contentment, for example, are distinct from the consumption of everyday goods and services. According to some sources, since the 1970s, while economic activity and consumption may have increased, levels of social welfare have, in fact, declined.[77]

The standardization of consumer spaces has not been confined within the U.S. There has been a massive globalization of shopping malls, fast food restaurants, hotels, resorts, and other urban spaces. Shopping mall designs have become generic—these enclosed spaces look strikingly similar in China, Ireland, Mexico, or Brazil. Malls have a standardized site plan and design concept—it includes the use of anchor stores, public areas for walking and sitting, food courts, movie theaters, and restaurants. Malls are designed to look like any one of various international architectural styles that are promoted by the mass media. The idea is to promote the notion that it is good to consume wherever one is, and that what is important is what you consume, and not where you are. In the words of one writer, "consumerism provides the defining set of practices and beliefs—in a word, shopping—that aspires to transcend the very real differences that exist between geographical, ethnic and cultural communities, at 'home' and 'abroad'."[78]

The twenty-first century is witnessing the evolution of more predictable commodified spaces in cities—privatized streets, festival marketplaces, airports, and giant mall complexes. It is believed that these consumer spaces, in part, replace the traditional downtown as the primary pedestrian scale gathering place for post-modern city dwellers.[79] Consider the example of a futuristic street such as "City Walk" on the west side of Los Angeles. The architects successfully re-created the scale and the feel of a pedestrian street in a privatized, closed mall; each store is visually presented as a separate façade, giving the impression of a street lined with individual buildings. City Walk promotes itself as a network of city streets where people can walk and interact. In fact, it is a large private shopping center disguised as a small village of pedestrian spaces, lined with restaurants, clothing boutiques, specialty stores, and movie theaters. This kind of new urban space reflects the evolution of entertainment-oriented public consumerist spaces, dubbed "architainment."[80] City Walk-type developments are being planned and built in other parts of the world, including China, Japan, and South Korea.[81]

Globalization of the American Suburb: from the Southwest Border to Latin America

American suburbs, with all their environmental challenges, have not been confined to our continent; the suburban model has spread across our southern borders, over the last three decades, to Mexico, then to Central and South America, and finally to other continents across the planet.[82] It's important to remember that the building of suburbs was one plank in the larger project of American modernity. Marshall Berman has defined modernism as "any attempt by modern men and women to become subjects as well as objects of modernization, to get a grip on the modern world and make themselves at home in it."[83] Thus, one must remember that as American cities grew after World War II, and as freeways and suburban communities were being laid out, the world was watching. In Brazil, architects Lucio Costa and Oscar Neimeyer were so enamored of the modernist project that they designed an entire city, the new national capital of Brasília, using the principles of modern urban design. That city, constructed in only three years, quickly revealed the dangers of designing with a limited palette of modernist ideals. In Berman's words, Brasília quickly became "immense empty spaces in which the individual feels lost, as alone as a man on the moon."[84]

The important point here is that America's suburb was part of what one scholar has termed a "global project."[85] Following World War II, the U.S. became the center of a global economy based on free trade. However, that global dominance was not only economic; it was also cultural. The U.S. made a conscious effort to build more spread out cities, in part because the Federal government saw the marketing value of projecting America as prosperous and the image of a family living in safe suburbs as the American dream, which nations all over the world might aspire to. So the suburb became a place that exemplified American freedom, security, and the promise of prosperity. At the same time, it has been argued that homeownership, mainly in the new suburbs, would be yet one more way to protect the values of capitalism against the tide of socialism. Suburban developer Levitt, who built the iconic Levittowns on the east coast, was quoted as saying: "No man who owns his own house and lot can be a communist."[86]

Across the planet, after World War II, America's image as a democracy and as world economic leader also became a cultural model for consumerism and community-building. American images and ideas central to the lifestyle of its new suburbs—supermarkets, automobiles, super-highways, and motels—were exported to other nations. The American post-war dream was concretized in the form of the single family suburban home, the cul-de-sac community, the local shopping center, and the family car, as opposed to the crowded, high crime, industrial cities.

The post-war suburb did not entirely live up to the idyllic marketing images of the 1950s and 1960s. Three important examples of colossal urban sprawl—San Diego, Las Vegas, and Phoenix—spread across the deserts and fragile ecosystems along the southwest border of the U.S. Suburbanization in Mexico, moving from the national capital Mexico City where the first experiments in building "suburbs" began in the 1940s and 1950s, to the border city of Tijuana, where American style suburbs burst on the scene in the 1990s, speaks to a larger phenomenon sweeping across that nation. After less than twenty years, new American style suburbs, which sought to copy U.S. trends in the construction of automobile-based, gated communities, are in trouble. Many of these new suburbs were poorly designed, isolated, and lacking services. In a few cases, entire subdivisions are either sparsely occupied or even abandoned. In Brazil, similar problems can be seen in the mega-coastal suburbs south and west of Rio de Janeiro.

It is important to point out that the periphery of most Latin American cities has been occupied by what anthropologists, development experts, planners, urbanists, and other social science researchers began calling "squatter settlements" or "shantytowns" as early as the 1950s.

When Latin America entered the modern era, experimenting with strategies of import substitution, as well as seeking giant international development loans to promote urban/industrial development during that period, massive waves of rural migrants flowed toward the cities in search of work. As we now know from more than five decades of research, these migrants arrived with virtually no liquid capital and no permanent source of employment. They soon became part of a booming "informal" street economy, which only provided temporary sources of wealth. Faced with no real prospect of renting or purchasing homes in the "formal" housing market, millions of city-ward migrants chose to squat on, or occupy, land, usually on the outskirts of cities and often in floodplains or canyons, on steep sloping hillsides, or other less desirable land isolated from the "formal city." Over time, these temporary encampments of shacks and cardboard or wooden homes morphed into permanent slums, which now crowd across the periphery of Latin America's urban areas, with few signs of going away.[87] What is new, however, is that the periphery has also begun to attract elite enclaves of upper and upper middle class residents seeking the typical lifestyle of the post-war U.S. suburb.

Is there an alternative to the fast world of mass-produced suburbs? In the end, I am arguing for the foundation of "slow urbanism," at the scale of city, community, and individuals. I stitch together several of the important rationales and movements for an alternative urbanism, one that moves away from the modern suburban design prototype. I argue that citizens want to be both actively and passively engaged with their living spaces.[88] Cities need to recapture a more human scale,[89] as reflected in the design of buildings and spaces. As a simple example, in France the arrangement of tables in cafes is permanently designed so chairs face outward toward the street. More generally, across the United States citizens are rising up to take back their streets and communities, whether it is women "taking back the night" by promoting safety in cities, or neighborhoods making streets more livable and promoting "placemaking."[90] The importance of public life and community is illustrated by the growing global movement to revitalize older public spaces in cities like New York, Chicago, Paris, Rome, London, Mexico City, and Rio de Janeiro, or to create vibrant new

Figure 1.6 The Parisian Cafe Is a Form of Slow Urbanism
Source: Photo by Lawrence A. Herzog

public places in cities like Barcelona, Portland, San Diego, and Denver.[91] These social movements to take back streets and other public places, or to become more engaged with local spaces and communities, represent the kind of "slow urbanism" we need to offset the mistakes of the late twentieth century legacy of fast, mass-produced suburbs.

Notes

1   Kevin Kruse and Thomas Sugrue, *The New Suburban History.* Chicago: University of Chicago Press, 2006.
2   Michael Pacione, *Urban Geography: A Global Perspective.* New York: Routledge, 2009, 84.
3   Anthony Flint, *This Land: The Battle over Sprawl and the Future of America.* Baltimore, MD: Johns Hopkins University Press, 2006.
4   I should point out up front that, as I mention later in the book, the peripheries of most Latin American cities are mainly covered with lower income settlements, which began as "squatter" settlements for poor migrants from the countryside and have become part

of what author Mike Davis has called the "planet of slums." In the last two decades, however, new middle and upper class enclaves, more like U.S. suburbs, have begun to emerge outside cities like Mexico City, Buenos Aires, Santiago, São Paulo and Rio de Janeiro, and these are the settlements I refer to in this book.

5   This textbook definition is found in a number of books on the subject; see, for example, Andres Duany, Elizabeth Plater-Zyberk, and Jeff Speck, *Suburban Nation*. New York: North Point Press, 2000; James Howard Kunstler, *The Geography of Nowhere*. New York: Touchstone, 1993.

6   I will leave it to anthropologists and sociologists to consider how this happened; this book is more about the results. And, as I will show in two Latin American cases (Mexico and Brazil), while the forms of "global suburbs" evolving on the peripheries south of the border are dispersed and sprawling, they don't look entirely like U.S. suburbs—architectural qualities (and densities) are distinct, though there is plenty of evidence of the influence of U.S. suburbs, from shopping malls to gating.

7   Lynn Hirschberg, "Sofia Coppola's Paris," *New York Times*, September 24, 2006, travel section.

8   James T. Mackenzie, Roger Dower, and Donald D.T. Chen, "The Going Rate: What It Really Costs to Drive," World Resources Institute, 1992.

9   Howard Frunk, Lawrence Frank, and Richard Jackson, *Urban Sprawl and Public Health*. Washington, D.C.: Island Press, 2004, Chapter 6.

10 R. Ewing, R.A. Scheiber, and C.V. Zeger, "Urban Sprawl as a Risk Factor in Motor Vehicle Occupant and Pedestrian Fatalities," *American Journal of Public Health*, 93 (9), 2003, 1541–5.

11 Traffic congestion is not unique to American cities. Mega-cities around the world have severe traffic congestion in places like Mexico City, Beijing, Johannesburg, Shenzen/Hong Kong, and Nairobi. See IBM Global Commuter Pain Survey, http://www-03.ibm.com/press/us/en/pressrelease/35359.wss, retrieved 3/7/13.

12 One of the landmark studies of urban sprawl devotes an entire chapter to traffic injuries. See Frunk et al., 2004. I offer further details in Chapter 2 of this book.

13 See Carl Honore, *In Praise of Slowness*. San Francisco: Harper Collins, 2004, and also see later discussions in this book about the Slow Food and Slow Cities movements.

14 See AT&T TV ad "Faster or Slower" at http://www.ispot.tv/ad/7AVh/at-and-t-faster-or-slower-featuring-beck-bennett, retrieved 3/7/13.

15 The concept of fast and slow urbanism began to emerge in the urban design and planning field in the early 2000s, in particular as a response to the Citta Slow (Slow Cities) movement in Italy. I address this in greater detail as part of an alternative policy response to the ecological problems of suburbs in Chapter 6 of this book. See also Heike Mayer and Paul Knox, "Slow Cities: Sustainable Places in a Fast World," *Journal of Urban Affairs*, 28 (4), 2006, 321–34; Paul Knox, "Creating Ordinary Places: Slow Cities in a Fast World," *Journal of Urban Design*, 10 (1), February, 2005, 1–11.

16 The author wishes to thank Sharon Zukin for clarifying this distinction.

17 John Dos Passos, *Manhattan Transfer*. New York: Houghton Mifflin, 1925. Thanks to writer/scholar Mike Davis for reminding me about this evocative novel.

18 Alex Krieger, "The Costs and Benefits of Sprawl," in William Saunders, ed. *Sprawl and Suburbia*, Minneapolis: University of Minnesota Press, 2005, 44–56.

19 James S. Russell, "Privatized Lives: On the Embattled Burbs," in Saunders, ed., 2005, 95.

20 Melanie A. Rapino and Alison K. Fields, "Mega Commuting in the U.S." U.S. Census, Social and Economic Housing Division, Washington, D.C., 2012.

21 Tim Ferriss, author of *The 4-Hour Workweek*, cited in Marco R. della Cava, "Time Flies: Having Fun?" *USA Today*, January 28, 2008, p. D-2.

22 Ivan Illich, *Energy and Equity*. New York: Harper and Row, 1974. Cited in Richard Register, *Ecocities*. Berkeley, CA: Berkeley Books, 2002, 140.

23 Ibid., 141–5.

24 "Smart Phones Can Increase Stress Levels, Study Says," *Huffington Post*, January 12, 2012. http://www.huffingtonpost.com/2012/01/12/smartphones-cause-stress_n_1202924.html, retrieved 10/21/13.

25 See Richard Louv, *Last Child in the Woods*. New York: Algonquin Books, 2005.

26 See, for example, Arthur Harris, *Sport in Greece and Rome*. Ithaca, NY: Cornell University Press, 1972.

27 Honore, 2004, 23.

28 While sundials and water clocks date back to ancient empires in Rome, Greece, China, India, Egypt, and elsewhere, the first mechanical clocks are associated with churches in medieval Europe around the thirteenth century. In fact, the word "clock" is said to come from the Celtic words *clocca* or *clogan*, which mean "bell," reinforcing the connection between clocks, time, and the sounding of church bells. See, for example, David S. Landes, *Revolution in Time: Clocks and the Making of the Modern World*. Cambridge: Harvard University Press, 1983.

29 Honore, 2004, 26.

30 This point is emphasized in Honore, 2004.

31 Thich Nhat Hanh, *Zen Keys*. New York: Doubleday, 1974.

32 See, for example, Jon Kabat-Zinn, *Full Catastrophe Living*. New York: Dell, 1990.

33 The ancient source was "Maxim" (c. 430 BC). See Stuart Flexner and Doris Flexner, *Wise Words and Wives' Tales: The Origins, Meanings and Time-Honored Wisdom of Proverbs and Folk Sayings Olde and New*. New York: Avon Books, 1993.

34 See James Vincent, "Yahoo Brands Nick D'Aloisio's Summly App for Mobile-News Focus," http://www.independent.co.uk/life-style/gadgets-and-tech/ces-2014-yahoo-rebrands-nick-daloisios-summly-app-for-mobilenews-focus-9045993.html, January 8, 2014, retrieved 1/9/14.

35 Of course, mobile devices are not equally available to all citizens on the planet. The poor and disadvantaged across the less developed nations are still economically limited in purchasing hardware and learning how to use rapidly changing digital technologies.

36 See, for example, Joshua Baruch, "The Reddit Phenomenon," http://psupopculture.wordpress.com/2011/02/01/the-reddit-phenomenon-how-social-news-reveals-what-we-really-care-about/, retrieved 1/9/14.

37 See www.fastcompany.com/magazine/117.

38 Richard Florida's book *The Rise of the Creative Class*, New York: Basic Books, 2002, also looks at cities as concentrations of creativity. Florida's thesis is that concentrations of "knowledge workers"—financial planners, doctors, lawyers, etc.—in large cities can stimulate creativity under the right conditions. But he also argues that these knowledge workers need to be less self-centered, and more part of a cohesive group with a social conscience.

39 Fast Cities 2007. http://www.fastcompany.com/magazine/117/features-fast-cities-intro.html.

40 Other similar time-saving websites have come along, including news summary sites like Newser.com, Google News, My Yahoo and Digg.com, as well as sites such as Reddit that consolidate entertainment and social media.

41 Marco R. Della Cava, "Time Flies. Having Fun? They Can Help." *USA Today*. January 28, 2008, D-1–D2.

42 See Carl Honore on his website, www.carlhonore.com.

43 Juliet Schor, *The Overworked American.* New York: Basic Books, 1992; Sara Robinson, "Bring back the 40 Hour Work Week," Salon.com, March 14, 2012, http://www.salon.com/2012/03/14/bring_back_the_40_hour_work_week/, retrieved 3/11/13.; G.E. Miller, "U.S. Is Most Overworked Developed Nation in the World," 20 Something Finance, October 12, 2010, http://20somethingfinance.com/american-hours-worked-productivity-vacation/.

44 I will suggest in the concluding chapter that policy changes to make cities more sustainable must be anchored by design efforts to fortify "slower urban" lifestyles, including livable streets, greater pedestrian access, locally based food, and greater neighborhood identity and sense of place.

45 See International Workers of the World, "More Time for Life," in Industrial Worker Supplement. www.iww.org, retrieved 3/12/13.

46 Ibid.

47 Robinson, 2012.

48 For example, writer Tom Peters' books became best-sellers; they extolled the virtues of the new high tech work ethic for the future of American business. See Tom Peters and Robert Waterman, *In Search of Excellence.* New York: Harpers Business, 1992.

49 Robinson, 2012.

50 Ibid., 5.

51 G.E. Miller, 2010.

52 Ibid.

53 See also Robert Putnam, *Bowling Alone.* New York: Touchstone, 2001.

54 This is documented in the next chapter.

55 See Leigh Gallagher, *The End of Suburbs.* London: Portfolio, 2013.

56 Shaila Dewan, "Is Suburban Sprawl on Its Way Back?" *New York Times*, September 14, 2013, SR7.

57 This point is reinforced in the work of Leslie Sklair, *Sociology of the Global System.* Baltimore, MD: Johns Hopkins University Press, 1991, and George Ritzer, *The McDonaldization of Society.* London: Pine Forge Press, 1996.

58 Sklair, 1991.

59 Advertising is just one example of how global decision-makers need rapid access to information, and the ability to bring together stakeholders in communication forums. The boundaries between global marketing and social media, however, are still being negotiated. For example, legal experts and users successfully challenged the attempt by the owners of social networking website Facebook to employ users' identities as a marketing tool, without respecting their right to privacy. See Somini Sengupta, "FTC Settles Privacy Issue at Facebook," *New York Times*, November 29, 2011, B-1, http://www.nytimes.com/2011/11/30/technology/facebook-agrees-to-ftc-settlement-on-privacy.html.

60 Sklair, 1991.

61 Jon Goss, "The Magic of the Mall: An Analysis of Form, Function, and Meaning in the. Contemporary Retail Built Environment," *Annals of the Association of American Geographers*, 83 (1), March, 1993, 18.

62 George Ritzer, 1996.

63 Ibid.

64 James Howard Kunstler, *The Geography of Nowhere.* New York: Touchstone, 1993.

65 Andres Duany, Elizabeth Plater-Zyberk, and Jeff Speck, *Suburban Nation.* New York: North Point Press, 2000, xx.

66 In the last two decades, some master planned communities have done a better job of providing more amenities (parks, trails, recreation spaces, schools) to suburban dwellers than the original "Levittowns" did.

67 Mitchell Schwartzer, "The Spectacle of Ordinary Building," in Saunders, ed., 2005, 86.

68 Mark Girouard, *Cities and People*. New Haven, CT: Yale University Press, 1985.

69 The Galleria Vittorio Emanuele II is considered the oldest shopping mall in Italy; the Galleria is named after Vittorio Emanuele II, the first king of the Kingdom of Italy. It was originally designed in 1861 and built between 1865 and 1877. The use of a glass and cast iron roof is consistent with design approaches used in nineteenth century arcades, such as the Burlington Arcade in London. In general, glass covered larger shopping arcades began with the Saint-Hubert Gallery in Brussels (opened in 1847), the Passazh in St Petersburg (opened in 1848), the Galleria Umberto I in Naples (opened in 1890), and the Budapest Galleria. See Johann F. Geist, *Arcades: The History of a Building Type*. Cambridge: MIT Press, 1982.

70 Susan Porter Benson, "Palace of Consumption and Machine for Selling: The American Department Store, 1880–1940," *Radical History Review*, 21, Fall 1979, 199–221.

71 Ritzer, 1996, 29.

72 Ironically, Gruen was worried about the soullessness of shopping centers and consumerism, and tried to make the Edina mall a more mixed use project. However, only the mall ended up being built, and Gruen later claimed his mall concept was "bastardized" into something more superficial that went against what he himself believed in. Alex Wall, *Victor Gruen: From Urban Shop to New City*. Barcelona: Actar, 2006.

73 Ashish Kumar Sen, "The Malling of America," *Span*, March/April, 2005, 4.

74 Bill Quinn, *How Walmart Is Destroying America*. Berkeley, CA: Ten Speed Press, 2005.

75 Walmart website at: http://corporate.walmart.com/our-story/our-business/locations/, retrieved 11/6/13.

76 Gregg Spotts, *Walmart: The High Cost of Low Price*. New York: Disinformation Books, 2005.

77 Avner Offer's study on the subject, using data from the Index of Sustainable Economic Welfare (ISEW), shows that: "If we regard society as a unitary actor, according to the ISEW, the growth of economic activity since the mid-1970s has been producing a reduction in aggregate welfare." See Avner Offer, *The Challenge of Affluence*. New York: Oxford, 2006, 20.

78 Leslie Sklair, "Iconic Architecture and Capitalist Globalization," in P. Herrie and E. Wegerhoff, eds. *Architecture and Identity*. Berlin: Lit Verlag/Habitat International, 2008, 207–19.

79 However, there is also evidence that in the U.S. downtowns are making a significant comeback and bucking this trend. From Portland, Oregon, to Austin, Texas, many cities have revitalized their centers and people are moving back. Even older cities like Newark or Oakland are finding ways to empower their old central business districts. See, for example, Susan Piperato, "American Cities Are Revitalizing Their Downtowns and Recreating Their Profiles," *National Real Estate Investor*, March 28, 2012, http://nreionline.com/city-reviews/new-jersey/american_cities_revitalizing_downtowns_03282012/. For a wider overview of how American downtowns, in different contexts, have tried to re-emerge, see Larry R. Ford, *America's New Downtowns*. Baltimore, MD: Johns Hopkins University Press, 2003.

80 Luis Fernandez Galiano, 2005. "Spectacle and Its Discontents, or the Elusive Joys of Architainment," in William Saunders, ed. *Commodification and Spectacle in Architecture*. Minneapolis: University of Minnesota Press, 2005, 1–7. See also Sklair, 2008.

81 See, for example, Norman Klein, "A Glittery Bit of Urban Make Believe," *Los Angeles Times*, July 18, 1993, http://articles.latimes.com/1993-07-18/local/me-14440_1_movie-set, retrieved 3/27/13.

82 As I discuss in Chapters 4 and 5, elite and middle class suburbs in Mexico, Brazil, and other Latin American nations are in no way identical to U.S. suburbs. They occur under different circumstances and in different land contexts. However, my argument is that they share many similar ecological, social, and urban planning challenges, and that we must begin to see them in this collective light, even given the different cross-cultural settings.

83 Marshall Berman, *All That Is Solid Melts into Air: The Experience of Modernity.* New York: Penguin, 1988, 5.

84 Ibid., p. 7.

85 Robert Beauregard, *When America Became Suburban.* Minneapolis: University of Minnesota Press, 2006.

86 Ibid., 156.

87 The literature on Latin American squatter developments and shantytowns is copious. See, for example, Janice Perlman, *The Myth of Marginality.* Berkeley: University of California Press, 1980; Mike Davis, *Planet of Slums.* London: Verso, 2007; Robert Neuwirth, *Shadow Cities.* New York: Routledge, 2004.

88 See Stephen Carr, Mark Francis, Leanne G. Rivlin, and Andrew M. Stone, *Public Space.* Cambridge: Cambridge University Press, 1992.

89 William Whyte shows that "people watching" is the number one activity on plazas in large cities like New York City. See William Whyte, *The Social Life of Small Urban Spaces.* Washington, D.C.: The Conservation Foundation, 1980.

90 See Project for Public Spaces, "Launching the Place-Making Movement," December 20, 2013, http://www.pps.org/blog/launching-the-placemaking-movement/, retrieved 1/09/14. More vital places can occur at a variety of densities, depending on the setting. In large cities, taller buildings are not necessarily a bad thing, especially if they can make housing more affordable. Also, in the U.S., given the high costs of purchasing housing, we may need to promote renting as a viable alternative for urban living.

91 See, for example, Lawrence A. Herzog, *Return to the Center.* Austin: University of Texas Press, 2006.

2

SPRAWL KILLS

ECOLOGICAL CRISIS ON THE URBAN PERIPHERY

The second half of the twentieth century can be called the era of the American suburb.[1] The urban form that preceded it, the late nineteenth and early twentieth century American city, was far more compact, a city of "streetcar suburbs" where people walked or used mass transit to move around. The image of those "mass transit" cities where formally dressed men and women walked everywhere or rode the trolley, while living at close quarters in brownstones or masonry apartment buildings, may seem old fashioned. Yet, the higher density design forms from these earlier periods deserve our attention when juxtaposed against the unsustainable ecologies of ill health, traffic fatalities, air pollution, and fast living that our late twentieth century urban sprawl produced.

Urban sprawl kills. The built environment of fast urbanism and suburbs has spawned traffic fatalities, road rage, air pollution, and documented threats to public health. Its auto-centric design causes us to walk less and has sparked an epidemic of obesity and higher rates of hypertension, heart disease, diabetes, and early death. Its wide open spaces have given us large yards and big front lawns, but that same luxury of space has mesmerized us into assuming we can just keep building further out, live in bigger houses, drive larger cars, and shop in bigger box stores, even as we deplete the earth's supply of precious fossil fuels. Its design emphasizes our individuality and encourages us to consume more and think less about our civic obligations. It saps our social capital, leaving us with less time and less ability to build communities of like-minded citizens who care about public health and ecology.

The construction of an automobile-oriented, decentralized metropolis, filled with low density single family developments in uniformly designed subdivisions with cul-de-sacs and curvilinear streets, was one of the pillars of the American modernist city-building project. Modernists in Europe celebrated the "machine age" city by focusing on mass produced high rise office buildings and apartment complexes at relatively high densities. America embraced the high rise architecture identified with Swiss architect Le Corbusier, and this shaped the central business districts of New York City, Chicago, and other large cities. But America also developed its own cultural agenda for a rational, orderly, auto-centric urbanism aimed at the open lands that lie beyond cities: the low rise suburbs. If the design pinnacle of rationalist, high rise modernity was the glass and steel skyscraper, then its counterpart for low rise modernity was the planned suburb, facilitated by the favored tool of post-war modernist planners—single use zoning.

The "machine" that anchored the urbanism of single family subdivisions, strip malls, and post-1950s suburbia was the automobile, not the skyscraper. Of one of the icons of utopian modern architecture, the planned city of Brasília, critic Robert Hughes wrote: "In the future, everyone would have a car and so the car, as in Corbusier's dreams, would abolish the street."[2]

Historian Kenneth Jackson posits four key factors that shaped the evolution of America's suburbs: transportation technology, changing cultural values, a romantic connection to nature, and Jeffersonian anti-urbanism.[3] Taken together, these elements would reconfigure the geography of American cities over the next century and half, with the United States shifting from being a nation of relatively compact cities to one of decentralized metropolitan form. As a result, the post-1950 spatial trends are quite startling: from one-fourth of the total population living in the suburbs in 1950, to two-thirds of Americans in suburbs after 2010.[4]

Think back to the 1800s. American cities were still densely populated and pedestrian in scale. People of all social classes and backgrounds often lived alongside each other. But, over the next half century, the introduction of new forms of transportation technology—the steam ferry, horse car, cable car, and elevated rail—forever altered the spatial form of American cities. Each technological innovation built the momentum for a wholesale exodus of city dwellers from the original urban core. In the 1870s and 1880s, the first "streetcar suburbs" of America, from Boston to San Francisco, allowed people to move away from increasingly crowded downtowns, with their congested warehouse and financial zones, factories, and densely occupied immigrant tenement districts. Rail suburbs initiated what became the driving theme for modern American city-building: escape from the congestion, noise, and pollution of the traditional urban core. Ironically, that original desire to escape the impending environmental crisis of rapid industrial growth in the central city—air pollution, traffic, and noise—would eventually reproduce another version of those problems on the urban periphery.

Developing technology also inspired a longing to reconnect with nature. In the late nineteenth and early twentieth centuries, utopian thinkers like Ebenezer Howard, Lewis Mumford, and others advocated the creation of "garden suburbs" or "rail suburbs"; these early utopian villages on the urban periphery included what would now be considered sustainable design practices—growing local food, encouraging mixed land use development, and locating residential and work locations in the same place. Unfortunately, most of these utopian suburbs were never realized at any large scale.

Another force historians believe fed the demand for suburban growth was a growing American cultural emphasis on domesticity and privacy. Following the massive densification of downtowns from the middle to late nineteenth century, American city dwellers yearned for both more aesthetic beauty and the introduction of nature back into urban life.[5]

These forces continued to feed the nation's fervor to get away from the increasing chaos and overcrowding of late nineteenth century industrial cities. Historians argue that the nineteenth century was also defined by the expansion of the American frontier, the move westward toward the wilderness, the opening of new lands, and the discovery of vast resources—mineral wealth, forests, fishing, and new fertile lands for agriculture. This "frontier spirit" and what was essentially a rural economy in colonial America led some American leaders to argue for a nation built around its rural, rather than its urban, heritage. In this Jeffersonian "anti-urban" view, cities were seen as mere necessities for housing government or trade operations or for the building of military bases. But most Americans, argued the "anti-urbanists," should strive for a family life close to the land in small rural villages or in the countryside.[6]

Rail and streetcar suburbs dominated the first waves of urban growth toward the periphery. This phase lasted about a half century. But by the early decades of the twentieth century, the invention of the automobile would slowly begin a second dramatic transformation in the outward growth of the American metropolis.

In the first phase of automobile urbanism, "elite auto suburbs" were built for the minority of wealthy people who could drive the early versions of cars from their new homes back into the city for work or recreation. The second phase, which started after World War II, was the one that has defined American cities ever since. This phase of "freeway automobiles" was ignited when the U.S. federal government passed the Interstate Highway Act in 1956, unleashing the construction of a national inter- and intra-city highway infrastructure; it also created the Federal Housing Administration, which organized a national financing program to grant low interest mortgages to working class and other war veterans. Millions of Americans flocked to the waves of mass produced suburbs, beginning in the 1950s and 1960s and continuing well up to the present day.[7]

One of the less obvious but critical shifts that occurred with this massive exodus was the dramatic separation of workplace and residence that became permanently ingrained by the suburbanization of the U.S. When cities were more compact, as factories were built during the early industrial revolution, it was possible for workers to live in close proximity to their place of employment. From a labor politics point of view, this helped empower workers, as they saw a connection between their job and their overall quality of life. Indeed, early industrialists actually built company towns to house their workers. However, once they realized that when workers lived near the factory, their discontent with industrial capitalism was intensified (for example by living close to industrial pollution), very quickly the phase of building company towns began to disappear.[8] Some large companies actually left downtown and moved outside the city to get away from the union politics of downtown.

Eventually, industrial capital found it more advantageous for workers to be dispersed, and not live in a single community close to the workplace. Of course, this job/housing imbalance would become one of the defining ecological dilemmas of urban sprawl, since highly dispersed workers require enormous supplies of energy to travel to equally dispersed work locations. Further, the only way to get to those locations is by car, the very machine that may not be sustainable in the future.

The Age of Sprawl Begins

With the dawn of the new millennium, there was a notable flurry of books and studies of suburbanization by scientists, architects, planners, urban scholars, journalists, and ecologists. The buzzword underlying the critiques of suburbs can be captured in a single word: "sprawl." "Sprawl" was defined in one study as "a process of large-scale real estate development resulting in low density, scattered, discontinuous, car-dependent construction, usually on the periphery of declining older suburbs and shrinking city centers."[9] The ecological problems of suburbs became the catalysts for new paradigms of thinking and for the creation of coalitions of architects, planners, and environmentalists to promote "new urbanism" or "smart growth." These terms have gradually become part of the mainstream of discourse within the city planning, architecture, and urban design professions.

Before we consider the various environmental and public health problems of urban sprawl, it's fair to recognize that not everyone believes America's suburbs are dysfunctional. Real estate consultants, conservative media, and what one author has labeled as "populist" academics represent what we might call a loose coalition of defenders of late twentieth and early twenty-first century suburban sprawl.[10] One simple argument used to defend this prototype of urban design is that if Americans want to live in sprawling communities, a free enterprise system should allow them to do just that. In the words of one advocate for traditional U.S. suburbs: "It is my view that people should be generally free to do whatever they want unless they inflict harm on their fellow citizens."[11] A variation on this theme is that, in a democracy, living in a sprawling community is a basic constitutional right or "freedom."

Another common pro-suburbia rationale might be termed the "real estate thesis," or the argument that, whether or not they are environmentally perfect, suburbs create value.[12] This view generally holds that suburbs are good because a larger share of American wealth is located there. An example of this optimism is found in a mid-2005 statement by a well known urban economist from southern California: "Instead of clustering in large, crowded cities, Americans are building bigger and bigger houses."[13] There have not been very many social scientific studies that defend suburban development. But in one of them urban sprawl is argued to be healthy for Americans because it allows privacy, mobility, and choice, and because a version of sprawl did, in fact, exist throughout history in some form or other.[14] On the latter point, however, the urban sprawl found during the Roman Empire, or in other ancient cities, is significantly dwarfed by the scale of twenty-first century sprawl, leading some to consider the contemporary version as an entirely distinct ecological phenomenon. As one Harvard urban design scholar wrote, "a billion sprawlers is a cause for worry."[15]

Beyond this small group of urban sprawl defenders, more overwhelming has been the early twenty-first century outpouring of books and scientific studies that address the environmental and design problems of the American suburbia-building project. In one key work of the era, the authors speak of five critical built components of sprawl: housing subdivisions, shopping centers, office parks, disconnected public buildings surrounded by parking lots, and roadways. They go on to say that "the problem with suburbia is that, in spite of all its regulatory controls, it is not functional; it simply does not efficiently serve society or preserve the environment."[16] Many of the scientific studies make another critical point about suburban sprawl—that you can debate whether it is culturally, aesthetically, or ideologically the right solution for urban living, but there is no doubt that the principal problem of suburban sprawl lies in its hidden public health costs: traffic congestion and air pollution, highway fatalities, obesity and diseases that result from lack of physical activity, overemphasis on private space, and the resulting lost social capital combined with greater socio-psychological stress. These five issues represent the public health ecologies of fast urbanism.[17]

Urban Sprawl and Air Pollution

The way suburbs are deliberately shaped forces people to drive more. The design of most suburbs has been termed a "loop and lollipop" configuration,[18] where residential, commercial, and office clusters or "pods" of housing subdivisions are isolated from one another, requiring separate automobile trips for every errand and every destination. Thus, the typical suburban resident makes numerous daily trips by car to work, shop, attend school, pick up a package at the post office, visit a friend, or eat dinner in a restaurant. Moreover, as new housing subdivisions have migrated further and further out, and with no attempt to match the workplace with the location of residences, Americans are driving even more miles, and the pattern of sprawl has become even more problematic. All of these trips and additional driving in stop-and-go traffic mean more auto emissions are being deposited across suburban regions of the U.S.

For example, in Atlanta, between 1982 and 1997, 571,000 acres of land were added to the urbanized region through the construction of new suburbs. During this period, 1.3 million new inhabitants moved into the urban region, and the total number of miles driven more than doubled. By 2001, the average Atlanta resident drove 34 miles/day, yet those numbers were even more skewed in the suburbs, where residents drove as many as 44 miles/day; meanwhile, the average number of miles driven by residents who lived in and near the inner city averaged 0–12 miles/day.[19] In another study of thirteen neighborhoods in Los Angeles and San Francisco, scientists found much lower rates of automobile commuting in high density, transit-oriented urban neighborhoods, as opposed to suburbs.[20] Further, in a national analysis of forty-four metropolitan counties with over one million population, the data shows that higher densities and higher incidence of mixed land uses generate lower rates of automobile commuting.[21]

When people drive more, there is a corresponding increase in auto emissions and air pollution. This produces measurable negative public health outcomes in the high commuting zones (the suburbs), including asthma and other respiratory diseases, cancer, and premature mortality.

Cars and trucks generate 77 percent of all the carbon monoxide pollution in cities, 56 percent of nitrous oxides, 30 percent of carbon dioxide, and 47 percent of volatile organic compounds.[22] A study of the Seattle metropolitan area demonstrated that neighborhoods with "sprawl characteristics" (low density, separated land uses, disconnected street networks) consistently tested out with higher levels of air pollution than neighborhoods not having sprawl elements.[23] A comprehensive analysis of air quality in forty-five major U.S. metropolitan areas used a sprawl index defined around four elements: centeredness, connectivity, density, and land use mix. Based on this index, the analysis found that sprawling regions of the U.S. have higher ozone levels than do compact regions.[24]

Exposure to toxic levels of air pollution produces respiratory health problems like asthma, especially among children. Air pollution can lead to early mortality, particularly exposure to particulate matters (PM); again, this is especially true for young children whose lung tissue is more vulnerable.[25] In general, polluted air from automobiles carries known carcinogens from volatile organic compounds such as benzene, styrene, and toluene. These chemicals evaporate from gasoline and are present in exhaust fumes that can be breathed in by those living near roads, and also by commuters sitting inside their cars in traffic. In fact, these carcinogen exposures are associated with higher rates of lung cancer, and studies show that people living near freeways are especially vulnerable.[26]

Automobile emissions are scientifically linked with several major air pollutants—ozone, PM, and nitrous oxides—all of which are associated with lung related health problems for people living in urbanized regions. Studies point to higher levels of acute or chronic respiratory illnesses for residents living near roads with heavy traffic. In Los Angeles, for example, scientists have shown that children living closer to air pollution sources have lower levels of lung growth than those living in less polluted neighborhoods.[27]

By consolidating growth in the future, new urbanist, higher density, mixed use communities would hopefully cut down on the need to drive. As people walk more to shops, schools, and even jobs, there would be some limited decrease in miles driven, and thus in air pollution levels. However, the higher density centers, for those using cars, might also cause some increases in traffic, and thus higher localized levels of air pollution. This would mean that any future planning in the outer suburbs would need to take greater steps to discourage automobile use and provide efficient alternative transportation (bicycle paths, jitneys, bus rapid transit, or well designed pedestrian zones).

Traffic Accidents and Road Rage

Another public health concern associated with urban sprawl lies in the statistical pattern of fatal and near fatal accidents that occur in suburbia. Automobiles cause an average of 40,000 deaths per year in the U.S. and 3.4 million injuries, and impose a cost of $200 billion dollars annually.[28] Not all of those deaths, injuries, and costs are linked to suburban locations. However, it's been suggested that one can use the epidemiological concept of "time at risk" to argue that, in sprawling suburbs, people are spending more and more time in their cars, due to increased congestion and the location of developments further and further out. Driving more means suburban dwellers are putting themselves at greater risk.[29] When people need to drive longer distances, and spend long hours in their cars, they become either fatigued or irritable, both of which can increase their risk of getting into an accident, not to mention other negative health impacts related to stress. With the addition of cell phones and the distraction of talking or texting while driving, there is even more risk today for those drivers who are spending longer amounts of time in their cars.[30] For example, in 2010, the National Safety Council released estimates that showed that about 28 percent of all traffic crashes—or at least 1.6 million crashes each year—involve drivers using cell phones and texting.[31] The National Highway Traffic Safety Administration says that the percentage of traffic deaths associated with "driver distraction" is on the rise. Between 2005 and 2010, the percentage of fatalities due to distraction, as a proportion of total traffic accident deaths, increased from 10 to 16 percent.[32]

The nature of highway and road design in sprawling communities often adds to the probability of traffic accidents. Cul-de-sac designs funnel residential loop and curvilinear roads into wider "feeder" roads that encourage faster speeds and higher volumes of traffic. Yet those feeder roads also feature design elements like excessive width, curb cuts, and driveways that allow quick access in and out of shopping centers, office parks, and other destinations. Many accidents tend to concentrate along these feeder roads due to high speed, congestion, and the aforementioned design elements. For example, a study of street widths in Colorado showed that, out of all the design elements on those streets—width, trees, building height, curb cuts—width was the highest predictor of risk of collision.[33]

Studies demonstrate that sprawl increases car-related deaths. The most comprehensive study of 448 metropolitan counties in 101 urban areas of the U.S. ranked all counties using a sprawl index. Controlling for age, income, and household size, it found a strong correlation between sprawl and traffic fatalities. In the most spread out, low density suburban counties of the U.S., the study found traffic fatalities ten times higher than in more compact counties.[34]

Aside from motorists being injured or killed by other motorists, pedestrians walking in urban sprawl communities are more likely to be

Figure 2.1 Freeway and Feeder Road Designs Contribute to Higher Traffic Accident Rates
Source: Photo by Lawrence A. Herzog

hurt or to die in car accidents than in non-sprawl communities. The higher accident rates in suburbs are attributed to road design features that apparently increase the risk of motorist accidents. Those features include: multiple lanes at high speeds, no sidewalks, long distances between intersections (which allow drivers in cars to speed up too much), and roadways lined with multiple large scale commercial facilities or residential complexes.[35] As an example, the rates of auto-induced deaths to pedestrians are far lower in New York City (2.2/100,000 inhabitants), Chicago (2.5), and Philadelphia (2.5) than they are in more sprawling urban regions like Dallas (3.0), Phoenix (4.), and Tampa (6.6).[36]

Interestingly, most families who move to suburbs do so because they view them as safer for their children. Parents especially fear that inner city neighborhoods have higher crime rates, including homicides. This idea was challenged in a study done by the University of Virginia. The study looked at the risk of dying in fifteen metropolitan areas over a fifteen year period, focusing on two causes of death: traffic accidents and being murdered by a stranger. It found that the risk of traffic fatality was highest in the counties in the U.S. with the greatest sprawl (using population density as an indicator). For each metropolitan area in the study, the risk of dying in a traffic accident in the suburbs was far greater than the risk of being murdered by a stranger in the central city.[37]

Americans now spend, on average, about fifteen hours per week in their cars (over two hours per day). One might suggest that driving mostly alone in an automobile makes people more self-absorbed and less civic. Marshall McLuhan once wrote that: "The car has become . . . an article of dress without which we feel uncertain, unclad, and incomplete."[38]

People not only spend time driving in their cars; they have also begun to live out many functions of their lives within the space of their cars. According to John Nihoff, a professor of gastronomy at the Culinary Institute of America, in the U.S. people are eating, on average, 19 percent of their daily meals in their cars, if you include snacks such as doughnuts. In fact, food-related auto accidents have become so commonplace that one Michigan-based insurance company compiled a list of the ten most dangerous foods to eat while driving. Drivers are distracted eating items that spill all over their clothes or car. These include fried chicken or barbecued foods, which drip, and jelly and cream filled doughnuts, which squirt.[39] The automobile can be like a "second home." Activities like eating, entertainment, putting on makeup, or doing office work are now considered part of life inside the automobile. Observing that texting, listening to expensive sound systems, and even watching TV are done in the car, one writer commented that "the car of the future is not so much a car as a mobile pleasure dome. And the driver of the future, with both hands free to ensure minimal cappuccino spillage, is hardly a driver at all."[40]

If the automobile is a self-enclosed extension of the home, social and environmental psychologists hypothesize that it may also be an extension of the self, and the ego. With city dwellers spending more and more time in their cars, especially those who live in suburbs, there is more time than ever for stress and other psychological illnesses to impact automobile driver behaviors. This has come to light in studies of "road rage." Experts on the psychology of rage have identified a continuum of behaviors. These range from simple frustration to expressions of rage that gradually become more violent. "Road annoyance" is defined as having negative thoughts towards another driver or verbalizing the negativity, for example by muttering, in a manner that is not communicated to the other driver. These actions are considered within the bounds of normal behavior by experts. "Aggressive driving"—speeding, weaving in and out of traffic, and deliberately disregarding traffic control signals such as red lights—crosses the line into unhealthy behavior. The aggressive driver may or may not be angry at others, but this conduct is obviously selfish, because it potentially endangers the safety of others. "Road rage" unfolds when someone acts in a way that triggers a highly dangerous response from another driver, for example pulling up alongside another motorist and making an obscene gesture. These more extreme behaviors—hostile stares, yelling, obscene gestures, pressing the horn, flicking headlights up and down, spitting, throwing objects, or retaliation by cutting off or tailgating—have even come to include felonious acts such as brandishing or actually firing a gun, ramming a vehicle as a weapon, and stalking with the intention of causing physical harm. One of the definitive national studies on road rage found that in more than half of a sample of over 500 road rage incidents the behaviors approached that of a psychological disorder.[41]

In the end, road rage may be one unfortunately unhealthy mechanism for acting out the anxieties and stress of driving in increasingly congested urban settings. It is known, for example, that some drivers develop a competitive attitude toward other drivers' performances, and then act out feelings of either superiority or insecurity. Drivers may use motoring in their car as a way to enhance their self-esteem—where they act out their need to take more risks than others or to criticize or harass those they consider to be inferior drivers.[42]

Sprawl and Obesity

One of the critical public health crises of our time is obesity. Over one-third of all adults on the planet, some 1.46 billion people, are reported to be obese or overweight. These numbers continue to grow steadily, in both wealthy nations and developing ones. According to one source, between 1980 and 2008, the number of obese or overweight adults in developing nations (in Africa, Asia, Latin America) rose from 250 million to 904 million, or more than a factor of 3.0; during that same period, the growth among high income nations increased by a factor of 1.7.[43] International development experts see a direct connection between obesity and disease: "Obesity, together with excessive consumption of fat and salt, is linked to rising global incidence of non-communicable disease including some cancers, diabetes, heart disease and stroke."[44]

Obesity is now considered a national health crisis in the United States. Excess weight and inadequate rates of exercise account for over 300,000 American deaths per year. This is second only to tobacco as a major killer in the U.S. By 2005, the U.S. government recognized that obesity was one of the most dangerous diseases in the country. Of nearly 120 million adults in the U.S., about 64.5 percent are overweight, and almost one-third (30.5 percent) are obese. The condition and the illnesses it produces are costing the nation an estimated $117 billion per year in direct medical costs and lost productivity.[45] Until very recently, Americans have been slow to confront the ways in which our culture and built environment are part of this crisis. While some forms of obesity are genetic, there is evidence that a significant percentage of obese people have become that way simply due to a lifestyle of overindulgence combined with a lack of physical activity.

As more adults and children become overweight, type 2 diabetes has evolved into one of the fastest growing diseases in the United States. At its present growth rate, the first quarter of the twenty-first century will witness a doubling of the number of individuals suffering from diabetes—to 300 million worldwide. In the United States alone, diabetes is the fifth leading cause of death. Particularly alarming is the rate of obesity increase among children, and the corresponding astronomical rise of type 2 diabetes among young children and adolescents, a growth rate of 5 percent per year since 1990. "It is disconcerting that childhood type 2 diabetes is a direct result of our society's long-term disregard for adequate nutrition, exercise and the problem of childhood obesity," comments one medical expert on the subject.[46]

Across the border in Mexico, diabetes is the leading cause of death. More than 71 percent of Mexican women and 66 percent of Mexican men are overweight, according to the latest national surveys. The health consequences of obesity include increased rates of diabetes, high blood pressure, and heart disease. A recent study showed that a quarter of Mexican children aged five to eleven are too heavy, a 40 percent increase since 2000. The Mexican Diabetes Federation estimates that 6.5 million to 10 million Mexicans have diabetes. Experts recognize that obesity and diabetes are fueled by the rising popularity of soft drinks and fast food restaurants.[47] Mexico, like many developing nations, imports not only U.S. products, but also the larger consumerist culture that accompanies those products.[48] It then imports the public health implications of those consumerist values.

The dramatic explosion of diabetes is considered to be caused by three factors—an aging population, a sedentary Western lifestyle, and rising obesity. A 2006 report by the Surgeon General of the U.S. linked physical inactivity to many killer diseases in the U.S.—diabetes being one of the most important (along with hypertension, colon cancer, arthritis, and coronary heart disease).[49] Yet, despite this fact, the report stated that 74 percent of adults in the U.S. do not get enough physical activity to meet public health standards. Further, one out of four adults is entirely inactive during their leisure time.

After decades of being ignored, however, in the late 1990s the problem of obesity, physical inactivity, and poor diet finally began to receive

Figure 2.2 Obesity Is a Global Phenomenon: Advertisement for Weight Reduction Surgery in Brazil
Source: Photo by Lawrence A. Herzog

more attention. Obesity, poor eating habits, and their projected threats to public health started to seep into the mainstream discourse in America; obesity joined such known killers as smoking and drug use. One media event that gave the public a jolt was Morgan Spurlock's 2004 film *Supersize Me*, which documented the ills of fast food consumption. In the film, Spurlock subsisted for one month entirely on food and items purchased only at McDonald's. He documented the fast food diet impacts on his physical and psychological well-being, while commenting on the fast food industry's corporate influence. He argued that fast food corporations essentially encourage poor nutrition for their own profit.

During the filming, Spurlock ate at McDonald's restaurants three times per day, sampling every item on the chain's menu at least once. He "super-sized" his meal every time he was asked. He consumed an average of 5,000 kcal (the equivalent of 9.26 Big Macs) per day during the experiment. After one month of following this extreme fast food diet, the film's protagonist (he was also the producer, director, and screen writer) suffered from serious weight gain, heart palpitations, and depression. His doctors were shocked at the deterioration in his health and worried that he may have done, in only thirty days, serious damage to his liver; had he kept up the diet and lifestyle, he would have been in serious medical danger.

A few years earlier journalist Eric Schlosser's acclaimed *Fast Food Nation* showed how the evolution of fast food in the U.S. contributed to a national public health tragedy. While it did not prove scientifically that there is a relationship between a nation's fast food consumption and its rate of obesity, it hinted at the connection. The book shows that regions in the U.S. where fast food chains experienced the highest rates of expansion are the same regions where rates of obesity have been rising.[50] Many of the counties with the highest obesity rates are suburban counties.

Obesity and overconsumption are strongly linked to the character and form of America's built environment, to its dispersed suburbs and exurban communities. Americans use automobiles for 90 percent of all urban trips, no matter what the distance. We walk or bike in our cities only 6 percent of the time. By comparison, Italians walk or bike 54 percent of the time, while Swedes do so 40 percent of the time.[51] These striking patterns pointed to a need for an analysis of the possible correlation between obesity, public health, and the quality of life in cities. In 2003, a team of doctors, scientists, and public health officials carried out the most comprehensive study to date on the public health impacts of automobile-dependent urban sprawl. Studying a sample of over 200,000 adults in 448 U.S. counties and 83 metropolitan areas, the research team put together a "metropolitan sprawl index," based on twenty-two land use and street variables including residential density, land use mix, and centrality. This index was then statistically co-mingled with the adult sample data sets on obesity and physical exercise. The results showed a clear pattern of excess weight, lack of physical exercise, and higher levels of hypertension and obesity skewed significantly toward the highest "sprawl counties" in the nation.[52] Conversely, higher density, "low sprawl" zones in inner city communities had significantly lower measures of obesity and poor health. The authors concluded that urban form (sprawl) has a critical impact on physical activity, and thus on health outcomes.[53] As an illustration of this pattern, the "Inland Empire" region of southern California, one of the fastest growing suburbs in America during the 1990s and early 2000s, has one of the highest obesity rates in the nation. According to a report by the Centers for Disease Control and Prevention in 2006, 33.1 percent of people in the Greater San Bernardino Area were overweight, and 30.8 percent were obese. *Forbes Magazine* ranked the area as the "fourth fattest" in the country.[54]

These urban sprawl findings are supported by national trends. For example, 70 percent of American adults have reported that they walked or rode their bicycles to school in their childhood, while only 10 percent of their children walk to school today. According to children in recent surveys, the main reasons for not walking or riding the bike to school are: a) school is too far away (66 percent of surveyed homes listed this as the number one reason); b) there is too much traffic or it is not safe to walk (17 percent reported this); c) it is not convenient (15 percent); d) children

Figure 2.3 Dependence on Automobiles in the American Suburb Contributes to Less Physical Activity and Higher Rates of Obesity

Source: Photo by Lawrence A. Herzog

don't want to walk (6 percent). In short, we have created a built environment that discourages walking.[55] In 2005, a Congressional Briefing on this issue was commissioned by the National Institute of Environmental Health Sciences. The study begins by observing: "Improvements in land use and community design could help moderate many of the chronic diseases of the 21st century—high blood pressure, obesity and asthma—by providing transportation options that increase physical activity and reduce air pollution." The report then states that "those living in the most sprawling areas are likely to weigh 6 more pounds than those living in the least sprawling areas."

The authors of the briefing propose a comprehensive list of policy changes that could counter the health problems embedded in the morphology of suburban sprawl—among those are some familiar urban planning recipes: building at higher densities, encouraging mixed land use and "transit-oriented" projects, creating stronger city centers and gathering spaces, making streets safer for walking, adding bicycle lanes, pedestrian facilities, and safer routes to schools.[56]

Figure 2.4 Social Scientists Report a Connection between Urban Sprawl, Obesity, and Poor Health in the U.S.

Source: Photo by Lawrence A. Herzog

Oversized Bodies and Super-sized Urban Space

The obesity pattern in the United States is part of a larger trend that can be termed "super-sizing." Americans are known for having a voracious appetite for larger and larger homes on generous parcels of land. For the last three decades we also began driving bigger vehicles and shopping in warehouse sized "big box" stores, while our suburbs continued to spread out into super-sized urban regions. According to the Global Footprint Network, the average national per capita ecological footprint worldwide is 2.6 hectares; the United States, however, consumes a startling 9.0 hectares per person, giving us the distinction of having one of the largest footprints on the planet. By comparison, France averages 4.6 hectares, Japan 4.1, and Mexico 1.9.[57] In the U.S. we no longer reside in "cities"; it would be more accurate to say that we live in mega-regions whose scale begets a cultural model built around "bigness."

Our super-sizing behaviors cover the full range of what we consume—land, housing, cars, and personal consumer goods. The average size of a new single family home in the U.S. has doubled since the 1950s—from 1,100 square feet to 2,340 square feet. One would assume that family size also grew during that period. Not so. Families have actually gotten smaller. During the baby boom (1950s to 1970s) household size was 3.7 members. By the decade of the 2000s, it had shrunk to 2.6.[58]

Meanwhile, we have been driving larger and larger vehicles. In 1985, only 2 percent of new vehicles were classified in the SUV category; fifteen years later, one in four new vehicles purchased were SUVs.[59] Statistically, the number of U.S. private vehicles considered to be "light trucks" (SUVs, pick ups, mini-vans) represents nearly 50 percent of all passenger vehicles.[60]

Over the last quarter century, we also began super-sizing the places where we buy our consumer goods. In 1980, the U.S. had 5 square feet of retail space per person; today the average is 20 square feet per person. When one compares the U.S. to other nations of the world, the next largest country to the U.S. is Sweden (3.3 sf/person), followed by the United Kingdom (2.5 sf/person), France (2.3 sf/person), and Italy (1.1 sf/person).[61]

Despite the recognition in the last two decades of the ill effects of obesity, poor diet, and lack of exercise, there is a countervailing problem in the U.S. of what might be termed the cultural acceptance of super-sized bodies. America finds itself in an era of abundance and consumerism. The nation has long celebrated its successes in the form of materialism, with advertising slogans such as "big is beautiful" or "more is better." Whether intentional or indirect, such thinking, over time, has been transferred to the American body. Marketing companies and the food industry itself have taken steps to minimize or divert attention, where possible, away from the reality of the obesity epidemic and its connection to the corporate food industry, fast food, and other forms of super-sizing behavior related to our American consumerism.

Simply put, corporate strategy, over the last few decades, evolved toward a goal of getting Americans to eat more.[62] A McDonald's executive introduced the culinary "super-sizing" concept to America. The executive reputedly learned from the experience of movie theaters, where owners in the 1960s faced the challenge of how to get movie-goers to consume more food at their concession stands. Over time, they discovered that most people would not return for "seconds" from the popcorn stands, because psychologically it made them feel like gluttons. However, in their initial purchase, people were willing to buy more popcorn and soda, *as long as it came in a single serving.* Thus was born the Big Mac, Jumbo Fries, and the Big Gulp. From a marketing perspective, McDonald's found the right approach when they concluded that social taboos against gluttony were holding people back. Fast food corporations needed to disguise the gluttony. They thus devised a marketing campaign to "super-size it." The ingenious marketing of the super-sizing idea turned a potential negative into something positive—super-sizing was reinvented as normal, even hip, as an American way of life.

Once this happened, it set off a chain effect. In the last decades of the twentieth century, cheap, abundant, and large food portions began appearing across the nation, in fast food hamburger stands, fried chicken outlets, diners, and chain restaurants. The corporatization and transformation of "super-sizing" into an iconic symbol of the good life in America (and then across the planet) no doubt have contributed to America's metamorphosis into a nation of overweight and obese people. Also, back in the 1970s, federal policy toward food changed. The Nixon administration of that period sought to keep the cost of food down, but it did so by loosening regulations on the food and agriculture industries, and subsidizing farmers. This ended up energizing the emerging fast food industry.[63]

It is striking how our culture has adapted to obesity rather than taking steps to wipe it out. As a nation, we have been slow to come to terms with our obese character, partly because our corporations and giant media outlets have, whether consciously or not, jumped on the super-sizing bandwagon, or else refused to challenge it. For example, at California's Disneyland, the signature "It's a Small World" ride began to break down regularly during the 1990s. In 2007, the Disney Corporation announced that it was temporarily shutting down the ride for a facelift. It reopened the ride in 2009. What it did not publicly acknowledge was that a possible reason the ride had been malfunctioning is that the channel depth, built to manage the average weight of boats in the 1960s, was no longer able to handle the average weights of Americans five decades later. In two places where the boat channel turned sharply, overweight people in the boat would cause it to get stuck, thus forcing operators to temporarily shut down the entire ride. While Disney employees were trained to guide people toward boats to distribute weight, they simply could not keep the burgeoning masses of overweight people out of enough boats to ensure their normal flow.[64] The average weight of an American in 1960, when the ride was built, was 166 lbs; in 2002, the average weight was 191 lbs. While it's true the ride needed to be renovated anyway, Disney apparently refused to admit publicly that overweight visitors were a major cause of the ride breakdowns. Ironically, even its own employees are now overweight; it has been reported that Disney has redesigned its costumes for more obese workers.[65]

This corporate refusal to admit to the culture's obese and overweight patterns shows up across many sectors of the U.S. economy. In the clothing industry, it is a well known fact that companies have changed sizes to

Figure 2.5 Overweight Americans Reportedly Caused Ongoing Malfunctions of the "It's a Small World" Ride at Disneyland; It Was Remodeled in 2009
Source: Photo by Lawrence A. Herzog

make heavy people appear smaller. For example, a woman's size 14 in the 1950s is a size 10 today. Airlines have quietly rebuilt interiors to include larger seats for overweight passengers. They have also had to increase weight allowances to carry the overall heavier passenger load on each flight. For example, the average passenger in 2007 weighed 21 lbs more than the average passenger in 1995. Airlines spend some $275 million/ year on burning 350 million more gallons of fuel to move increasingly large Americans and others around the globe. The environmental impact is such that an additional 38 million tons of carbon dioxide are now released into the air every year, just to provide the additional energy to move planes through the skies with larger people, according to the U.S. Center for Disease Control and Prevention.[66]

The cultural acceptance of being overweight, combined with its corporate management, are striking features of the obesity crisis in America.

They suggest a nation in denial, and a private sector willing to go to any length to construct a denial disguised in an acceptable and attractive form. Indeed, the food industry must also be singled out for its role in creating larger and larger portions for consumers in restaurants, supermarkets, and take-out food outlets. Muffins, to cite just one example, are now 33 percent larger than recommended by the USDA. Pasta portions served in restaurants are 48 percent larger than recommended.[67]

The list goes on. A "medium" sized popcorn today consists of 16 cups of popcorn, or over 1,000 calories. Package size has an impact on what we consume. Clearly, we are being given too many oversized packages. When continually bombarded with oversizing, many people simply become accustomed to that kind of packaging and soon consider it the norm, even if, in reality, super-sizing and overeating are profoundly unhealthy and can lead to deadly disease. In one scientific study on eating, it was shown that physiological "satiety cues" (how much human bodies really need food) are often overridden by "food cues" (larger portions and ready availability). We are thus fooled into super-sizing, fooled into overconsuming, and possibly even fooled into believing there may be healthy qualities to what is essentially unhealthy food.[68]

While portion sizes have been inflated, there has also been a steady explosion of places where one can find food in American cities today—shopping malls, movie theaters, airports, gas stations, big box stores, sports arenas, stadia, and amusement parks. We are a nation well stocked with oversized candy bars, all you can eat buffets, and super-sized fast food outlets. Government and private firms should be working together on a larger scale to craft policies to overcome obesity and diabetes. This could include taxes on junk food, regulating portion sizes, better labeling, and controlling what is sold in public schools. Yet, in 2012, when New York City Mayor Bloomberg's administration floated the idea of banning giant soft drinks in restaurants, movie theaters, and street vendor carts, critics accused the city government of infringing on personal freedoms, and a media frenzy ensued.[69] While policy changes end up being very slow to evolve, marketing firms selling items to obese people continue to take steps to disguise the physical condition of the very people they are marketing to. For example, in 2007, the nation's largest chain of men's plus-sized clothing—Casual Male Big and Tall—changed its name to Casual Male XL. According to sources, the company decided to drop the use of the word "big" because they thought it was seen as a code word for "fat." Casual Male also reportedly purchased a Vancouver-based catalogue called "Supersize World.com," and launched an online catalogue that celebrates products for the growing population of oversized people. The catalogue includes giant lawn chairs that claim to "support 800 lbs" (they sell for $139.95) and a Big John toilet seat with a 1,200 lb capacity that sells for $124.95.[70]

Mental Health and the Decline of "Social Capital" in American Suburbs

There are a number of ways in which suburban sprawl negatively impacts mental health, and contributes to depression, anxiety, and attention deficit disorder. For example, as discussed above, sprawl typically leads to a lack of physical activity. A sedentary lifestyle can, in turn, be a trigger for depression. Suburbs spread people out and sometimes contribute to feelings of social isolation, and to lost opportunities for social interaction.[71] Arguments are also made that the increasingly private worlds of suburbs lead to a loss of the advantages of traditional community life.[72]

Mental health problems and loss of social capital are one of the more difficult ecological problems to document, since their patterns are more subtle and indirect. Author Robert Putnam's work has provided some important insights on this issue. Putnam described an America where we are "bowling alone," where we belong to fewer social organizations, know our neighbors less than ever before in U.S. history, and socialize with friends less often.[73] His work distinguishes between two levels of trust: "thick" trust and "thin" trust. "Thick" trust refers to personal relations and strong connections to one's community and extended networks of friends. "Thin" trust speaks more to politeness and the general sense of trust one experiences among strangers. Putnam sees a loosening of both forms of trust, leading to a decline in the benefits that traditionally accrued from social interaction in U.S. cities. This loss is further exacerbated by changing technology (computer, TV, smart phone, social media), which replaces face-to-face encounters. As one observer notes: "Sprawl has sliced through the moorings that traditionally connected Americans to each other, and has set adrift those values that extend beyond the self."[74]

Researchers point out that suburbia's overall lack of a sense of place may also contribute to inhabitants' isolation.[75] Suburbs are not even the safe refuges they were once thought to be. As suburbs grew, the social problems of inner cities began to migrate outward into the inner belt of sprawl. This has caused suburbs to become even more inward looking and isolated from each other, and in some cases engaged in political battles. For example, in suburbs north of New York City and Los Angeles, there have been battles fought over big box stores: where to locate them, who absorbs their environmental costs, and who benefits from the tax revenues.

Are the social costs limited to loss of interaction, or do they extend further to the damage inflicted on children by being raised in places that foster isolation and social alienation? In the words of one journalist: "Increasingly, the newest, largest suburbs are being criticized as landscapes scorched by unthoughtful, repetitious building, where . . . the isolations of larger lots and a car-based culture may lead to disassociation from the reality of contact with other people."[76] Describing a setting like Columbine, the suburban high school and site of the 1999 mass shooting tragedy, outside of Denver, Colorado, Charles Blosten, community services director for nearby Littleton's city planning division commented that:

> Typical of the Denver metro area are the new suburbs, where "downtown" is a four-way intersection with three shopping centers and a condo development . . . Highlands Ranch, Denver's largest suburban development, has its own ZIP code, nothing but rooftops and miles and miles of nothing, it's got to affect people.[77]

A Gallup Poll taken in 1999 showed that 46 percent of suburban teenagers could see a fellow teen turning violent. Just 29 percent of city teens said the same. Child psychologists report that the design of suburban life makes young people feel "left out, ignored and alienated."[78]

A psychologist from a suburb near the Columbine tragedy, Dr. Brian Brody, was reported to have been warning about the hidden dangers in the suburbs for a decade prior to the massacre. His office in Littleton,

Colorado, looks out onto Columbine High. He cited the lack of outlets for teenage energy, coupled with the absence of supervision by too busy adults, as a bad combination. "I think in the suburbs we have tried to give our children everything," Brody reported.

> We've moved further away from the cities trying to get bigger houses, more material things—a safer environment for our kids. And I think parents are running themselves ragged. If it's all structure and buildings without the connection and the teaching kids of self-discipline and the coping skills they need—without that, this all crumbles. The great suburban dream has been shattered.[79]

Teenagers too young to drive feel trapped. What they want are places to gather, to call their own—somewhere other than the mall or school. One mom from outside Atlanta, Georgia, thought she had found the perfect living environment for her children. But, she says: "They became depressed—they were isolated, and basically surrounded by their loneliness."[80]

Figure 2.6 American Suburbs: Could Isolation Contribute to Social Dysfunction?
Source: Photo by Lawrence A. Herzog

Another observer notes that: "In most suburbs, there's not even a decent park, because everyone has a backyard. But older kids never play in the backyard. They'll find even the crummiest piece of park."[81] Typically, the students at Columbine High School went to Southwest Plaza, a two level mall that has video arcades, food courts, and stores, supervised by security guards and closed by 9 P.M. "Like any suburban community, there's not a lot of places to go and hang out," said a resident of Littleton.[82] Of course, not having social outlets cannot be the sole explanation for the decline in social opportunity in suburbs, but it is a contributing factor. Many believe that places like malls are not adequate gathering spaces for teenagers. They typify most suburban communal nodes—commercially and environmentally "controlled spaces." As one architects points out: "They are not places for free expression or hanging out."[83] Shopping malls are, in the end, spaces that are "intensive landscapes of control, privately owned spaces where freedom of speech barely exists, where young people grow up as consumers in a mall instead of as citizens in a democracy."[84]

Psychologists have studied the mental health implications of suburbia and the values of its residents. UCLA professor Peter Whybrow describes the emerging behavioral condition of U.S. consumers as a "mania," where Americans have grown addicted to "acquisitive pleasure-seeking behaviors," a pattern of self-indulgence that is unsatisfying and leads to irritability, confusion and depression.[85] "In our relentless pursuit of happiness," he writes, "we have overshot the target and spawned a manic society with an insatiable appetite for more."[86] Citing troubling increases in the rates of obesity, drug use, and diseases and ailments related to high blood pressure, Whybrow argues that self-restraint is disappearing, replaced by what he calls "a new demand driven environment for ourselves, a Fast New World."[87] Further, he points out, the America of neighborliness, empathy, and social mores that was part of Adam Smith's checks and balances on a society with an open marketplace is disappearing. In its place a different America has evolved, a place where self-interest reigns supreme, corporate greed is the norm, and anxiety-related illnesses continue to grow.[88]

Figure 2.7 Building Spaces to House Consumerism in a Fast World
Source: Photo by Lawrence A. Herzog

The Privatization of the Built Environment

Contemporary American urban culture feeds individuality and a greater emphasis on private space, while de-emphasizing city dwellers' sense of community and civic responsibility. Writer Richard Sennett's seminal work *The Fall of Public Man* (1978) traced the origins of America's shift away from a public culture, showing how the civic model of urban life began to lose its sway. He interprets the decline of "public" or civic man as rooted in the cultural definition of what public and private means to citizens. Ancient Romans had a specific higher social purpose in their privacy—to seek religious transcendence beyond the everyday (public) world. By contrast, Sennett observes, in the contemporary U.S. our privacy merely serves as a time to reflect and search for authentic meaning in our feelings: "We have tried to make the fact of being in private, alone with ourselves and with the family and intimate friends, an end in itself."[89] Yet Sennett, too, concludes that this shift toward individual space has left people feeling empty and unfulfilled.

The social organization and physical layout of the earliest cities were built around civic life. In ancient Rome and Greece, cities were designed with a grand civic space at the epicenter—the *agora* (square) in Greece and the *forum* in Rome. Greeks believed that, in an ideal democratic city-state, the town square (agora) was a place accessible to all, where strangers could mingle, and where politics could unfold in an open manner. "Agora" means assembly in Greek, and is said to derive from the practice of Greek warriors gathering in a circle to express feelings of common concern. Town squares epitomized public life for many centuries after the Greeks and Romans, through the Middle Ages and Renaissance—where they continued to house a variety of civic functions, from the gathering of water to public markets, civil tribunals, intellectual debate, and political speech-making. Being in public was essential to citizens' sense of their own identity; for example, eighteenth century Parisians used the very public "promenade" and modes of dress to act out their social class identity and to negotiate their position in society.[90]

The decline of public life can be traced, in part, to changes in the design of our cities. In the late eighteenth century, public places became more privatized and were designed for privileged groups. For example, elite squares for the rich were often gated. Plazas were built to celebrate royal families or powerful church hierarchies. Public life also moved indoors, to privately owned cafes and pubs, or to more isolated parks that did not foster civic spirit or political gatherings. This gave way to even more privatizing trends later in the nineteenth century; as industrial development increased, people began to reorient their lives toward family and home, moving further away from their civic duties and responsibilities. Physically this can be viewed in the new cafe lifestyle where people became passive observers of the street, rather than active participants in town square politics.

In the twentieth century, the shift from public to private reached its peak—urban citizens had moved out of squares and cafes into the private world of their homes and family spaces. Bolstered by electronic media and printed news publications, the need for oral exchange and information gathering in public places gradually disappeared, along with the sense of defining one's life in both civic and private fashion. "Public man" fell into permanent decline. The physical expression of that decline could be seen in cities with empty plazas and gardens, replaced in America by a new culture of cars, suburbs, and private shopping malls.[91]

Indeed, the quintessential public place of cities—the "street"—took on a pejorative meaning in post-World War II America. Although in Latin America public places were viewed as the "rivers of life" in a city, in America they were called "mean streets." From the 1960s, it became trendy for city governments to look for ways to defend public places, while citizens were busy fortifying their private domains.[92] Americans were losing their hold on the very thing the ancient Greeks had celebrated about the city—the democratic enjoyment of sharing a public square with other strangers. As Sennett laments about contemporary U.S. culture: "The stranger himself is a threatening figure, and few people take great pleasure in that world of strangers, the cosmopolitan city."[93]

The growing shift from the public arena to ourselves, our personal and family identity, along with the increasing importance of therapy, self-help, anti-depressants, and personal consumption, have been accompanied by a host of new personal technologies—smart phones, Blackberries, and iPads—that keep us in our individual cocoons.[94] The American retreat into personal space runs parallel to the growing sense of fear of public places—crime, terrorism, and fear of "mean streets."[95] That fear drove citizens toward privatized and non-public realms such as gated communities, luxury condominiums, and walled spaces. This has been documented in the United States and in other parts of the world.[96] Some 30 percent of all new suburban homes are now gated. The master planned/gated community has become an icon of American cities; it was featured in a 1998 Hollywood film, *The Truman Show*, starring Jim Carrey.

One might argue, however, that Americans still find ways to live public lives in public places; they have just shifted to different venues in suburban communities. The huge role of shopping malls as public spaces has already been mentioned. But, in addition, thousands of American families gather at Little League sports events across America, especially in the suburbs. Even larger crowds regularly attend high school and college sports events in their communities. There are many indoor public spaces that continue to attract Americans—from mega-churches to bars and saloons, although it has been pointed out that the number of neighborhood taverns in the U.S. dropped from about 90 percent of the total that existed in the 1940s to about 30 percent forty years later.[97] Some of this decline has more recently been offset by a surge in new kinds of neighborhood nighttime gathering places, such as wine bars, and taverns and breweries that serve locally made "craft" beers. However, the majority of these are located in urban, rather than suburban, areas.[98] Oldenburg's work in the 1980s argued that the shift to the suburbs had left Americans lacking an informal public life, beyond family, job, and what he called "passive consumerism." He believes the nation's shift toward suburbs has not been accompanied by an evolution of viable "third places," informal locales for "hanging out" such as the cafe in France or the pub in the United Kingdom.[99]

Figure 2.8 Public Space and Local Government Regulations
Source: Photo by Lawrence A. Herzog.

The Rise of Gated Communities

Meanwhile, studies show that Americans are retreating further into private space. The startling proliferation of gated communities in America, according to one study, is exacerbating segregation. Gated neighborhoods exude an illusion of security but may not actually enhance real security, since gated communities are only as good as the security personnel or companies that operate them. In the end, what gated communities really seem to do is serve as "symbols of exclusion" in an increasingly privatized and exclusive American metropolis.[100] By walling themselves off, parents with children, young married couples, "empty nesters," and retirees collectively express a larger national phobia about safety, driven by a subtle fear of a more ethnically diverse America; the gated community reinforces a desire to recapture the close knit, picket-fenced communities of childhoods past. But studies are showing that these communities are no safer than other suburbs, and many who move to gated developments report feeling disheartened by their insularity and restrictive rules.[101]

By the late 1990s, over eight million Americans (6 percent of national total of housing) had sought refuge from perceived crime and other problems of urban living by installing gates and fences to limit access to their communities. A decade later these numbers continue to rise. Some 40 percent of all new homes built in California are inside gated complexes.[102] New towns built on the urban periphery are increasingly gated; in some places entire incorporated cities feature guarded entrances. Not only have new residential developments been putting up walls, but many existing neighborhoods have been installing barricades and gates to seal themselves off. Gated communities physically restrict access so that everyday public spaces are privatized. They differ from apartment buildings with guards or doormen, which exclude public access to the private space of lobbies and hallways. Instead, gated communities exclude people from traditionally public areas like sidewalks and streets. They give the illusion of being a small, independent city, but in reality there are not enough services or activities to keep people inside.

What does gating tell us about American cities? Moving behind walls is yet another illustration of Americans rejecting a more civic life over a neighborhood life that favors the self (or the family). It is also a reaction to the "ecology of fear" that is instilled in Americans both at the urban level, through fear of crime and the streets, and at the national and global level, through the post-9/11 focus on homeland security. There is in addition a sense of wanting to recover control over one's destiny, when confronted with the many layers of real and imagined global threats. The world seems a riskier place to some. As one author notes, commenting on the trend toward working at home: "There's a great deal of retreating into ourselves . . . The only environment I can control completely is my living room."[103] Writer Mike Davis argues that much of Los Angeles' built environment and people's relation to it is defined by fear—fear of difference (a real estate machine that encourages segregation), fear of ecological disaster or dangerous animals, and ultimately fear of each other. Davis goes so far as to envision a future LA he describes as "beyond Blade Runner," where neighborhood geography is defined by a series of concentric rings: a homeless inner core, blue collar crime watch suburbs, affluent gated communities, and, just beyond the urban edge, a gulag of prisons.[104]

Today, technologies increasingly enhance Americans' ability to stay in their homes, away from the public realm, thus reinforcing the idea of a "fortress America." Online supermarkets allow customers to order goods that are then delivered to the home. Online or on-demand movie companies, as well as cable TV firms, allow films to be delivered or sent electronically to the home, thus eclipsing the once public act of going out to the movies. Online chat rooms and social media allow city dwellers to remain at home instead of meeting face-to-face. Many other publicly consumed goods can also be ordered online and delivered—dry cleaning, gourmet food, or books. People seem to want more inside the house what they used to get on the outside. This, in turn, reinforces the increasing privatization of the American city, especially in the periphery.

The patterns I have documented in this chapter—obesity, diabetes, sprawl—not only damage public health; they are tied to a larger problem of eco-disaster in our urban regions. Urban sprawl can make wildfires worse, increase the toxicity of the air, and use up scarce water.[105] This problem is central to my critique in this book. In the next chapter, I focus this critique on three specific examples of metropolitan areas at the interface between the U.S. and Latin America—the southwest U.S. border region—to illustrate some of the specific ecological problems of urban sprawl today.

Notes

1 Throughout this book, I speak of the 1950s "American suburb," as opposed to "suburbs" in general. European suburbs evolved much earlier; in fact, historians trace the first suburbs to the late eighteenth and early nineteenth centuries in the United Kingdom. See, for example, Robert Fishman, *Bourgeois Utopias: The Rise and Fall of Suburbia.* New York: Basic Books, 1982.

2 Robert Hughes, *The Shock of the New.* New York: McGraw Hill, 1980, 209.

3 Kenneth Jackson, *Crabgrass Frontier.* New York: Oxford University Press, 1985.

4 Kevin Kruse and Thomas Sugrue, *The New Suburban History.* Chicago, IL: University of Chicago Press, 2006; John R. Short, B. Hanson, and Thomas Vicino, "The Decline of Inner Suburbs: The New Suburban Gothic in the U.S." *Geography Compass*, 1 (3), 2007, 641.

5 Two examples of early suburban design experiments that emphasized beauty and nature would be Llewellyn Park (outside New York City in the state of New Jersey) and the village of Riverside (outside Chicago); the latter was designed by Frederick Law Olmsted.

6 Thomas Jefferson, a rural landholder from Virginia, was the most outspoken proponent of the idea of "anti-urbanism."

7 Jackson, 1985.

8 Mike Davis writes about the steel city of Fontana, on the outskirts of Los Angeles, which fostered worker solidarity until the city incorporated in 1952, leaving the factory outside the city limits. See Mike Davis, *City of Quartz.* New York: Verso, 1990.

9 Dolores Hayden, *A Field Guide to Sprawl.* New York: Norton & Co., 2004, 8.

10 Writer James Howard Kunstler points out these distinctions in a book review; see J.H. Kunstler, "Review of Sprawl: A Compact History," in *Salmagundi Magazine*, Skidmore College, no. 152, Fall 2006.

11 Wendell Cox, "The Crusade against Urban Sprawl: Assaulting the American Dream," *Demographia*, February, 1999, www.demographia.com.

12 James Howard Kunstler, "Sprawl," *Salmagundi Magazine*, no. 152, Fall 2006.

13 Joel Kotkin, "Rule Suburbia: The Verdict in, We Love It There," *Washington Post*, February 6, 2005.

14 See Robert Bruegmann, *Sprawl: A Compact History.* Chicago, IL: University of Chicago Press, 2005.

15 Alex Krieger, "Review of *Sprawl: A Compact History*," *Harvard Design Magazine*, Fall 2006/Winter 2007.

16 Andres Duany, Elizabeth Plater-Zyberk, and Jeff Speck, *Suburban Nation: The Rise of Sprawl and the Decline of the American Dream.* New York: North Point Press, 2000, 14.

17 The following sections draw heavily from the most comprehensive study on the subject; see Howard Frumkin, Lawrence Frank, and Richard Jackson, *Urban Sprawl and Public Health.* Washington, D.C.: Island Press, 2004. This fine work serves as a kind of handbook on the problems of contemporary urban sprawl in North America.

18 Frumkin et al., 2004.

19 Ibid., 10. It should be noted that income, household size, and personal preference also impact the number of miles households drive each day, though these variables do not impact miles travelled differently in suburbs vs. inner city neighborhoods.

20 R. Cervero and R. Graham, "Commuting in Transit versus Automobile Neighborhoods," *Journal of the American Planning Association*, 61, 1995, 210–25.

21 R. Cervero, "Mixed Land Use and Commuting: Evidence from the American Housing Survey," *Transportation Research Part A*, 30 (5), 1996, 361–77.

22 Frumkin et al., 2004.

23 Ibid.

24 Brian Stone, "Urban Sprawl and Air Quality in Large U.S. Cities," *Journal of Environmental Management*, 86, 2008, 688–98.

25 It is not always clear where particulate matter (PM) comes from—industry or motor vehicles; however, recent studies in the Netherlands show that three times as much PM comes from motor vehicles as from coal burning (industrial) sources. Lawrence Frank and Peter Engelke, "Multiple Impacts of the Built Environment on Public Health," *International Regional Science Review*, 28 (2), April, 2005, 193–216.

26 Ibid.

27 W.J. Gauderman, R. Melonnel et al., "Association between Air Pollution and Lung Function Growth in Southern California Children," *American Journal of Respiratory and Critical Care Medicine*, 162 (4), 2000, 1383–90, cited in Howard Frunk, Lawrence Frank, and Richard Jackson, *Urban Sprawl and Public Health*. Washington, D.C.: Island Press, 2004.

28 Frumkin et al., 2004, 110.

29 Ibid., 111.

30 See, for example, J.M. Violanti, "Cellular Phones and Traffic Accidents," *Public Health*, 111 (6), 1997, 423–8.

31 National Safety Council website. See http://www.nsc.org/Pages/ NSCestimates16millioncrashescausedbydriversusingcellphonesandtexting.aspx, retrieved 3/21/13.

32 See Jeff Bertolucci, "Cell Phone-Related Driving Deaths on the Rise," *PC World*, September 20, 2010, http://www.pcworld.com/article/205795/cell_phone_related_ deaths_on_the_rise_govt_study.html, retrieved 3/1/13.

33 Frumkin et al., 2004, 111.

34 Reid Ewing, R.A. Scheiber, and C.V. Zegeer, "Urban Sprawl as a Risk Factor in Motor Vehicle Occupant and Pedestrian Fatalities," *American Journal of Public Health*, 93 (9), 2003, 1541–5.

35 It should be noted that if more suburban dwellers, for health reasons, begin walking and bicycling more, then even more fatalities will occur unless these street designs are not modified.

36 National Highway Traffic Safety Administration, *Traffic Safety Facts 2001: A Compilation of Motor Vehicle Crash Data*. Washington, D.C., 2002. It should be noted there are a couple of statistical exceptions—sprawling Los Angeles had a lower fatality rate (2.6), while more compact San Francisco had a higher rate (3.8).

37 W.H. Lucy, "Mortality Risk Associated with Leaving Home: Recognizing the Relevance of the Built Environment," *American Journal of Public Health*, 93 (9), 2003, 1564–9.

38 Marshall McLuhan, *Understanding Media*. New York: McGraw Hill, 1964.

39 Liane George, "North Americans and Their Cars," *MacLeans Magazine*, February 27, 2006.

40 Ibid.
41 See U.S. House of Representatives Hearing, "Road Rage: Causes and Dangers of Aggressive Driving," July 17, 1997, Washington, D.C.
42 Ibid.
43 Overseas Development Institute, leading UK think tank on international development issues; see http://www.odi.org.uk/future-diets, retrieved 1/09/14.
44 http://www.odi.org.uk/sites/odi.org.uk/files/odi-assets/publications-opinion-files/8773.pdf.
45 Trust for America's Health, *F as in Fat*, Washington, D.C., 2005.
46 Jose F. Cara, M.D., "Type 2 Diabetes in Children—A Concern about a Growing Threat," *American Academy of Pediatrics*, 1999, cited at www.medscape.com.
47 Franco Ordonez, "Mexico Is Second-Fattest Nation after U.S.," *San Diego Union Tribune*, March 24, 2008.
48 Also, since 1990, Mexico has imported the U.S. model of suburban development—see Chapter 5 of this book.
49 U.S. Surgeon General, *Physical Activity and Health*. Washington, D.C.: U.S. Department of Health and Human Services, 2006.
50 Eric Schlosser, *Fast Food Nation*. New York: Harper, 2005.
51 Trust for America's Health, 2005.
52 One study, however, argues that the suburb/obesity link might also be partly caused by obese people choosing to live in suburbs so they can avoid walking. See Andrew Plantinga and Stephanie Bernell, "The Association between Urban Sprawl and Obesity," *Journal of Regional Science*, 47 (5), (2007), 857–79.
53 Reid Ewing, Tom Schmid, Richard Killingsworth, Amy Zlot, and Stephen Raudenbush, "Relationship between Urban Sprawl and Physical Activity, Obesity and Morbidity," *American Journal of Health Promotion*, 8 (1), September–October, 2003, 47–57.
54 Andrew Edwards (November 29, 2007), "I.E. Sees Heavy Growth—in Fatness," *San Bernardino County Sun*, http://www.sbsun.com/search/ci_7585339.
55 Surface Transportation Policy Project, *American Attitudes toward Walking and Creating More Walkable Communities*, 2002.
56 Naomi Friedman and Ray Minjares, "The Public Health Effects of Sprawl," *Congressional Briefing Summary*, Washington, D.C.: Environmental and Energy Study Institute, 2005. See also R.C. Brownson, C.M. Hoehner, K. Day, A. Forsyth, and J.F. Sallis, "Measuring the Built Environment for Physical Activity," *American Journal of Preventive Medicine*, 36 (4), 2009, S99–S123.
57 One hectare equals about 2.5 acres. See Global Footprint Network at http://www.footprintnetwork.org.
58 Alex Wilson and Jessica Boehland, "Small Is Beautiful: U.S. House Size, Resource Use and the Environment," *Journal of Industrial Ecology*, Winter/Spring, 2005, http://www.greenbiz.com/news/2005/07/12/small-beautiful-us-house-size-resource-use-and-environment.
59 U.S. Bureau of Transportation Statistics, U.S. Department of Transportation, 2006.
60 As oil prices have steadily inched up, however, there is evidence that smaller and more efficient cars are now being considered by many Americans. For example, by 2011 the small car market had risen to over 17 percent of the U.S. market. See Doron Levin, "Why Small Cars Are Actually Selling Now," CNN Money, August 4, 2011, http://tech.fortune.cnn.com/2011/08/04/why-small-cars-are-actually-selling-now/. But it will take some time to undo the dominance that larger vehicles and light trucks have held in the U.S. market for several decades.

61 James Howard Kunstler blog commentary, June 25, 2007, http://www.kunstler.com/mags_diary21.html.

62 Greg Critser, *Fat Land*. New York: Houghton Mifflin, 2003.

63 Ibid.

64 Meg Marco, "Obesity: We're Too Big for Disneyland's It's a Small World," *Consumerist*, October 29, 2007, http://consumerist.com/2007/10/29/obesity-were-too-big-for-disneylands-its-a-small-world/, retrieved on 4/8/13.

65 "It's a Larger World after All," www.miceage.micechat.com/allutz/al100907c.htm.

66 Daniel Yee, "Big Bottoms Crushing Airlines Bottom Lines," *Tucson Citizen*, November 5, 2004.

67 Martha Coventry, "Super-sizing America: Obesity Becomes an Epidemic," University of Minnesota *UNM News*, Winter, 2004.

68 L.R. Young and M. Nestle, "The Contribution of Expanding Portion Sizes to the U.S. Obesity Epidemic," *American Journal of Public Health*, 92, 2002, 246–9.

69 See Michael Grynbaum, "New York Plans to Ban Sale of Big Sizes of Sugary Drinks," *New York Times*, May 30, 2012, http://www.nytimes.com/2012/05/31/nyregion/bloomberg-plans-a-ban-on-large-sugared-drinks.html?pagewanted=all; Martine Geller, "Coke, McDonalds Slam NY City Bid to Ban Big Soda Cups," Reuters, May 31, 2012, http://www.reuters.com/article/2012/05/31/us-usa-sugarban-reaction-idUSBRE84U1BN20120531.

70 Mark Jewel, "Revamped Retailer Steps into Niche for Plus-Sized Items," *Washington Post*, August 25, 2007, F13.

71 One can point to health benefits associated with living in suburban communities. Since the 1950s, residents have left the inner city to relieve the stress of overcrowding, and the hectic pace of the urban core. They also came in search of larger homes with backyards to house larger families with children. Further, the suburbs represented feeling closer to nature—trees, grassy yards, and more open spaces. But "nature" in many suburbs became a somewhat artificial construct—since the original natural elements—hills, canyons, forests—were bulldozed away during construction. The new housing subdivisions were then decorated with artificial grasses, shrubs, and non-native trees.

72 As early as the 1960s, scholars warned of a U.S. culture of "privatism" due to an emphasis on individuals' pursuit of happiness via personal independence and material wealth. See Sam Bass Warner, *The Private City*. Philadelphia: University of Pennsylvania, 1968.

73 Robert Putnam, *Bowling Alone*. New York: Touchstone, 2001.

74 Douglas Morris, *It's a Sprawl World after All*. Canada: New Society Publishers, 2005.

75 James Howard Kunstler, *The Geography of Nowhere*. New York: Touchstone, 1993; Morris, 2005; Jackson, 1985; Duany et al., 2000.

76 William Hamilton, "How Suburban Design Is Failing Teenagers," www.nytimes.com, May 6, 1999.

77 Ibid.

78 John Roberts, "Do Suburbs Create Teen Rage?" *CBS News Reports*, www.cbsnews.com, June 7, 1999.

79 Ibid.

80 Ibid.

81 Peter Lang, professor of architecture at the New Jersey Institute of Technology, quoted in Roberts, 1999.

82 Hamilton, 1999.

83 Lang, quoted in Roberts, 1999.

84   Matt Lassiter, "Apathy, Alienation, and Activism: American Culture and the
     Depoliticization of Youth," Golden Apple Lecture, January 28, 2004, cited on http://
     www.personal.umich.edu/~mlassite/applelecture.html.
85   Peter C. Whybrow, *American Mania: When More Is Not Enough*. New York: W.W.
     Norton, 2005. Whybrow's observations are based on his analysis of patients he saw
     over the years in his own practice in mainly suburban southern California, as well as
     thousands of cases he researched in the psychiatry field.
86   Whybrow, 2005, 4.
87   Ibid., 10
88   Not all consumers come from the suburbs I write about in this book; however, I
     am arguing that the built environment of suburbs, perhaps more than elsewhere, is
     constructed to encourage consumerism.
89   Richard Sennett, *The Fall of Public Man*. New York: Alfred Knopf, 1976, 3.
90   Ibid.
91   The evolution of public space is also described in Lawrence A. Herzog, *Return to the
     Center: Culture, Public Space and City Building in a Global Era*. Austin: University of
     Texas Press, 2006.
92   Mike Davis wrote about this need to create "fortress cities" in the U.S. See Mike
     Davis, *City of Quartz*. New York: Verso, 1990.
93   Sennett, 1976, 3.
94   Indeed, consider the iRony of the use of "i" in many of these new personal
     technologies—iPod, iPhone, iTouch, iPad, etc.
95   See, for example, Davis, 1990; Setha Low and Neil Smith, eds. *The Politics of Public
     Space*. New York: Routledge, 2005.
96   Teresa Caldeira shows the same pattern of fear among middle and upper class
     residents of São Paulo, Brazil. In São Paulo, people find safety by living in heavily
     guarded, luxury high rise condominiums. See Teresa Caldeira, *City of Walls*. Berkeley:
     University of California Press, 2000.
97   Ray Oldenburg, *The Great Good Place*. New York: Marlowe and Co., 1999, 9.
98   Most of the wine bars and taverns/breweries are built around the demographic of
     younger, more footloose city dwellers. For example, in San Diego, only two out of
     the top eight most celebrated wine bars were in suburbs, the rest either downtown or
     in older urban neighborhoods just beyond downtown. See Keli Dailey, "Eight Great
     Wine Bars," *San Diego Union Tribune*, February 26, 2013, http://www.utsandiego.
     com/news/2013/feb/26/best-wine-bars/?print&page=all, retrieved 4/10/13.
99   Oldenburg, 1999.
100 Setha Low, *Behind the Gates: Life, Security and the Pursuit of Happiness in Fortress
     America*. New York: Routledge, 2003.
101 Ibid.
102 John Jay College of Criminal Justice/CUNY, "Gated Enclaves Are Not Just for the
     Well-Heeled," *Law Enforcement News*, May 15, 1997.
103 Marian Salzman, advertising executive and author, quoted in G. Wayne Miller, "No
     Place Like Home," *San Diego Union Tribune*, June 11, 2007, D3.
104 Mike Davis, *The Ecology of Fear*. New York: Vintage, 1999.
105 The problem of water scarcity is particularly acute in the southwestern United States,
     the subject of the next chapter. Recently, experts observed that drought is seriously
     depleting the water supply in the Colorado River, which is the major source of water for
     most of the southwest's large cities, in Texas, Arizona, New Mexico, Utah, and southern
     California. See http://www.nytimes.com/2014/01/06/us/colorado-river-drought-forces-
     a-painful-reckoning-for-states.html?hpw&rref=us&_r=0, retrieved 1/09/14.

3

FAST SUBURBS IN THE
SOUTHWEST BORDERLANDS

In late October of 2007, the San Diego, California, metropolitan region was nearly wiped out by one of the most devastating urban fires in modern U.S. history. Hot, dry "Santa Ana" winds,[1] combined with seasonal drought conditions across southern California, led to the outbreak of two mega-scale wildfires. One fire broke out in the suburban hills of northern San Diego County, the other at the southern edge of the county, near the town of Potrero, just north of the U.S.–Mexico border town of Tecate.

Over the next four days, like two pincers moving closer from each corner of the region, these wildfires roared across San Diego County, scorching a combined 300,000 acres of land and prompting the largest mandatory evacuation in the region's history. One-half million men, women, and children had to pack up and leave. More than a thousand homes were destroyed, and hundreds more damaged. Twelve thousand people were rendered homeless; some ended up sleeping in cots at Qualcomm Stadium, home to the San Diego Chargers football team, which was set up as a temporary evacuation center. Then California Governor Arnold Schwarzenegger flew in and quickly declared a state of emergency. In Washington, D.C., then President George W. Bush ordered federal emergency funds to supplement state and local response efforts. Over 6,000 firefighters came to San Diego and other parts of southern

California to fight the blazes; they were aided by units of the United States Armed Forces, United States National Guard, as well as sixty firefighters from the Mexican cities of Tijuana and Tecate.

Like the rest of California, San Diego had experienced wildfires before, including a huge one only four years earlier. But the 2007 event was different—it was poised to become an ecological catastrophe on a much larger scale, one that might have deeply wounded one of the nation's largest cities. Powerful winds were thrusting the firestorm directly toward the most heavily populated center of the metropolitan area. Thick smoke and ash made it difficult to breathe; residents across a region with over three million inhabitants were advised to stay indoors. At this point, city and county officials began evacuating thousands of citizens in suburban communities along the region's major freeway corridors, mainly to the northeast but also in the southeast suburbs. Of the remaining population spared evacuation, tens of thousands had their bags packed, or valuables stored in their cars, and were ready to flee the region at a moment's notice.

On the Mexican side of the border, more than 15,000 acres of land was burning near the cities of Tecate, Tijuana, and Ensenada. This wildfire was now both a regional and an international emergency, and was spreading south of the border. What most San Diegans and others probably never realized, even to this day, was how close the 2007 wildfire event came to literally destroying a significant portion of the urbanized core of the region. Tens of thousands of homes could easily have been damaged, and many residents might have perished if the winds had continued blowing from the eastern desert back toward the heart of the urban region. But, by chance, on the third day the winds shifted to the south, and later toward the east (a more normal flow, except during fall Santa Ana conditions), slowing the wildfire's path toward the urban core. Once the wind direction changed, it carried more humidity from the Pacific Ocean, giving firefighters a chance to control the crisis.

The wildfire should have been a huge wake-up call about the dangers of San Diego's emerging peripheral settlement pattern, its connection to the natural ecosystem and to the ecology of wildfire. But, to this day, the wake-up call has been largely ignored. This is a region blessed with a Mediterranean climate and physical beauty on the southern end of California's coastline; it has been one of the fastest growing metropolitan areas in the U.S. since the 1970s. Even though land shortages and housing costs have slowed growth considerably in the new millennium, San Diego's population of 3.2 million is expected to increase to 3.5 million by 2020. By 2030, its population will have grown by one million inhabitants since 2000.[2]

Most of this growth will occur in the eastern fringes of the region, in an arc of suburban growth of inland cities and towns—in what San Diegans used to call the "backcountry," and what ecologists now term the "wildland–urban interface" (WUI). This suburban growth pattern has unfolded with far too little attention to the dangerous implications of poorly managed, low density, sprawl type growth in a semi-arid region where wildfires are part of the natural ecological cycle. But the pattern of ignoring nature is symptomatic of a larger growth culture where super-sized metropolitan regions are being constructed over desert terrain and semi-arid regions along the southwestern U.S. border with Mexico. This is the fast urbanism that must be halted.

Disastrous Sprawl

Three salient examples of disastrous "southwest sprawl" are San Diego, Las Vegas, and Phoenix. Between 2000 and 2006, the ten fastest growing metropolitan areas in the U.S. included Las Vegas (29.2 percent increase) and Phoenix-Mesa-Scottsdale (24.2 percent),[3] and San Diego was not far behind, especially if one measured only the growth of its inland fast suburbs, which expanded at rates similar to Las Vegas and Phoenix.[4] These mega-urban regions typify the boom of cities in the warmer latitude "sunbelt" states within the southwest border region—Texas, Arizona, California, Nevada, and New Mexico. Vast metropolitan regions have spread across these open lands in states on or near the border with Mexico.

What these regions have in common is rapid growth that occurred in the last four decades of the twentieth century and in a distinctly dispersed suburban pattern. That growth continues. More than cities on the east coast, the "sunbelt" cities of the southwest grew much later, and thus a greater proportion of their total metropolitan population resides in the low density spaces on the urban periphery, with auto-dependent, isolated, mostly single family or semi-attached condominium housing developments and master planned communities. All three cities also share the common attribute of limited public transit or other alternative forms of circulation.[5] Until very recently, most of the peripheral urban growth in these three cities lacked the kind of higher density, mixed use development with dynamic activity centers and walkable public places that is the hallmark of "new urbanism."

Las Vegas grew so fast that it now covers 39,719 square miles, rendering it nearly three times as large physically as the New York-New Jersey-Long Island metropolitan area, and about the same size as one of the first U.S. sprawl regions—Los Angeles-Riverside-San Bernardino. The Phoenix region covers almost half of the land area of Los Angeles, while its population is only one-fourth the size of L.A. These regions also share a common physical geography: scarce and expensive access to water due to arid and semi-arid ecosystems that are increasingly vulnerable to the ecology of wildfires.

Wildfires, Suburbs and the San Diego Region

Wildfire ecology is no longer an occasional natural hazard in America's largest U.S.—Mexico border metropolis, San Diego, California. It is a permanent part of the regional landscape, as the mega-scale wildfires of 2003 and 2007 made clear. In an era of global warming and climate change, attention to inland suburban ecology in semi-arid lands must become a priority, especially given the acceleration of urban growth here. The inland region of this part of North America sits in a shifting ecosystem of "chaparral" draping the hilly topography, leading toward the mountains, a warm semi-arid climate between the cool foggy coast and the hot desert. The very limited supply of land along the coast for development, especially within the city of San Diego, has added to the pressure to build inland. This trend has been further exacerbated by greater home buyer interest in larger homes on larger lots, only affordable in southern California by moving away from the coast. Many of the towns that are booming in the WUI were once rural villages.

The wildland–urban interface (WUI) is where most of the new growth in the San Diego region has unfolded—suburbanization literally within the zone of cyclical, but predictable wildfire. Between 2010 and 2030, the cities projected to experience the largest amount of growth in San Diego County mainly fall within this region.[6] Most of the predicted growth of the last vacant parcels of land within the city of San Diego will be also along the edges of the wildland–urban interface zone.[7] And it must not be forgotten that the stakes for protecting this zone are high, since it is here that an estimated three million acres of land were scorched by fire and nearly 10,000 homes were destroyed in 2003 and 2007.[8]

Wildfires in both 2003 and 2007 swept through rural towns, burned semi-rural inland suburbs, and then spread across inland master planned communities. The wildfire pattern was almost as unpredictable as the fragmented layout of suburban development across San Diego's periphery, which has continued to expand toward the east and north. Three out of four homes built in San Diego since 1990 lie in the wildland danger zone that lies between the coastal foothills and the mountains further inland. As one writer has commented: "through the foothills, free range McMansions often castellated in unconscious self-caricature occupy rugged ocean view decks surrounded by what foresters grimly refer to as 'diesel stands' of dying pine and old brush."[9]

The loss of agricultural foliage has been put forward as a partial ecological explanation of the sudden wildfire crisis in San Diego and southern California in the last decade. In the past, orange, lemon, and avocado groves served as firebreaks for the seasonal wild conflagrations. But even more critically, global warming poses greater problems: rising temperatures and decreasing rainfall create the perfect conditions for larger scale wildfires than normal. The natural ecology of wildfires has been disturbed; as a result, wildfires in a globally warmer San Diego interior burn hotter and spread faster. Higher and higher temperatures combined with the dry, hot winds of seasonal Santa Ana conditions are producing a landscape that is riper than ever before for more devastating wildfire conflagrations.

Yet perhaps the least noted element of changing wildfire ecology lies in the flammable nature of fast urbanism in the southwestern United

States. Sprawling, mass produced suburban developments have been built quickly and are poorly adapted to the dry ecology and wildfire tendencies of the U.S. southwest. Both the scale and form of cookie cutter suburbs work against wildfire safety. Wildfires burn intensely and are driven by high winds that make them spread in unpredictable ways. When you build tens of thousands of homes and disperse them at consistent densities along the edges of cliffs precisely where the fires arrive when winds blow from the east, you are creating the ingredients and fuel for much larger scale wildfires, and much more extensive damage.

Politics, Lifestyles and Inland Wildfires

Natural disasters like wildfires challenge us to rethink our lifestyles. They remind us of the boundless power of the earth, the heavens, the wind and rain. They renew our connection to the ecological cycles of this planet. But we live mostly cocooned from nature. Our automobiles cushion us from the spaces we pass through as we zoom from one part of the region to another. Our homes block out nature. Inside them we make a beeline for our machines—television, DVD player, computer—and blast off into channel surfing, cyberspace utopia. The natural world outside disappears. We take all this for granted.

The reactions of many San Diegans to the October 2003 firestorm exposed some of the contradictions in what writer Mike Davis later called "stupid urbanization that conspired to create the ingredients for one of the most perfect firestorms in California history."[10] In 2002, the year before this wildfire, election data showed that most residents of the inland suburbs hit hardest by the fire voted for the recall of then-California governor Gray Davis, a Democrat, because they stood "against the oppression of an out-of-control public sector." In general, the biggest supporters of Proposition 13 and every other attempt to downsize California government have been upper middle class suburbanites in southern California. And yet, on the day the Crest fire roared down the canyons toward the bastions of suburban sprawl in east and north San Diego County, these same citizens were calling for more helicopters, more firefighting planes, more fire engines. Suddenly, they wanted government to help them.

In Alpine, an inland San Diego suburb hit by the 2003 wildfire, during the second day of the fires a woman called into a local radio talk show complaining that "it was criminal" that her electricity was out and her water pressure low. This same woman also wanted "less government intervention and less taxes." But she expected that firefighters and utility workers would be there immediately when she needed them during a crisis. With huge budget deficits driven by twenty-five years of voting out new taxes, how can inland residents expect California to provide the colossal fire protection it now appears will be needed to protect millions of inland residents from the inevitable Santa Ana-induced fires that come each fall?

An irate resident near the inland suburb of Ramona told a reporter: "Screw the tree huggers. They're a bunch of city people telling us what we can do with the land we pay taxes on."[11] But does paying property taxes actually give landowners the right to do anything they want with their parcels? In fact, the private right to build on land or improve existing structures, whether in the backcountry or in exurban spaces, is not constitutionally guaranteed. For more than a century of decision-making in land use, environment, and property law in the U.S., the courts have sought to provide a balance between the private property rights of individuals and the larger "public interest."[12] For example, the federal government restricts urban development in the floodplains of some regions of the U.S. because, during rainy seasons, it is not in the public interest to endanger the lives of hundreds of thousands of city dwellers who reside in low-lying river valleys. The arid hills and canyons of southern California's backcountry encompass what is now understood to be a fire danger zone; this danger must then be weighed against the rights of developers to build sprawling cul-de-sac suburbs.[13]

To put this in legal terms, the threat of massive wildfires may pose greater harm to the public interest than the private right to build master planned suburban communities. This simple notion of public interest was forgotten during the public debates in the aftermath of the worst fire disasters in San Diego and California history. The loss of more than 2,400 homes and 375,000 acres of natural landscape in San Diego County in 2003 alone should have jolted public officials to reconsider allowing unregulated suburban growth in fire-prone, semi-arid danger areas. Yet by 2007, aside from new brush clearing requirements and the purchase of a few more fire engines or helicopters, the San Diego region did little to craft new design approaches or controls on its land use patterns in the most fire-prone suburbs; nor did it significantly expand local firefighting capabilities. As a result, the damages caused by the 2007 wildfires was even worse than in 2003.

Meanwhile, residents are quick to defend their suburban lifestyle, with little thought to the larger public interest it may compromise. They express outrage at the idea of building at higher densities in existing towns, both back in the urbanized core as well as in the traditional centers in the rural county. In the words of the "tree hugger" critic from the suburb of Ramona: "There are people like me who don't like city life. I say leave people alone, let them live their life without government intervention."[14] It's one thing to reject city life and go live in the wilderness of Alaska. It's another to live in Ramona, a suburban community that lies solidly inside the urbanized region of San Diego. One of the fallacies held by exurban residents is that they should be able to enjoy the benefits of proximity to the city without taking responsibility for being part of its ecological area of influence. They want to exist apart from the public interest. The Ramona resident's response: "We have to live somewhere, and I'm not going to live like a bunch of animals in the high-rises downtown." Instead, residents like this one prefer twenty-first century sprawl.

Geography vs. Architecture

Fire ecologists believe an important factor in the proliferation of wildfires in the San Diego region is the way houses are sited, designed, and built. Most homes lack what is called "defensible space," cleared swaths of land free of flammable vegetation. Not only are too many homes being built in the arc of wildfire country, but developers often completely ignore the natural landscape in creating site plans and community designs. For more than three decades, there has been almost no recognition within the developer community, or even in government, of the risks of wildfires and the fragility of inland southern California's

Figure 3.1 Wildfire Prevention Sign, California
Source: Photo by Lawrence A. Herzog

arid ecosystem. Developers purchase blocks of land, then bring in giant soil moving machines to level off the topography. They then plunk down cul-de-sac type subdivisions on top of the leveled off hills and mesas, whose layout seeks to maximize views of the wilderness, while ignoring ecological design errors such as building on steep slopes or on the eastern facing ridges that directly face into the path of periodic wildfires. The Spanish and Mediterranean style homes look innocent enough, until they lie in the path of a roaring wildfire.

Developers also pay too little attention to the effects of canyons on the spread of wildfires. Canyons are generally regarded as an open space amenity that attracts suburban residential development; the general strategy is to build houses alongside canyons. But when located too close to canyons suburban housing is endangered—because canyons can become wildfire heat funnels during fall "Santa Ana" conditions, when fires start and burn out of control. When housing is constructed up against natural canyons and, even worse, along the edges of cliffs overlooking steep sloping hillsides below, the danger is even more pronounced.

The reason is that the movement of wildfires typically advances up hillsides and is fed by flames that grow stronger as they reach the tops of hills. When houses are sited at the very top of sloped hills (as they often are in southern California suburbs), they become fuel for the fires, are immediately engulfed, and end up feeding the wildfires, and increasing their heat level. This causes them to spread with more power and volume. From a site planning perspective, homes in suburban developments should be located to avoid natural "fire chimneys" like canyons, saddles, and slopes.[15]

Suburban building designs have often fed the wildfires, too. For many decades, suburban homes were built with wooden shingle roofs—these easily ignite when wildfires shoot sparks into the air—and many homes were destroyed because of this. Studies have shown that homes with wooden roofs have a twenty-one times greater chance of burning than a home with a non-wood roof.[16] Homes made of less flammable material—like stone, brick, or concrete block—always withstand wildfires better. Some fire experts note that in nearby Baja California, just south of the Mexican border from southern California, a region with exactly the same ecosystem, considerably less damage has occurred from wildfires. They believe this is attributable to a culture that allows more natural burns than north of the border. But it may also be the case that when wildfires enter urbanized areas, the Mexican homes are generally built from reinforced concrete or prefabricated stone and tile. This slows down the spread of the fires, and limits the extent of destruction.

Rooflines, eave vent reduced overhangs, double-pane windows, non-flammable shutters, and even swimming pools are construction details that can further limit the spread of wildfires in urbanized zones. Even more helpful, as noted above, is the creation of "defensible space" around homes—a green belt of 100 feet where fuel sources (shrubs, trees, grasses) are thinned out around the home to keep the fire from burning hotter, and from entering the home itself, or spreading faster to surrounding homes. However, developers sometimes refer to "defensible space" as the "magic bullet" solution, which they wrongly conclude frees them to build unlimited low density suburbs anywhere. In fact, defensible space designs will only work if combined with better site planning, zoning that prevents precarious and ecologically dangerous developments along canyons and near east facing slopes, and better coordination of local fire-fighting capability with land use and traffic circulation plans.

The Media Miss the Story

Generally in the suburban, fire-prone regions of San Diego's inland suburbs, politicians, developers, local government officials, and the media have responded to the wildfire problem in a surprisingly limited fashion—by focusing mainly on firefighting equipment, tactics of fire fighting such as water drops from airplanes or helicopters, or emergency preparedness. If one examines the media coverage of the southern California wildfires in 2003 and 2007, one theme that dominated media attention was the fact that water drops were limited by visibility or jurisdictional difficulties. Some military planes did not take to the air until trained "spotters" were brought in to accompany them. This issue was continually discussed by local politicians and covered by local newspapers and TV stations.

In 2007, elected officials took pride in making a football stadium the symbol of their overall policy response to the wildfire event. In the midst of the 2007 crisis, politicians gathered at the local football stadium—Qualcomm—in San Diego's Mission Valley. The atmosphere was tense due to the fear that the fire was spreading toward downtown and the coast. High winds and low visibility were hampering air drops on the fire, and damage was said to be worse than in 2003. The public needed to be reassured. Mayors, county supervisors, the governor, and firefighters collectively presented a "military style" policy approach. The wildfire was portrayed as if it were an enemy that needed to be conquered. The language of policy decisions was principally couched in terms of how soon helicopters and air tankers could take to the skies, and where the "wounded" would be evacuated to. The football stadium served to sustain the metaphor of firefighting as a battle between two "teams," government/communities on one side and nature (wildfire) on the other. This inaccurate metaphor allowed government to avoid addressing the larger ecological problem.

As important as it was to manage evacuations and firefighting strategy, local and state officials avoided the theme of wildfire ecology and prevention, both during and in the aftermath of the crisis. Meanwhile, there was non-stop discussion of aerial water drops as a critical need. But, in fact, local fire experts say the importance of aerial drops of water on firefighting is exaggerated.[17] Yet, on the third day of the wildfires, when the helicopters got off the ground, the city's principal newspaper, the *San Diego Union Tribune*, carried the headline "Help from Above: Air Fleet Grows."[18] This was a hopeful message coming after the first two days' headlines that read "Wildfires Rage" and "300,000 Flee Fires."

If elected officials missed the opportunity to address the ecology of wildfires, the media largely failed too. One would think that local journalists would cover other stories and all points of view. But, in San Diego, a media industry strongly oriented toward protecting the regional fast urbanism "growth machine"—developers, politicians, real estate, construction, and other businesses that rely on growth—glossed over the causes of the wildfires, and subsequent long-term policies needed to address them.

Another striking example of the media missing the larger story occurred at the national level. When CNN first reported on the 2007 southern California wildfire story, at one point its lead story spoke of a rumored arsonist who may have set a fire in eastern Orange County, California. This fire destroyed only fourteen homes. It was one of the least important fires going on at that point—a minor conflagration that was but a tiny fraction of the dozens of communities and thousands of homes on fire in San Diego County. Yet the tag line "Arson in Southern California" designated the headline story at a critical juncture in the reporting of this event.

A second distortion of media understanding of the ecology of wildfires, and one that is sometimes echoed by policy-makers, is what might be termed the "demonization of chaparral." Chaparral is natural vegetation that grows wildly in the eastern hills at the edge of southern California's urbanized regions. "Fuel centrists" like to claim that by eliminating vegetation (chaparral, brush, shrubs) wildfires will diminish. This plays well with public fear of wildfire and offers an oversimplified solution to a more complicated problem. As it turns out, it is a somewhat misguided notion. In fact, fire ecologists say the two most important factors in determining whether a wildfire becomes dangerous are fuel moistures (humidity) and wind. Vegetation will not carry the flames unless other conditions are in place.[19] Further, a more powerful fuel than vegetation is buildings—especially houses built from wood. The media tends to underplay the role of housing and suburban development, while it overplays the role of vegetation.

Thus media sources and elected officials basically ended up echoing the views of pro-development politicians, the developer lobby that gets them into office, and the myriad businesses that benefit from uncontrolled growth. Every attempt is made to steer the narrative away from the growth itself—its form, scale, location, and design. This is the real story behind the wildfires. The escalation of wildfire events in the southwestern U.S. must also be understood in the context of global warming, and the degree to which the increase in temperatures, as well as in extreme weather conditions, may also exacerbate the scale and frequency of the more dangerous wildfires.

Figure 3.2 Lack of Planning for Wildfires: Home Burned in the Rancho Bernardo Community of San Diego
Source: Photo by Lawrence A. Herzog

Local and regional government officials are not immune to echoing these same misconceptions. For example, during the 2007 wildfires, in a *New York Times* interview, the Interim Deputy Director of the San Diego County Department of Planning and Land Use was asked about the wisdom of building in suburban subdivisions in the wildland urban interface area. He responded that "the idea is not that we create goals and policies to slow growth, that's not the intent. It's to make sure that people are safe during a wildland fire."[20] Here, one of the highest ranking planning officials in regional government was unwilling to address the wildfire problem with the basic tools of urban planning—land use regulation or site plan restrictions—nor willing to question the pattern of unsustainable development in the unincorporated regions of San Diego where fires were burning the hottest. A second example of this comes from another county official, one of the members of County Board of Supervisors. When questioned by critics about building patterns in the path of Santa Ana winds, too close to canyons or on the edges of cliffs, being part of the wildfire problem, the Supervisor refused to accept this point, stating that "there will always be some kind of threat. All of San Diego is fire-prone."[21] The "all of San Diego" reference is a convenient way to avoid land regulation in designated fire safety zones.

Another example of the media avoiding stories that address suburban growth came during the 2003 wildfires in the San Diego region, when a local radio host, covering the "Cedar fire" that was spreading west from the hills toward the city of San Diego, created a stir with what was presented as a late breaking story. The talk show host claimed that the Cedar fire was halted from spreading further toward the city because its movement was pointing toward a military base—Miramar Airfield, the place where the nationally popular film *Top Gun* starring Tom Cruise was filmed in 1986. According to this radio host, U.S. Marines went out with shovels and bulldozers to stop the fire, while "corrupt and featherbedding firefighters from the San Diego Fire Department did nothing." Sources later revealed that this story was a complete fabrication.[22] But it illustrates the degree to which the media will pursue a sensationalized story and miss the deeper truths about wildfires.

Underlying these misdirected narratives from the media, the ideology espoused by politicians and government officials is that "growth in any form is good." By sticking with this point of view, its logic leads to the idea that the way to solve the wildfire problem is not by slowing down or changing the way the region grows, but rather by allocating bigger and better technology toward firefighting—armies of helicopters, air tankers, modern trucks, more fire personnel, and high tech equipment. This is an extension of the twentieth century ideology of "modernity"—that better technology and science can solve all problems.

These narratives tend to underplay or ignore the role of nature in the suburban periphery—the natural cycles and ecologies of fire, the importance of wind, topography, climate, and seasonal drought which create the environment in which fire occurs, and which should be the factors that drive alternative growth policies in light of the now critical importance of wildfires and residential survival in suburban settings like southern California. One rarely heard "nature" mentioned as a factor in regulating growth as a form of fire prevention during the public discussions and debates that unfolded during both the 2003 and 2007 eastern San Diego wildfire disasters. As one writer surmised during the 2007 wildfire event in San Diego County: "The question is never—why am I building here on this hillside, that predictably catches fire every few years . . . it is instead, how can technology and new materials—how can progress—protect me from the dangers inherent in living where I have chosen to live?"[23]

In short, public policy makers and the media have constructed a knee-jerk approach to wildfires in the suburbs. As the wildfire phenomenon grows in scope, instead of looking at the deeper reasons for wildfires, they have tended to simply lump them into a category—"natural disasters that are inevitable"—like hurricanes or earthquakes, and therefore must be addressed with better equipment, coordination between different government agencies, and efficient evacuation plans. Meanwhile, there is a distinct sense of denial about the broader picture. It is easier and safer to blame the problem on vegetation or equipment or even on the firefighters themselves, than it is to step back and question the pattern and scale of the growth itself. Is the forest burning our homes or are our homes burning the forest?

Urban Planning and Wildfires

Too often "fire plans" do not link up with local comprehensive plans. Indeed, two of the most comprehensive studies of fires within the U.S. reached this conclusion. An American Planning Association's 2005 technical report is the most comprehensive recent study of the subject. It argues that wildfires tend to be "very much a people-triggered hazard," since 80 percent of fires are ignited in some way by humans. It further suggests that the extent of wildfire destruction depends heavily on development decisions—including building design, subdivision design, land use regulations, landscaping, and management of biological fuel loads. It goes on to state that development in the wildland urban interface is a direct consequence of land use policy. The problem is that, under current practices, wildfire plans "attempt to mitigate the outcomes of land use planning without trying to change its direction." What is lacking, the study concludes, is a more direct connection between fire planning and comprehensive planning.[24]

That study later cites the city of Santa Barbara for having one of the most comprehensive wildfire plans in the nation, because the city went beyond suppressing and preventing wildfires to understanding the ecological conditions that create risk—such as flammable vegetation. However, that study also went on to observe a main weakness of the Santa Barbara wildfire plan: "An omission in this plan is its lack of relationship to the city's comprehensive plan."[25]

A second seminal work on the subject is a technical report commissioned by the U.S. Forestry Service back in 1991. That project concluded that local governments needed to increase the role of fire protection in the planning process; it further suggested that the costs of fire planning and fire-sensitive urban planning needed to be born equally by developers, local government, and fire protection agencies—under the watchful management of state legislatures.[26]

One of the major unresolved issues lies in the question of who should pay for wildfire protection. When CALFIRE, the State of California Department of Forestry and Fire Protection, responds to a serious wildfire in the backcountry of San Diego County, along with local and regional firefighting units, as well as supplementary helpers, including military personnel, police, and federal emergency management teams, the costs of all this emergency assistance have traditionally been passed on to all taxpayers. But, in the wake of the 2007 catastrophe, state and local officials have begun talking about charging rural and fire-prone "wildland" backcountry residents a special "fire protection" fee that would create a permanent fund to pay for the expenses of fire protection in the most vulnerable subregions. State officials have proposed a fee of between $100 and $200 per year, plus a sliding scale for properties either more or less vulnerable, based on a variety of factors including location, whether any steps have been taken to make the home more fire-resistant, and so forth. The point is that rural and inland owners of McMansions who live in sprawl and fire-prone developments must fully fund their own fire protection, rather than shifting the costs to taxpayers who live in the city or along the coast.[27]

Fast Suburbs in the Mojave Desert

It has been said that the Las Vegas strip is so lit up at night that it can be seen from outer space.[28] Las Vegas is a city best known for a lifestyle of excess, gambling, and the celebration of materialism. Its identity is symbolized by the corridor of casinos and hotels that define the tourism, entertainment, and gambling business center, known as "the Strip." The urban cultural landscape here is one of profoundly gaudy signage, dependence on automobiles, and a general buzz of consumerism and worship of money. Where once Las Vegas was merely a gambling destination, by the late twentieth century it began to urbanize dramatically. It became a magnet for Americans seeking the lifestyle of fast urbanism, and businesses willing to relocate to a place that symbolized these values. Designers struggled to make sense of this new kind of urban place—the electronics and fluidity, the buzz, sense of movement, and automobile-oriented lifestyle—and asked whether architecture could adapt to a new, fast urbanist, sprawl-like growth pattern in the Mojave Desert.[29] The biggest challenge to Las Vegas is that the business side of fast urbanism is now on a collision course with the physical environment.

Las Vegas began as a 1920s transshipment town and railroad repair center. It benefited from 1930s New Deal monies for reclamation of the

Hoover Dam. The dam and subsequent investment in military facilities fueled the beginning of a speculative growth strategy for what would become one of the centers of fast urbanism in the nation. In this regard, 1931 was an important date for Las Vegas—the year gambling was made legal in Nevada. During the 1930s and 1940s, crusades to limit prostitution and gambling were prevalent in California; meanwhile a different cultural norm was emerging for Las Vegas. It would become the city where "anything goes," and thus a magnet for investors from outside the state. Not only was gambling legalized in 1931, but in that same year divorce laws were liberalized in Nevada, making Las Vegas the place to obtain a divorce after only six weeks of residency. Just after World War II ended, resort hotels and gambling casinos opened, and by the early 1950s tourism and entertainment were the largest employers in the valley.

When the Federal Highway Administration began building interstate highways in the 1950s, the connection between Las Vegas and Los Angeles was strengthened. This link would become a catalyst for the post-1960 boom in Las Vegas. The development of air conditioning technology, the siting of an air base and nuclear testing ground nearby, and the location of new industrial activity all contributed to this process. By the 1960s, Las Vegas was a "divorce town" and an entertainment city for southern Californians.[30]

From the 1950s to the 1980s, casino and hotel development was still largely in the hands of underworld (mob) financing, and thus other mainstream investors and companies shied away from doing business there.[31] Even when huge corporations began to invest in the Las Vegas region, they did everything they could to disguise their location there. For example, Citibank's giant service center was given a fictitious address—"The Lakes, Nevada"—to avoid alienating customers.

The late 1980s marked a transformation of Las Vegas, as external capital discovered a huge asset of the region—its glitter and potential could make it a global entertainment center in tune with the late twentieth century "fast world" of electronics, media, and fantasy.[32] Steve Wynn, a developer and former liquor distributor, opened a mega-hotel, the Mirage, using financing from the most important global investment center in the world—Wall Street (he financed with junk bonds). The Mirage Resort was opened in 1989 with 3,000 rooms, at a cost of $630 million, the most expensive hotel in history up to that moment, and also the largest casino in the world. It featured a fifty-four foot volcano, which erupted every half hour after dark. This revealed the new power of "spectacle" in the invention of global entertainment cities. The Mirage Resort became a landmark that soon exceeded the Hoover Dam as Nevada's most visited attraction. The "mega-hotel/resort" ushered in a new corporate era for Las Vegas in the 1990s. Many of the older iconic resorts from the 1950s and 1960s, including the Dunes and the Sands, were demolished. The mob was replaced by corporate capital from Wall Street, and a reinvented city began to attract a global market of consumers.

The success of the Mirage unleashed a fervent boom of mega-hotels, resorts, and casinos in the 1990s. Las Vegas' gambling base was mainly concentrated along the aforementioned 4.1 mile section of Las Vegas Boulevard—"The Strip." The parade of glamorous, giant hotels included Excalibur, Luxor, Treasure Island, New York-New York, Bellagio, Mandalay Bay, Paris, and the Venetian. Over eight billion dollars was invested in the Strip, and by the late 1990s Las Vegas became the world's most visited tourist site, outdistancing Mecca in Saudi Arabia. When the dust from all these investments had cleared, eighteen of the world's twenty-five largest hotels by room count were now on the Strip, with a total of over 67,000 rooms.

The post-1980 Las Vegas boom coincided with the emergence of new forms of global cities built around creating giant high tech urban centers of consumption, in an age of advertising, electronics, and fast paced spectacle. After 1980, developers in Las Vegas were able to blend gambling with entertainment, allowing the city to cash in on a specialized form of fast urbanism—the co-mingling of entertainment and culture. The creation of a global electronic city of gambling, night clubs, and a sense of the fantastic points to the emergence of a new iconic model that celebrates fast urbanism.

An extreme illustration of this trend is the mega-hotel-casino complex "City Center," a sixty-seven acre $9 billion multi-use resort. The

Figure 3.3 The Las Vegas Strip: Architecture of Spectacle and Consumption in a Global Era
Source: Photo by Lawrence A. Herzog

first phase was completed in 2009. It was advertised as the largest hotel in the world with nearly 5,000 rooms and 2,500 luxury condominium units. Also promoted as "a city within a city," estimates of the total square footage range as high as seventeen million square feet, including some 500,000 square feet of retail space, and another 300,000 square feet of convention center space.[33] In effect, Las Vegas became a twenty-first century "media-metropolis," a place of glitz and glitter used by the media, and which used the media to grow. It had transitioned smoothly out of the mob era into a world of entertainment driven fast urbanism. What this "architainment" facilitated most of all was growth.

The Mega-suburbs Boom

As billions of dollars poured into Las Vegas, another important story was emerging behind the hype and the glitz and glitter: the making of a booming, massively spread out, cosmopolitan region, the twenty-first century's fastest growing American metropolis. The Las Vegas region virtually doubled its population in every decade since 1960. In that year, its population was 139,126, but by 1970 it was up to 304,744; it reached over a half million in 1980, 852,732 in 1990, and 1.56 million in 2000. By 2007, its population had reached 1.8 million, then climbing to an estimated 2.2 million by 2010.[34]

What accounts for the massive population influx in a city that was once merely a holiday escape in the middle of the desert, but hardly a place people would want to live in year round? The answer is: jobs, affordable housing, and changing cultural values. The multi-billion dollar tourism and entertainment industry turned Las Vegas into a magnet for service industry investors, retired people searching for an affordable paradise in the sun, and wealthy entrepreneurs looking for second homes. The City Center complex alone was projected to create 12,000 new jobs. All of this new development was a catalyst for an explosion of the construction sector. The "legitimizing" of Las Vegas by Wall Street also meant that respectable corporations could now relocate activities here. Las Vegas gradually became its own glitzy advertisement for new residents and investors. It offered a sense of the exotic and cheap housing that attracted migrants fleeing expensive southern California. Some forty million people visit Las Vegas each year, and many are now returning to live there permanently. During its peak growth period in the 1990s and the first half of the 2000s, Las Vegas was building a new house every twenty minutes, and 5,000 new residents were arriving every month.[35] But this housing boom later led to bust. By the end of the first decade of the 2000s, Clark County (the Las Vegas metropolitan area) was either number one or in the top five in the list of U.S. cities with the highest foreclosure rates.[36]

Las Vegas became the new national symbol of an emerging American urban prototype—the iconic "fast city"—no longer just a gambling and casino town, but a place of entrepreneurial spirit, innovation, economic opportunity, and change sustained by electronics and digital media. Growth occurred relatively quickly in a state (Nevada) not accustomed to giant cities and the problems of rapid expansion, a state known to defend the rights of landowners, and a state not known for its progressive politics, with the exception of organized labor in the visitor industry sector.[37] Las Vegas, already tied to Los Angeles culturally and demographically, may have also borrowed from southern California's "growth machine" politics—where land investors, real estate companies, and builders are courted and protected by local elected officials, all in the interest of maximizing growth and profit, and driving the regional economy upward.[38] At the same time, "growth machines" are notoriously unwilling to prioritize environmental protection, socio-economic equity, and affordable housing.

Could the real significance of Las Vegas be that, in the end, it simply offered a place for southern Californians to continue their already less-than-sustainable lifestyle (consumption of large automobiles and pattern of suburban dispersal) at a lower cost? As one L.A. observer wrote a decade ago: "As LA becomes increasingly crowded and expensive, Las Vegas is holding itself out as the last frontier of the California dream."[39] Las Vegas, like L.A., believes in its "Manifest Destiny"—the destiny to build a great city in the remote and forebidding desert.

As Las Vegas mushroomed beyond two million people, it has taken on the form of a giant amorphous suburbanizing blob of low and medium density condo complexes, townhomes, and single family cul-de-sac developments that stretch across hundreds of squares miles of Nevada desert, from Boulder City and the Hoover Dam in the southeast to North Las Vegas and Summerlin in the northwest. The sprawling region touches the foothills of mountains and the edges of desert wilderness. Much of the scattered, diffuse development takes the form of master planned or gated communities, fragmented and separate from each other, and placed in exurban "pods" spread around the core of the city of Las Vegas, the Strip and along the freeways (I-15 and I-95) that facilitate mobility in the region. Two of the biggest "pods" of exurban development in the northwest and southeast are anchored by two mega-projects, Summerlin and Green Valley. These mega-scale master planned communities are largely copied from earlier models like the Irvine Ranch in southern California.

Irvine Ranch was one of the largest and most spread out suburban master planned subregions in the U.S. in its time, and set the cultural and economic standard for all those that followed, especially in the western United States. The Irvine Ranch is 94,000 acres in size and encompasses almost one-fifth of Orange County, California. Its properties overlap six cities including Laguna Beach, Anaheim (Anaheim Hills), Irvine, Tustin (Tustin Ranch), Orange, and Newport Beach. It was originally a Mexican land grant (owned by James Irvine and others) of 185 square miles.

In Las Vegas, the sprawl of Summerlin approached that of Irvine Ranch, with some forty square miles of area and a projected population of nearly 200,000. So large was Summerlin that, like Irvine Ranch, it is divided into numerous "villages," many with artificial lakes. While the subdivided sections are called "villages," there are few community centers that can be reached on foot, and few activities that residents can walk to. One planner describes Summerlin as creating a "suburban-style quality of life not by accentuating the environment, but by nearly obliterating it."[40]

There are signs, however, that these planned communities have taken steps to become more sustainable. Many include trails, open space, and access to nature for residents. Newer master planned communities are being held to environmentally higher standards,[41] but those standards cannot be retroactively imposed on the multitude of existing planned communities and their hundreds of thousands of residents. Also, critics question the extent to which these features are fully embraced by a majority of residents. In many communities, trails and open spaces are neglected. Older communities display ecologically insensitive design elements, including concrete block walls between homes for privacy, which make people feel isolated and not part of a community; lack of neighborhood centers; and over-reliance on the CC & Rs (Community Codes and Regulations), which give too much power to only a few decision-makers (the Homeowners Association officers).[42] Many of the older master planned communities are gated, and some have walls built around their perimeters, which adds to their sense of isolation. Las Vegas does not have a regional transit system that links suburban planned communities with activity centers. This makes residents completely dependent upon their automobiles.

A critical flaw in the development of Las Vegas' master planned communities is that they were built on a piecemeal basis; this leads to fragmented land management, where separate communities are dropped into different locations within existing floodplains, forest zones, and wildlife habitats. This haphazard imposition of privately owned communities makes it difficult to preserve ecosystems that require coordinated efforts across space.[43] Native plants are disturbed, water quality is compromised, and noxious plants and weeds from residential subdivisions are introduced and can invade local ecosystems. Localized septic systems threaten groundwater.

Figure 3.4 City of Summerlin, Las Vegas, along the I-215

Source: Photo by permission of Landiscor Aerial Information, Phoenix, Arizona, www.landiscor.com

By the 1990s, Las Vegas sprawl stretched farther and farther into the desert wilderness in a series of master planned housing developments, many lacking an identity, or a sense of community, or a connection to their surrounding ecology. In the late 1990s, some of the new developments were gated. A trend toward building enormous single family homes also started; these homes were referred to in some circles as "palaces of nineteenth century barons." At one million dollars and upward, they suggested a new kind of Las Vegas migrant: billionaires who simply built homes because they could afford them and, in some cases, did not necessarily expect to live there full time. Thus, the landscape would be dotted with 5,000 to 10,000 square foot homes that would lie vacant for much of the year. "I probably won't live there at all," one wealthy Californian reported, after he had purchased a three million dollar condo. "I thought Las Vegas would be a good place to go on occasion—to see a show, dine in elegant restaurants, or play a little golf."[44] This same

Figure 3.5 Sprawling Suburb of North Las Vegas along the US 93/I-15

Source: Photo by permission of Landiscor Aerial Information, Phoenix, Arizona, www.landiscor.com

Californian also admitted he already owned homes in Tiburon and Pebble Beach, California.

Such high end residential development speaks of the larger cultural values that allow someone to feel entitled to build a three million dollar condo they will only use for an occasional golf weekend. It enhances the idea of Las Vegas as a place where people can flaunt wealth and luxury independently of place or ecology. Both Green Valley and Summerlin are self-contained living spaces—giving residents a feeling of being in a protected cocoon, insulated from both the city of Las Vegas and the harsh desert environment that engulfs them. As we saw in the San Diego region, sprawl is destroying the very human society that created it.

Unsustainable Las Vegas

> I've heard Las Vegas touted as the American City of the Future . . . the prototype habitat for a society in which the old boundaries between work, leisure, entertainment, information, production, service and acquisition dissolve, and a new colorful, pleasure-laden home emerges. But the trouble with Las Vegas is not just that it is ridiculous and dysfunctional, but that anybody might take it seriously as a model for human ecology.[45]

While the development community markets Las Vegas by selling the image of playful, leisure-oriented cityscapes, these same ingredients impose a heavy footprint on southern Nevada. The Las Vegas valley grew so quickly that it took urban planning observers by surprise. The problems of urban growth were hidden behind the larger social discourse of Las Vegas as a center of gambling, casinos, night life. As one observer notes: "Like Disneyland, Las Vegas encapsulates what we are. Every year, millions come to bask in its reflection. No one thinks Las Vegas is real; it is an illusion, but visitors willingly suspend belief and pretend."[46] It is as if the dazzle of the Strip is sacred; no one wanted to give up the fantasy; no one was willing to step in and impose regulations on Oz. So citizens simply allowed Las Vegas to grow without bounds and without regard to the environment.

Recently, however, Las Vegas has been forced to confront its ecological challenges. While the region's ozone air pollution has improved since it ranked fifth worst in the U.S. in the 1980s, it remains a concern in a metropolis that is growing so rapidly. Clark County created an Office of Sustainability in 2009. One of its missions is better monitoring of air quality. It is also enforcing permits and land use regulations, including the promotion of "transit-oriented development," where future residential projects would need to be linked to alternative transit. This is a relatively new idea for the Las Vegas region, and has not been seriously put into play yet.

The consumption of water per resident in Las Vegas exceeded most other cities in the southwestern U.S. during its boom growth years in the 1990s and early 2000s: the per capita rate of consumption in Las Vegas during that period was 300 gallons/day; in Los Angeles it was only 22 g/day, and in Oakland, California, 110 g/day. In another desert city similar in size to Las Vegas, Tucson, Arizona, residents only used 160 g/day.[47] To its credit, Las Vegas has begun to address the water issue. Between 2000 and 2009, the metropolitan area decreased its water use by over 20 percent, and now uses less water per capita than the Phoenix, Arizona, region.[48] Average per capita water use dropped from 347 gallons per day to 248 gallons per day. This was achieved through better management of water in government facilities, by public bans on front lawns, assigned watering days, and citizen education, especially in the use of smart landscapes, turf replacements for grass, and low water household fixtures. However, it is also true that the recession of that period may have lowered water consumption, as thousands of foreclosed families moved away.[49]

Water remains the biggest challenge to urbanization in the Las Vegas valley. Landowners with artesian wells draw water from the giant aquifer that sits under the Las Vegas region; that aquifer siphons water out of Lake Mead, which, in turn, draws down the Colorado River. This chain of water loss threatens to turn the Colorado River into a "deficit river," where more water is allotted to users than is replenished through the natural cycles. The regional water agency, the Southern Nevada Water Authority (SNWA), claims that it will address the water deficit by tapping regional groundwater supplies in alternative sources, including neighboring watersheds like the Virgin and Muddy Rivers, or Three Lakes Valley. However, environmentalists say that tapping these watersheds will negatively impact agriculture, wetland habitats, wildlife, and endangered species.[50]

Global warming and continuous drought have significantly depleted the main source of water to the region—Lake Mead, which is fed by the Colorado River. The lake needs a high enough level of water to produce power at the Hoover Dam, and to supply the growing population of the Las Vegas urban region. Despite the aggressive water conservation efforts in the Las Vegas metropolitan region, hydrologists still estimate that there is a 50 percent chance Lake Mead will run dry by 2020, if the current drought patterns from the last decade persist.[51] It is a very delicate balance, and as the general manager of the Southern Nevada Water Authority said back in 2010: "If the river flow continues downward and we can't build back up supply, Las Vegas is in big trouble."[52]

Still, the city of Las Vegas is not ignoring the warning signs of climate change. For example, it initiated a program called "Sustainable Las Vegas" that seeks to promote programs like recycling, solar energy, green building, and water stewardship.[53] Most of what is done falls into one of two categories: educating and encouraging (though not requiring) homeowners to lower their water consumption, and greening the government's buildings and facilities (installing solar panels on city-owned parking garage roofs, for example). Beyond this, city government is also seeking to encourage water reclamation on golf courses, turf conversion on public properties, and enforcement of a drought ordinance. It has converted its fleet to fuel efficient vehicles and is proposing a "complete streets" program to pedestrianize more streets in the city. There are plans for a Bus Rapid Transit system in the future.

The "Sustainable Las Vegas" program was officially established by the City Manager in 2007. A website was built,[54] and the Las Vegas 2020 Plan created. The plan is a serious policy commitment to make the urban region more sustainable. It calls for long-term commitments to transit-oriented development, the use of "form based codes,"[55] and new guidelines for infill and new developments. This latter point was strengthened by the signing in 2007 of an environmentally progressive

Development Agreement for Kyle Canyon, a 1,700 acre future development area. That agreement sets new standards for future master planned communities, including: requiring mixed-use development, pedestrian friendly streets, and extensive trail systems. It limits gated communities to 25 percent of all residential development. As mentioned, however, the policies and guidelines for new master planned communities are not necessarily being applied to existing ones.

Meanwhile, Clark County has also taken steps to match the City of Las Vegas. In 2008, the region started the first Eco-Initiative, whose goals included improving the county's air quality, water, land management, waste recycling, transport design, green building, and renewable energy. The county's approach follows the city's lead: to provide information for residential greening, while improving its own facilities. One of its goals is to improve citizen recycling rates from the current rate of 8 percent to 25 percent. Clark County does have one of the world's largest private solar energy production companies, Solar One, which creates incentives for the region to move toward solar energy.

There is, however, a feeling of institutional "window dressing" in these well articulated but limited programs at the city and county level. The initiatives are long on providing information, but short on hard-hitting regulations that will institutionalize larger changes. Most of the projects are voluntary, rather than enforced. The vast majority of large scale green projects are on government-owned properties, and not in the privately owned communities, where most of Las Vegas' two million residents live. Indeed, the only other notable green building outside of government-owned properties has occurred on the Strip, in the form of hotel and casino complexes seeking to lower their carbon footprint. Caesar's Hotel invested in low flush toilets and low water showerheads, while also improving its outdoor irrigation system. In a promotional slide show by a university research center, Las Vegas is praised for having "radical new urban design." That design, however, is limited to the new high rise hotels on the Strip. Some of these LEED-certified buildings, particularly in the new City Center complex, are owned by MGM Mirage, which has a natural gas fired power plant, and low energy air conditioning in the casinos. Sources report that

Figure 3.6 Unsustainable Growth Spreads across the Fragile Desert Landscape: City of Henderson along the US93/US95/I-515

Source: Photo by permission of Landiscor Aerial Information, Phoenix, Arizona, www.landiscor.com

the construction of so many green buildings on the Strip was inspired by millions of dollars in tax breaks available after the state of Nevada passed green building legislation in 2005.[56]

The well-meaning government programs to make Las Vegas sustainable are a reaction to what happened during the region's three decade boom period, from 1980 to 2010. During that era, Las Vegas grew in a dispersed, low density manner that was not coordinated at the regional level. Over the last decade, environmental planning efforts to address the ecologies of sprawl created here have been limited.[57]

Las Vegas' urban development in those boom years was built around privatized mega-resorts and master planned "lifestyle communities"—giant, sprawling developments that marketed themselves as luxury homes set in the perfect setting of sun, desert, and palm trees. Most of the palm trees one sees in Las Vegas are not native to the southwestern deserts; nor are the artificial lakes. Las Vegas has been called many things—a frontier city, a place where people go to reinvent themselves, a place where a laissez faire spirit thrives. It is often celebrated for its adaptability, for being a shining example of the shift in America toward global trade, and non-natural resource, non-place-oriented economies. Las Vegas is seen as the city of the future—an economy built around information, entertainment, and even the internet, the true "quaternary" information economy capital of the western United States.

Yet one can argue that this vision of Las Vegas lacks an ecological conscience. It fails to consider the long-term costs of pollution. "Brown haze" is the local name for the air pollution that sits over southern Nevada. Once thought to be seasonal, over time it became a year round phenomenon, made worse by the over-reliance on automobiles and limited government intervention in land use or zoning to prevent or slow down sprawl. In 2010, the American Lung Association gave the region an "F" for the number of days with dangerous ozone levels (sixty-six per year), ranking it number twenty-one in the nation for ozone pollution.[58] Since 2010, the ozone levels have improved, but, without an alternative transit plan, the continued dependence on the automobile remains a concern, as does the problem of particulate (dust) pollution.[59]

Las Vegas is one of the last major metropolitan areas in the West that has virtually no mass transit, with the exception of two limited tram lines that move people between hotels along the Strip, and a limited bus system. Meanwhile the number of cars flowing through the Las Vegas valley has skyrocketed over the past decade, from 298,000 in 1980 to nearly a million by 2000. In 2007, *Forbes Magazine* rated Las Vegas as America's third most sedentary city (after Memphis and New Orleans)—that is, cities where people are least likely to walk. It also claimed 64 percent of Las Vegas residents are overweight or obese (this is slightly higher than the national average) and watch thirty-eight hours of TV per week.[60]

Las Vegas is not a pedestrian scale place, except perhaps for tourists strolling along the Strip, although residents do not consider the Strip a public space they use regularly. In fact, legally, the city of Las Vegas considers the only public spaces along the commercial Strip to be the overpasses. For a metropolis with almost two million people, Las Vegas has a striking scarcity of parks and open spaces. Many of the master planned communities are devoid of activity nodes that people can walk to. There may be paths or trails, but there are no centers, and no gardens or parks to walk to. Even the famed Strip discourages active public lives outside the casinos, since, in truth, the goal of the Strip is to get people inside the casinos, "along scripted, glassed in corridors where you can feel the cybernetic hum of slot machines,"[61] and not out on the streets. Reality lies inside the casinos, and street life is discouraged.

Figure 3.7 Public Life Is Discouraged Even on the Las Vegas Strip: The Idea Is to Get People inside the Casinos

Source: Photo by Lawrence A. Herzog

An anecdote about life on the Strip is illustrative of the disdain for vibrant civic spaces along a corridor dominated by privatized, consumerist casinos. A college professor was assembling his video crew to film a segment about one of the Strip's hotels—Treasure Island. He set up on what he thought was a public space—the sidewalk facing the casino from the main avenue. Wrong. He was ordered by hotel management to leave—and informed he was on private property! When he protested and asked, "Isn't this street right in front of your hotel a public space for pedestrians?" he was told that the "public" sidewalk was actually a narrow strip of concrete virtually below ground and with no view of the casino. Meanwhile, inside the casinos, people sit at slot machines. "The new Vegas Strip enhances the interior narrative, not the communal process."[62]

If Las Vegas emphasizes a narrative of gambling casino interiors, rather than the public space outdoors, this tends to diminish awareness of the natural environment. Indeed, the hotel-casino culture speaks to an architecture of fantasy—it negates natural light, nature, and the outdoors. Instead it uses artificial light to mask the time of day and create a timeless world where people can gamble. Interior spaces are defined by artificiality and techno-noise—bells ringing, slot machines buzzing, a fever pitch atmosphere to make people feel excited, so they will gamble more. The immediate spaces outside are also part of the Las Vegas stage set of "architainment." The "eye candy" facades of the mega-hotels along the Strip give the impression of grandeur, wealth, and total pleasure, a Disneyland-like effect. Of course, as in a theme park, the fantasy runs out at some point—and beyond the stage sets lie the trailer parks, abandoned lots, parking garages, and cheap apartments. And beyond that lie the vast suburbs. But back inside the casinos fantasy is alive and well, not on real city streets but in fake, miniaturized movie sets that produce a "happy imprisonment," as one writer terms it.[63]

The sense of artificiality that pervades Las Vegas also spills into the outdoors and the use of nature. At the Bellagio hotel, people jet ski on an artificial lake; nearby at The Venetian they ride gondolas along fake canals in a theatrically lit city. These fake uses of water belie the fact that water supply and water quality are grave environmental problems

Figure 3.8 Artificiality Defines Las Vegas Architecture
Source: Photo by Lawrence A. Herzog

in the southern Nevada valley. The nearest giant reservoir, Lake Mead, is contaminated by toxic waste from pesticides and industrial runoff. And, as mentioned, the Southern Nevada Water Authority is immersed in a political struggle to siphon away more than its legal share of Colorado River water, or other adjacent watershed sources.

The Las Vegas region also faces other pollution problems. A proposal to build a nuclear waste storage facility at Yucca Mountain, only one hundred miles from Las Vegas, came close to being seriously considered, until it was rejected by the incoming administration of President Barack Obama in 2008; but there are still political and economic interests that want to resurrect it.[64] There are reports of groundwater contamination from a former magnesium-titanium processing plant in nearby Henderson. Most of Las Vegas' electric power is still generated by coal-fired plants, especially on the Moapa Indian reservation northeast of the city.

One prominent writer has called Las Vegas "an environmentally and socially bankrupt system of human settlement."[65]

A Troubled Metropolis in the Valley of the Sun

The Phoenix urban region, known locally as the Valley of the Sun, is the fastest growing desert metropolis in the United States, and one of the fastest growing urban regions in the nation. Maricopa County encloses most of metropolitan Phoenix—its population climbed from 120,000 in 1940 to 331,770 in 1950, then over two decades ballooned to 2.1 million (1990), and to over 3 million in early 2012. Phoenix is projected to expand to 4.5 million by 2020, and as high as 7 million by 2050.[66] The Phoenix Metropolitan Statistical Area, as defined by the U.S. Census (it is officially called Phoenix-Mesa-Scottsdale MSA)[67], is the thirteenth largest in the U.S. with 4.0 million. Like Las Vegas, Phoenix was at the peak of its demographic and economic boom before the recession hit in 2008. From 2000 to 2006, it grew by 24.2 percent, placing it in the top ten in the U.S.[68]

How does a city in the middle of the Mojave Desert, far from either coast and distant from major natural resource concentrations, become one of the largest metropolitan regions in America? Like Las Vegas, Phoenix does not owe its growth to traditional resource-based or heavy manufacturing. Nor has it relied on having a regional pool of resources (energy, water, minerals) to sustain it. Typical of sunbelt cities, Phoenix grew in spite of its physical environment. The relocation of aircraft companies and technology firms jump-started the Phoenix economy in the 1960s and 1970s. Then, as momentum started to build, Phoenix took advantage of the growing information economy, as well as tourism, retirement, and real estate. It is also the state capital of Arizona, home to seven Fortune 1,000 companies, and the major headquarters of national corporations like U.S. Airways, U-Haul, and Best Western.

But what distinguishes this desert metropolis is its spatial growth pattern—massive, horizontal sprawl that stretches over endless flat desert valleys, canyons, and mesas sitting within the Salt River basin and its hinterland. The physical scale of Phoenix is extraordinary. Maricopa County alone has an area of 1,226 square miles, the size of the state of New Jersey! The city of Phoenix covers some 470 square miles; the larger metropolitan area encompasses 800 square miles.[69] It has been said that until the recession slowed its growth, Phoenix was expanding outward at the rate of 1 acre per hour.[70] The U.S. Census' Metropolitan Statistical Area of Phoenix, mentioned earlier, measures 14,598 square miles, making it the third largest metropolis in physical area after Las Vegas and L.A.-Riverside-Orange County.

Metropolitan Phoenix is a textbook example of post-1970 "leapfrog" growth. "Leapfrogging" describes the condition of discontinuous urban growth toward the fringes of urban areas. Typical growth would break out all over in unconnected locales on the outer edge of the city, without any significant linkage either between new growth zones or between those young suburban enclaves and the existing city. Growth would erupt wherever developers could induce it, and the question of how to tie it all together was left for another time.

This irregular pattern of growth unfolded in the Phoenix area for at least two important reasons. First, the city of Phoenix's aggressive annexation policy increased city size from 17 square miles in 1950 to 331 square miles in 1980. It also left 40 percent of the land inside the city vacant by 1980. Second, for many years Maricopa County government allowed developers to build master planned communities on the urban fringe with minimal guidelines or regulations. This has changed in the last decade. Some of the peripheral developments eventually were annexed into what have become the booming suburbs—Scottsdale, Tempe, Peoria, Mesa, and Glendale. These suburbs have, in fact, become cities unto themselves, yet another example of the sprawl ecology of fast urbanism.

As Phoenix grew between 1950 and 1960, its population increased and its density decreased—from 6,000 people per square mile in 1950 to 2,000 people per square mile in 1962.[71] Much of that decreasing density was the harbinger of the next forty years of suburban expansion with almost no regional coordination of growth, land use allocations, transportation, employment, walkability, or sustainability. Phoenix's sprawl was part of an urban culture where land development was the holy grail of the city's economy. The mantra of the land development industry was "you can never get hurt in dirt."[72]

Figure 3.9 Aerial View of Master Planned Suburbs, City of Glendale, Northwest Phoenix
Source: Photo by permission of Landiscor Aerial Information, Phoenix, Arizona, www.landiscor.com

By 1972, greater Phoenix already had sixteen mega-planned communities arising on its outskirts, some as far as twenty or twenty-five miles beyond older suburbs like Scottsdale. These included Fountain Hills, Rio Verde, and Sunlakes, among others. Land on the periphery was quite cheap in the 1980s and 1990s (especially compared with growth areas in California). Developers thus employed a well-worn land investment strategy—buying fringe property (flat desert land in this case) cheap, and then convincing masses of home buyers to purchase homes in their new "paradise," even if it happened to be located in the middle of nowhere. Like Las Vegas, the primary marketing tool for Phoenix is the climate—and all of its allusions to "sun drenched paradise," swimming pools in the winter, palm trees, mountains, desert, and open space.

Mega-land deals were easier to put together in fringe locations; more centrally located infill sites might entail complex politics or even local opposition to growth. Even as early as the 1950s and 1960s, Phoenix was cited favorably as a prime example of discontinuous urban growth.

This became a driving theme in the city's expansion, especially in the 1970s and after, when booming master planned developments, ranging from 640 to 10,000 acres, were built in the remote outskirts. Of some sixteen major new projects between 1970 and 1990, only four were within five miles of Phoenix.[73]

While the planned communities were promoted as new centers that would combine jobs and housing, in fact, most of them never really became self-contained. Indeed, they are essentially giant bedroom communities, whose citizens, each morning, join the growing army of commuters who fill the freeways and roads in the congested regional journey-to-work marathon. In one example, a development called "Belmont" projected building homes for a population of 150,000 people thirty-five miles west of the incorporated boundary of the city of Phoenix. Developers claimed there would be on-site employment nodes. However, one county supervisor saw that very few communities on the urban fringe were actually building job locations in these planned developments, and thus voted against approving the Belmont project. He was quoted as saying: "This is not leap frog development . . . it's leap frog Olympics."[74]

Another egregious example of peripheral development skirting land use law is the community of Anthem, thirty-five miles north of Phoenix along I-17. Anthem's master plan was approved by Maricopa County in 1995, despite strong opposition. The developer, Del Webb, claimed Anthem would create local jobs—with its own retail stores, offices, and a hospital. But by 2000, nearly all of Anthem's residents commuted to other parts of Phoenix, thus adding to the already heavy rush hour traffic pouring into the city from the north. Anthem typified the clever, unsavory tactics of developers. It was marketed as a "community" with a long tradition of local family history, which local experts say never existed.[75] Instead, what was built was a "designer desert" look—artificial landscaping using high tech engineering and intensive irrigation to "green" the flat, sandy, arid desert environment.

Further, it turns out that Anthem should not have been built for another reason—the Arizona Groundwater Management Act of 1980 requires that any new development must demonstrate one-hundred-year water supplies without depleting existing water tables. This law was put in place to keep developers from sinking wells into regional groundwater networks, and then depleting existing supplies. Instead, developers were supposed to negotiate new municipal water infrastructure to supply projected new residents. The mega-developer Del Webb got around this requirement by arranging to lease water rights from a local indigenous community—which had separate water rights through the Central Arizona project.[76]

By 1997, twenty-one large scale exurban projects (over 1,000 acres) were under construction in the Phoenix region, and another ten were proposed. One new suburb, Buckeye, is projected to grow from 18,000 to 430,000 residents by 2050.[77] Future peripheral developments include Foothills, Estrella, Sun City, and Desert Ridge. The market for these projects was not only external—some 60 percent of new fringe residents came from the Valley of the Sun itself. Apparently, people in Phoenix wanted more land and more space, and they were willing to drive hundreds of miles more per week to get it. As we move forward, however, energy costs will no doubt begin to transform people's perception of housing location, car consumption, and daily commutes.[78]

The Phoenix metropolitan area leaves a huge footprint on the central Arizona desert. It grew physically from 273 square miles in 1975 to 732 square miles by 1995. The urban region is projected to add 3.3 million inhabitants by 2040, creating a metropolitan area with some 6.5 million people. Based on current land occupancy data, one study argues it will take about 367 square miles more land to accommodate just the residential space needed to house the new population. That figure does not include land needed for streets, schools, parks, shopping, and employment. Adding that land means about 700 square miles of new land will be consumed by the projected population for the region. This would make the Phoenix region some 1,500 square miles in land area, larger than the Los Angeles metropolitan area with far less than half L.A.'s population.[79]

One scholar has defined sprawl as "to cause to spread out carelessly and awkwardly."[80] Clearly, Phoenix fits this definition. Infrastructure for alternative transit (bikeways, bus rapid transit, light rail) has been slow to catch up with the sprawl pattern. However, some changes have begun to address this problem. Valley Metro is the regional transportation agency that has taken on the task of redefining mobility for the twenty-first century. It built a $1.4 billion light rail transit system that opened in 2008 and now serves the central area of Phoenix, including downtown, the airport, and the cities of Tempe and Mesa. By 2013, the system covered twenty linear miles, had twenty-eight stations, and served about 40,000 daily riders. The agency projects that it will build thirty-seven more miles of rail line by 2032, expanding its reach further to dispersed areas of the region.[81]

Yet, even with its expansion, the number of users of the light rail system remains small (40,000), considering that more than one million laborers travel to work every day in the Phoenix region. Although the regional planning agency has supported transit-oriented projects recently, and proposes to continue to do so in the future,[82] the fact is that the region remains so massively spread out that it will be challenging and expensive to service residents with intra-regional transit. At the same time, the continual peripheral growth has channeled residents, more and more, into socially isolated enclaves, creating an urban archipelago that further strains regional sustainability.

To take just one example of the massive social fragmentation, in some fringe retirement developments, such as Sun West, zoning ordinances were actually created to keep younger people out. The Senior Citizen Overlay District (SCOD) ordinance sets rules such as: a) every dwelling unit must have at least one person over fifty; and b) children under the age of eighteen are not allowed to reside in a residential unit for more than ninety days. Sun West is reportedly one of five retirement communities where the SCOD ordinance is in effect. Local observers report that this trend toward "age zoning" and age-restrictive codes in Phoenix's suburbs is on the rise.[83]

Eco-disaster in the Central Arizona Desert

The irony of contemporary Phoenix is that it was once a major destination for people suffering respiratory ailments—from allergies and asthma to tuberculosis. But beginning in the 1990s, air pollution became a major concern to residents. The American Lung Association gave Maricopa County its lowest grade for air quality—in the categories of both ozone and particulates. According to a 2005 "State of the Air" report, 79 percent of Maricopa County residents (2.6 million people) are at high risk for respiratory complications due to air quality—this includes people with asthma, bronchitis, cardiovascular disease, and diabetes.[84] The Phoenix region has an estimated 260 miles of freeway, with over 300,000 inhabitants who live too close, according to planning studies. They are subjected to toxic air poisoning from ozone and dust particles. While carbon monoxide levels have been reduced through monitoring and intervention, experts point out that the main agency designated to plan for air pollution regulation, the Maricopa Association of Governments (MAG), actually has a conflict of interest. MAG is the principal transportation planning agency as well, and builds a lot of highways, which may compromise its ability to plan for land uses away from densely used freeways. Further, there is a tendency for agencies to simply meet minimum federal standards for air quality, without addressing whether only meeting minimum standards will be sufficient to protect citizens in the long term.[85]

The "Brown Cloud" that descends over the Valley of the Sun is caused by nitrogen dioxide gas and small particles of carbon. All large urbanized regions create pollution—it is formed through auto emissions from millions of vehicle trips, construction-related dust, power plants, lawn mowers, and factories spewing chemical and other waste into the air. When you put these ingredients into a setting like that in Phoenix—the basin of the Salt River with its pattern of hot, dry weather—and you keep funneling more toxic inputs through urban growth, the result is a lethal brew. Local geography creates and enhances the conditions that lead to danger: inversions of cool air at night cause the ground to cool, but a second layer of cool air hovers over the valley and traps the warm, polluted air in the middle, right over the valley where millions of people live. Each morning, as air warms over the valley, particulates swirl and rise, forming a brown cloud over the entire metropolitan region. One local illness that has emerged is termed "Valley Fever," a lung infection caused by a fungus that becomes airborne when dust near construction sites or agricultural zones is blown about by desert winds. When these fungal spores are imbibed, Valley fever results. Another phenomenon is called a "haboob," a windstorm of dust and sand that is usually caused by the collapse of a thunderstorm cell. These storms threaten public safety for anyone on the road or in the air when they occur.

The Phoenix region draws 60 percent of its water supply from the Colorado River, through the Central Arizona project, whose canals and pipelines have been operating since 1984. About 35 percent of the water supply comes from the Salt River project, which draws from the Salt River and Verde River watersheds. Drought, however, could sharply reduce the amount of low altitude water from the Salt and Verde rivers. Moreover, under severe drought, Arizona's rights to 2.8 million acre-feet of water flow from the Colorado River (according to the 1922 Colorado River compact) are what is legally termed "junior" to the rights of adjacent states, Nevada and California. Under current law, 1.7 million acre-feet (out of Arizona's 2.8 million allocation) have this "junior" standing, meaning droughts and cutbacks could take away 1.7 million acre-feet of Arizona's total allocation, in favor of Nevada or California.[86] In short, Arizona's water supply is highly likely to dry up.

A desert city like Phoenix relies on dams and groundwater to supply water to nearly four million people. Surface water is limited, due to heat and evaporation and limited rainfall. Thus groundwater is essential in central Arizona. But groundwater can only be extracted in proportion to its replenishment through natural processes. Unfortunately, as in the Las Vegas example, what is happening in the urbanized valleys of Arizona, around Phoenix and Tucson, is that groundwater has been overpumped for decades. More water is taken out than is replenished by natural processes. The result is that there are now well documented, long-term declines in underground water levels; there is also a pattern of land subsidence. This puts even more pressure on importing Colorado River water—which is expensive because it must be transported long distances. But, given cost issues and the threat to the Colorado River supply from Arizona's legal "junior" status, groundwater remains the most important, but troubled, future source.

Like so many major cities in the U.S., Phoenix has also had a tendency to dump its toxic waste problem on those least able to defend themselves from such land use policies—low income minorities in south Phoenix.[87] South Phoenix already has a high proportion of heavy industry. Out of seven hazardous waste storage facilities in the Phoenix region, six are located in south Phoenix, and one on an Indian reservation. Over the last decade, a noxious new waste storage complex was located in south Phoenix and has announced plans to expand. Waste is brought into the neighborhood by trucks, and then dumped in the south Phoenix facility. In 1992, a toxic chemical fire in south Phoenix burned for twelve hours, irritating the eyes and lungs of many residents. Tests after the incident revealed high levels of zinc in many homes. In 1994, the Arizona Department of Environmental Quality (ADEQ) began allowing California to send hazardous waste (including DDT and lead) to be dumped in south Phoenix facilities.[88]

One other measure of Phoenix's impact on the natural landscape is offered in a recent study of growth in twenty-five global cities in different parts of the world. Out of these twenty-five cities, Phoenix had the second highest consumption of land for new growth, and yet it also had the lowest density. It was classified at the upper end of a scale on spatial sprawl, and labeled an "expansive growth city" that was found to be three times as dispersed as most cities in the world. The authors argued, in general, that "sprawl" is a condition peculiarly unique to Canada and the U.S., and not replicated to the same degree in other parts of the world.[89]

A window into the quality of life and culture in Phoenix's new mega-suburbs is found in a new suburb called Surprise, Arizona, forty-five miles northwest of downtown Phoenix. Along with several other satellite towns in the central Arizona urban region, Surprise is one of the fastest growing suburbs in the U.S. Its population soared from 32,342 in 2000 to over 100,000 by 2008, a 300 percent increase! At build out, Surprise is projected to have as many as 650,000 people by 2040.[90]

Surprise can best be described as a landscape of non-descript cul-de-sac suburban tract complexes sitting under the hot desert sun. It has one main avenue of "strip malls" filled with all of the usual suspects— Target, Home Depot, and Walmart. The culture of place in Surprise

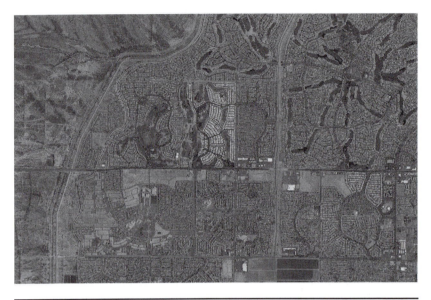

Figure 3.10 Mega Land Deals and Sprawl: City of Surprise, Arizona, in Northwest Phoenix
Source: Photo by permission of Landiscor Aerial Information, Phoenix, Arizona, www.landiscor.com

is perhaps typified by one phenomenon that has been observed—the evolution of mega-churches that appeal to those who want a limited religious experience in between trips to Starbucks and the shopping malls. The new mega-churches are built to look almost more like malls than spiritual spaces.[91] One such example is a church called Radiant. Radiant started small but grew to a congregation approaching 10,000 people. It built a 55,000 square foot church building which is said to have fifty plasma screen TVs in the foyer, a cafe with Starbucks-trained staff, and a drive-through latte stand. Krispy Kreme doughnuts are for sale, as well as Xboxes for kids while parents are in the church sanctuary. The leader of Radiant told a writer: "We want the church to look like a mall. We want you to come in here and say, Dude, where's the cinema?"[92]

Can the Phoenix Region Become Sustainable?

Leading Arizona climatologists believe the central part of their state (the urbanized Phoenix valley region) lies at the epicenter of global warming shock. They argue that, with climate change, the region is growing hotter, while its water sources are drying up, due to both warming and overuse as a result of the growing demand from a larger population. In addition, urbanization creates a heat island effect from buildings, roads, asphalt, and concrete, all of which absorb heat and transfer it to the land. In the words of one writer: "In a sense the whole city is a thermal battery, soaking up energy by day, and releasing it at night."[93]

Andrew Ross's ethnographic study of Phoenix argues that the city's culture and politics have been driven by the "growth machine," even when there was clearly not enough water to sustain its incessant growth. He found that city leaders were unwilling to make the big changes that could shift the development away from its emphasis on single family housing and sprawl, and toward a different model.

There have been a few success stories, however. One is the downtown area, where activists, artists, and others have energized neighborhood revitalization, including new transit lines, which has gotten thousands of residents out of their cars. There is also the case of Native American groups, like the Gila River community, who are fighting to take back their water rights and return to traditional agriculture. This would offer the hopeful model of local food production and indigenous land rights as a future way of life in the region.

To their credit, both the city of Phoenix and the surrounding Maricopa County have launched efforts to promote sustainable development over the last decade. The City of Phoenix produced a Climate Action Plan for Government Operations in 2009, and an accompanying website for its Sustainability Program.[94] The latter is aimed at improving air quality through dust control, managing landfills, and promoting biking and water conservation. Most of the programs are voluntary. Maricopa County initiated the "Green Government" program, which focuses mainly on making government facilities more sustainable, including installation of solar panels, waste recycling, and use of hybrid vehicles for its fleet. It also has a partnership with Arizona State University's Global Institute of Sustainability to establish what is called the Sustainable Cities Network to enhance dialogue between city governments in the region.[95] Better regional transit planning might begin to craft alternatives to the severe auto-dependence here.[96]

There are powerful forces working against the growth of a greener economy in the Valley of the Sun. Arizona is a state dominated by Republican legislators who not only don't believe in global warming, but also display what has been termed "a grade school misunderstanding of basic environmental science."[97] Anxious to take back political control after their homegrown candidate John McCain lost to President Obama in 2008, Arizona legislators lashed out and voted to disallow their own state environmental agency from regulating greenhouse gases, withdrew from the Western Climate Initiative, a multi-state pact to lower carbon emissions, and passed SB 1070, one of the harshest anti-immigrant laws in the U.S.[98]

So, although then Phoenix Mayor Phil Gordon claimed in 2009 that his goal was to make Phoenix "the greenest city in the U.S.," the facts about Phoenix begin to sound more and more like Andrew Ross's 2011 book title: "the world's least sustainable city." As we saw in Las Vegas, the recent changes in government have thus far been more cosmetic than substantial. At the same time, as Ross writes, "across that valley lies one thousand square miles of low density tract housing, where few signs of greening are evident."[99] While there may be a few pockets of "ecotopia," communities that can afford solar roofing or xeriscaped yards in places like north Phoenix, the larger reality is a region of middle and lower class residents living in tract housing and car-dependent suburbs. Water remains a scarce resource that larger populations continue to deplete. The region grows hotter, while the violent winds and desert ecology are mixing a brew of toxic dust pollution. So far, stakeholders in the region have not demonstrated the political will to profoundly interrupt the pattern.

In this chapter, we've seen that three of the fastest growing regions in the southwestern U.S. sunbelt—San Diego, Las Vegas, and Phoenix—are becoming victims of the very feature that helped create their growth—the physical environment, the sun, canyons, mesas, and spectacular desert landscapes. Sunbelt cities grew because people and jobs relocated for the climate and physical setting. This has pushed growth farther into the fringes, causing greater automobile dependency and subsequent environmental stress. Yet, it will be these places where we ultimately will determine if we can change our political and cultural behaviors enough to live there sustainably: to quote Ross's study of the Phoenix region: "If there is any hope of reversing the pattern of desertification, species loss, and ice-cap melt in the more remote locations, then the culture that produced 'Phoenix Man' will have to be transformed."[100] But, as the next two chapters demonstrate, even as we struggle to cope with the environmental problems of our fast suburbs in the southern U.S. borderlands, the basic model of urban sprawl has spread across the Americas.

Notes

1 Santa Ana winds are strong, extremely hot and dry offshore winds that affect coastal southern California and northern Baja California in autumn and winter, and have frequently led to wildfires. The origins of the term are not entirely clear, though it's thought they may be traced to the Santa Ana canyon in Orange County, which late nineteenth century reporters believed was the source of regional winds.

2 San Diego Association of Governments (SANDAG), *Regional Comprehensive Plan for 2030*, SANDAG, 2009, www.sandag.org.

3 U.S. Bureau of the Census, metropolitan growth statistics, 2000–6.

4 Many of the inland suburban towns in the San Diego region—such as Poway, Rancho Bernardo, Escondido, Chula Vista—grew between 15 percent and 25 percent during this period. See SANDAG, population projections, www.sandag.org.

5 The San Diego metropolitan area built a light rail transit system in the late 1970s. The trolley began service on July 26, 1981, and today operates three primary lines named the Blue Line, the Orange Line, and the Green Line, as well as a supplementary downtown circulator known as the Silver Line on weekends and holidays. About 96,900 riders use the trolley; the region plans to expand the trolley to serve northern San Diego County in the future. See San Diego Metropolitan Transit System, http://www.sdmts.com/.

6 They include Carlsbad (65 percent projected growth rate for that twenty year time period), eastern Chula Vista (60 percent), San Marcos (56 percent), the inland unincorporated county (54 percent), and Santee (34 percent).

7 Growth projections are from SANDAG, 2009.

8 Fire Safe Council background document for Senate Bill 838, Fire Prevention and Protection, www.firesafecouncil.org.

9 Mike Davis, "Diary: California Burns," *London Review of Books*, November 15, 2007.

10 Ibid.

11 Lawrence Herzog, "Rebuilding San Diego: Fires, Suburbs and the Public Interest," *San Diego Union Tribune*, op-ed., November 14, 2003, B-7.

12 "Public interest" is loosely defined as the wider health and welfare of the mass of people who live in a region.

13 In fact, since 2007, the state fire protection agency CALFIRE (California Department of Forestry and Fire Protection) has been building state and regional maps showing "Fire Safety Hazardous Zones." Local governments are seeking ways to charge citizens in those districts a fee to provide a higher level of fire protection. But the state does not have jurisdiction over this matter, and, in an era of anti-tax sentiment, there is resistance to this policy approach. It remains a work in progress.

14 Ibid.

15 This point is eloquently made in Richard Halsey, *Fire, Chaparral and Survival in Southern California*. San Diego, CA: Sunbelt Publications, 2008.

16 Ibid., 75.

17 Ibid., xi.

18 *San Diego Union Tribune*, October 24, 2007, 1.

19 Halsey, 2008, xiii.

20 K. Johnson and J. McKinley, "Rethinking Fire Policy in the Tinderbox Zone," *New York Times*, October 28, 2007.

21 Mike Lee, "Building Patterns to Blame," *San Diego Union Tribune*, October 25, 2007, A-7.

22 Halsey, 2008, xii.

23 Christopher Hawken, "Ignoring Nature, We Build Our Way into Fire's Path," *Los Angeles Times*, October 20, 2007, A-1.

24 J. Schwab and S. Meek, "Planning for Wildfires," American Planning Association, Planning Advisory Service, Report No. 529/530, 2005.

25 Ibid.

26 Carol L. Rice and James B. Davis, "Land Use Planning May Reduce Fire Damage in the Urban Wildland Intermix," General Technical Report, U.S. Department of Agriculture, Forest Service, Pacific Southwest Research Station, 1991.

27 See, for example, Michael Gardner, "Back Country's Fire-Protection Fee Advances," *San Diego Union Tribune*, April 10, 2008, http://legacy.utsandiego.com/news/metro/wildfires/20080410–9999–1m10firefee.html, retrieved 4/11/13.

28 Sadhbh Walshe, "Las Vegas: The Reinvention of Sin City as a Sustainable City," *Guardian*, April 25, 2013, http://www.theguardian.com/sustainable-business/las-vegas-sin-city-sustainable, retrieved 10/28/13.

29 Robert Venturi, Denise Scott Brown, and S. Izenour, *Learning from Las Vegas*. Cambridge, MA: MIT Press, 1997. Las Vegas was one of the places that inspired an urban discourse on post-modernism. See Michael Dear, *The Postmodern Urban Condition*. Oxford: Blackwell, 2000.

30 The evolution of Las Vegas is discussed in several useful sources. See Hal Rothman, *Neon Metropolis: How Las Vegas Started the 21st Century*. New York: Routledge, 2002; M. Gottdiener, Claudia C. Collins, and David R. Dickens, *Las Vegas: The Social Production of an All American City*. Oxford: Blackwell, 1999; Hal Rothman and Mike Davis, eds. *The Grit beneath the Glitter: Tales from the Real Las Vegas*. Berkeley: University of California Press, 2002.

31 Ibid.

32 An interesting comparative study of Las Vegas and Coney Island (Brooklyn) tracks the ways in which urban entertainment evolved from the early and mid-twentieth century to the late twentieth century. Brooklyn's Coney Island epitomized the notion of urban entertainment for the masses, and its populism was celebrated in its time. Yet, by the post-World War II period, as New Yorkers moved to the suburbs, that form of city spectacle became less attractive. By contrast, Las Vegas became the symbol of late twentieth century upward mobility; with all its glitter, speculation, and excess, it played to the American psyche of the era. See Sharon Zukin et al., "From Coney Island to Las Vegas in the Urban Imaginary," *Urban Affairs Review*, 33 (5), 1998, 625–53.

33 See the MGM City Center website at http://www.citycenter.com.

34 U.S. Census of Population and Housing data from various sources and projections from State of Nevada, Demographer's Office.

35 Rothman, 2002. It should be noted that, by 2010, the national recession slowed the housing boom in Las Vegas; in fact, a new trend began—people moving away to seek job opportunities elsewhere.

36 "Real Estate in Crisis," *Las Vegas Sun*, October 10, 2013, http://www.lasvegassun.com/news/topics/real-estate/, retrieved October 10, 2013.

37 While Nevada is considered a conservative state, an exception has to be made when it comes to labor. Las Vegas is home to the powerful Culinary Workers Union Local, a labor union for some 44,000 hospitality and service workers mainly employed in hotels, casinos, and restaurants in and around the gambling district.

38 William Fulton, *The Reluctant Metropolis: The Politics of Growth in Los Angeles*. Point Arena, CA: Solano Press, 1997.

39 Ibid.

40 Ibid., 314.

41 Those standards, as I discuss later in this chapter, must conform to the Las Vegas 2020 Plan, and in particular to a 2007 Development Agreement for Kyle Canyon, which set more sustainable design standards for future master planned communities.

42 Richard Malloy, "Dialogue on Development," in Richard Malloy, John Brock, Anthony Floyd, Margaret Livingston, and Robert H. Webb, eds. *Design with the Desert*. CRC Press, 2013, http://books.google.com/books, retrieved October 9, 2013.

43 Marko Salvaggio and Robert Futtrell, "Environment and Sustainability in Nevada," in Dmitri N. Shalin, ed. *Social Health of Nevada*. Las Vegas, NV: UNLV Center for Democratic Culture, 2012.

44 Mel Durco, quoted in Rothman, 278–9.

45 James Howard Kunstler, "Las Vegas: Utopia of Clowns," unpublished essay, www.kunstler.com.

46 Rothman, 2002, xii.

47 Mike Davis, "Las Vegas versus Nature," in Mike Davis, *Dead Cities: And Other Tales*. New York: New Press, 2002, 85–105.

48 Robert Lang and Arthur Nelson, "Megapolitan America," Places: Forum of Design for the Public Realm, November 14, 2011, http://places.designobserver.com/feature/megapolitan-america/30648/.

49 Henry Breen, "Southern Nevada Water Conservation Efforts Heralded," *Las Vegas Review Journal*, June 3, 2011.

50 Salvaggio and Futtrell, 2012, http://cdclv.unlv.edu/healthnv_2012/environment.pdf, retrieved 10/30/13.

51 Salvaggio and Futtrell, 2012.

52 Felicity Barringer, Pat Mulroy, quoted in "Water Use in the Southwest Heads for a Day of Reckoning," *New York Times*, September 27, 2010, http://www.nytimes.com/2010/09/28/us/28mead.html?_r=2.

53 See the "Sustainable Las Vegas" document at http://lasvegasnevada.gov/files/Sustainable_Las_Vegas.pdf.

54 See http://www.lasvegasnevada.gov/sustaininglasvegas/.

55 Form-based codes are regulations that seek to guide the relationship between the mass and form of buildings and the spaces around them, to achieve more street friendly, walkable neighborhoods. They are seen as replacements for traditional zoning regulations which only focused on separating categories of uses of land.

56 Sadhbh Walshe, 2013.

57 Aside from the public policy efforts mentioned above, there have also been public/private initiatives seeking a sustainable approach to managing growth in the region. See, for example, *Envisioning Nevada's Future: Goals and Strategies for Advancing Our Quality of Life*, Nevada Vision Stakeholder Group, 2010; see also the various publications of the Brookings Mountain West program, University of Nevada, Las Vegas at http://brookingsmtnwest.unlv.edu/publications/.

58 Kyle B. Hansen, "Las Vegas Gets Failing Grade in Air Quality Report," *Las Vegas Sun*, April 28, 2010, http://www.lasvegassun.com/news/2010/apr/28/las-vegas-gets-failing-grade-air-quality-report/.

59 Salvaggio and Futtrell, 2012.

60 "America's Most Sedentary Cities," *Forbes Magazine*, October 28, 2007, www.forbes.com/2007/10/28/health-sedentary-cities.

61 Klein, in Rothman and Davis, 18.

62 Rothman, 2002, Introduction.

63 Klein, in Rothman and Davis, 23.

64 See Steve Hargreaves, "Nuclear Waster Back to Yucca Mountain?" *CNN Money*, July 11, 2011, http://money.cnn.com/2011/07/06/news/economy/nuclear_waste/index.htm.

65 Davis, 2002, 91.

66 County of Maricopa, "Eye to the Future," 2001.

67 It includes Maricopa and Pinal counties.

68 U.S. Census, 2008. Phoenix also ranked in the top U.S. metropolitan areas in terms of the actual numerical growth during the 2000–2006 period—it gained 787,306 over that period, just behind Atlanta, Dallas, and Houston (all sunbelt cities too). The city of Phoenix, apart from the larger region, is itself the fifth largest city in the U.S. with 1.5 million, behind New York, Los Angeles, Chicago and Houston.

69 Patricia Gober, *Metropolitan Phoenix: Place Making and Community Building in the Desert*. Philadelphia: University of Pennsylvania Press, 2006.

70 John Mitchell, "Urban Sprawl," National Geographic Magazine online, July, 2001.

71 Joel Kotkin, "Phoenix Rising: A City of Aspiration," *Goldwater Institute Policy Report*, April, 2005.

72 Gober, 2006, 104.

73 Carol Heim, "Leapfrogging, Urban Sprawl and Growth Management: Phoenix, 1950–2000," *American Journal of Economics and Sociology*, January, 2001, 3.

74 Heim, 2001, 3.

75 Gober, 2006.

76 Ibid.

77 Ibid.

78 See, for example, "General Motors, Others Decide the SUV Is Dead," *U.S. News and World Report*, June 4, 2008; James Howard Kunstler, "Driving Toward Disaster," *San Diego Union Tribune*, Opinion, May 28, 2008, B-7.

79 Gober, 2006.

80 Dolores Hayden, *A Field Guide to Sprawl*. New York: W.W. Norton, 2004.

81 See website for Valley Metro light rail system, http://www.valleymetro.org/metrolightrail/.

82 Ibid. See http://www.valleymetro.org/metro_projects_planning/transit_oriented_development.

83 Gober, 2006.

84 American Lung Association, State of the Air, Phoenix, 2009, www.stateoftheair.org. These numbers have gone slightly up or down over the last decade, but Phoenix generally continues to suffer from poor air quality.

85 Shaun McKinnon, "The Air We Breathe: Surrounded by Pollution," *Arizona Republic*, January 29, 2012, http://www.azcentral.com/news/air-quality/?content=1-overview.

86 John Hazlehurst, "Arizona Would Bear Brunt of Water Restrictions," *Colorado Springs Business Journal*, October 5, 2007.

87 An excellent discussion of the inequities of environmental pollution within the Phoenix region can be found in Andrew Ross, *Bird on Fire*. New York: Oxford University Press, 2011.

88 Sarah Brooks, "Innovative Waste Utilization and the Concerned Residents of South Phoenix, AZ," http://www.umich.edu/~snre492/Jones/Sarahbrooks.htm.

89 Annamarie Schneider and Curtis Woodcock, "Compact, Dispersed, Fragmented, Extensive? A Comparison of Urban Growth in Twenty-Five Global Cities Using Remotely Sensed Data, Pattern Metrics and Census Information," *Urban Studies*, 45 (3), March, 2008, 659–92.

90 Jonathan Mahler, "The Soul of the New Exurb," *New York Times Magazine*, March 27, 2005, 30–7.

91 Mahler persuasively makes this argument in his 2005 *New York Times* magazine essay.

92 Ibid.

93 William DeBuys, "The Least Sustainable City: Phoenix as a Harbinger for Our Hot Future," March 17, 2013, http://grist.org/author/william-debuys/.

94 See the link at http://phoenix.gov/greenphoenix/sustainability/index.html, retrieved 11/4/13.

95 See the link at http://www.maricopa.gov/greengovernment/, retrieved 11/4/13.

96 Unfortunately, the key regional planning agency, the Maricopa Association of Governments, still has highway planning as its central mission. See Emily Talen, "Sprawl Retrofit: Sustainable Urban Form in Unsustainable Places," *Environment and Planning B: Planning and Design*, 38, 2011, 952–78.

97 Ross, 2011.

98 Ross, 2011.

99 Andrew Ross, "The Dark Side of the 'Green' city," *New York Times*, November 6, 2011, http://www.nytimes.com/2011/11/07/opinion/in-phoenix-the-dark-side-of-green.html?_r=0, retrieved 11/4/13.

100 Ibid., 15.

4

SPRAWL SOUTH OF THE BORDER
FROM MEXICO CITY TO TIJUANA

By the beginning of the twenty-first century, while US suburbs were struggling environmentally, their basic lifestyle and flawed design features were spreading across the planet. Today, one can speak of a globalization of suburbs, and the formation of what I am calling a "global suburb,"[1] an elite or middle class community on the periphery of cities across the Americas, as well as on other continents. These developments were partially influenced by the American suburb of the 1950s, though they took on different forms and evolved in different contexts in Latin America. The profile of the American suburb, as we see it in Los Angeles, San Diego, Las Vegas, or Phoenix, consists of low density, single family, detached housing, often on the outskirts of an urban core, and relies on the automobile to move people around. Similar versions have been built on the urban periphery in Australia, New Zealand, and South Africa. And now, for the first time, they are also becoming an important part of the sprawling urban landscape that stretches from the Mexican border to the southern cone of South America. These new suburbs blanketing the outskirts of Mexican cities display the same troubling ecological flaws and public health challenges we find in U.S. suburbs.

Around the world, global suburbs often employ the cultural branding of United States prototypes, for example through their place names. One of the most affluent suburbs outside Cairo, Egypt, is called "Beverly

Hills." An upper class enclave on the northern edges of Beijing is named "Orange County." One of Hong Kong's wealthy peripheral residential districts calls itself "Palm Springs." Similar global suburbs have risen outside Jakarta, Manila, Lagos, and Johannesburg.[2]

In South Africa, "security villages" emerged as a way for upper and upper middle classes to further fence themselves off during the period of apartheid or in the uncertainty of the post-apartheird era. The sprawling suburb of "Somerset West" outside Capetown, South Africa, has a state-of-the-art electric fence around it. More recently, a new kind of suburb has emerged in South Africa, the "eco-estate" or "nature estate." According to observers, it is still a suburb whose underlying motive for existence is affluent residents' fear of crime, and it has all the elements of a gated community—walls, razor wire, and other fortification motifs. However, these far-flung communities are designed to be closer to nature, as both a form of marketing as well as a way to give the often criticized idea of "gating" more social credibility by connecting its existence to nature.[3]

All of this also reflects a fundamental reorganization of space in urbanized regions, in which wealthy and poor are ever more separated, either geographically or via technology, walls, and fences. The term "global suburb" thus captures the idea of this sprawl, and the socio-spatial reorganization that has spread across the globe, a new form of escape within the metropolis of the twenty-first century, a post-modern expression of evolving personal tastes and identities.[4] These emerging social and cultural hybrids are part of the evolution of an evolving social model of cities. One wonders whether this new world simply reinforces the conditions of inequality, allowing wealthy classes to further distance themselves from the realities of urban life.

The suburban design model, albeit in different forms adapted to each cultural setting, has diffused globally to other nations over the last four decades. More importantly, what I would call its "socio-cultural design narrative" has also spread across the planet, and, I will argue, that narrative is a driving force behind the evolution of global suburbs. I should make it clear that I am not suggesting it is the only determining factor shaping gated communities and middle or upper middle class suburbs in Latin America; however, I am arguing it is a significant one that has not received enough attention. This "suburb" narrative is driven by a set of values that include: social exclusivity, an increasing desire for private over public space, fear of crime, a preference for predictable, homogeneous built environments, and a greater emphasis on consumerism and shopping within artificially constructed spaces. These values, either directly or indirectly, underscore the emerging "fast world" that I am also arguing has come to define urban spaces in the new century.

In this chapter, I explore the nature of the new periphery forming at the edge of Latin American cities. This new periphery is displaying many of the same troubling patterns of urban sprawl as in the United States. It has been shaped by the forces of fast urbanism from the north, which have diffused into Mexico, and which are producing car-oriented, highly dispersed, and unsustainable hinterlands south of the border.

As mentioned earlier in this book, since the post-World War II period, the outskirts of cities south of the border have been mainly occupied by waves of poor rural migrants seeking cheap temporary shelter away from the formal rental markets in the urban core. They built shantytown and squatter settlements that blanketed most urban peripheries. But, beginning in the 1990s, a new era of peripheral urbanization dawned. We can call it the era of the global suburbs.

An Overview of Global Suburbs in Latin America

For most of the second half of the last century, the urban periphery of Latin America was dominated by *asentamiento irregulares* (irregular settlements)—squatter settlements and shantytowns that evolved as poor rural migrants began arriving in cities in the 1950s. Thus, to speak of suburbs on the outskirts of Latin American cities is to recognize that most of that terrain is already occupied by the legacy of nearly a half century of spontaneous colonization and informal settlement construction by the most disadvantaged citizens of Latin American nations. Thus the global suburbs that are locating on the edges of large cities in Mexico or elsewhere in Latin America are communities wedged into squatter-dominated spaces of the periphery—along rivers or coasts, on land owned by the government, or on properties where residents are evicted or otherwise driven away to make way for more profitable uses of land.

The rise of global suburbs in Latin American cities must be understood within the context of cities that evolved under unique circumstances, ones that were very different from those in the United States. U.S. cities were historically influenced by the colonial traditions of British town planning, and also by the anti-urban Jeffersonian philosophy that favored agrarian life. American cities grew during the industrial age of the nineteenth century, and quickly evolved under the influence of, first, land speculators and then a sophisticated growth industry. Eventually innovation in transport technologies like rail, automobile, and highway building produced streetcar and later freeway suburbs for the middle and upper classes. A national housing program with federally backed mortgages fortified the mass suburbanization of the middle classes after World War II.

Latin American cities, by contrast, were more profoundly influenced by their Spanish colonial origins. The Spanish imperial system for colonizing Latin America was organized around the sixteenth and seventeenth century "Royal Ordinances for the Laying out of New Towns." These ordinances, established by the Spanish royal family, were dictated to the colonies through the imperial administration of viceroys and governors. They involved strict urban design and planning codes that ordained in great detail how all cities across Spanish America would be laid out. Among the laws and standards, for example, were design strategies requiring the use of a grid-iron plan anchored by a main plaza and several other secondary plazas which became the critical nodes around which the functional apparatus of the city would grow. Centrality would remain as a vital force in defining the socio-spatial structure of Latin American cities into the late twentieth century.[5]

Latin American cities evolved through three phases prior to the twenty-first century. In the first phase, from around 1500–1800, cities were compact and residential status defined by proximity to the main plaza. In the second phase, the nineteenth century, European immigration increased, and linear corridors extending from the downtown core defined the new zones of high status and upper income residence. Meanwhile, the poor remained in emerging slum quarters close to the city center or nearby industrial districts. During the third phase, from the 1940s onward, giant waves of rural to urban migration brought millions of landless peasants to the cities. This eventually produced a large-scale socio-spatial polarization of rich and poor, with the poor funneled into squatter settlements and shantytowns, mainly isolated in districts on the urban periphery, while the rich lived in a cone shaped area roughly defined by downtown and an elite corridor that connected the city center to a second high status zone on the periphery. These two zones for the wealthy were served by streetcars, and later by automobiles.[6]

By the late twentieth century, a geographic segregation between rich and poor defined the spatial form of most Latin American cities. Also, unlike in the U.S., only a small middle class existed and was not yet a significant factor in overall urban form. During the fourth phase of urban evolution, which began in the first decade of the twenty-first century, globalization began to reshape the spatial form of cities. The forces of globalization and the neoliberal model of economic development brought the elements of "fast urbanism"—heightened consumerism, the expansion of shopping spaces, advertising, high technology, business parks, and other sectors—to the urban periphery. These forces combined to create metropolitan regions characterized by fragmentation and by the formation of what has been termed an "archipelago" of gated spaces and fortified centers, all served by the automobile and all disconnected from each other. These closed off "islands" of activity included gated suburbs, malls, private schools, and social and recreation clubs. The archipelago of increasingly spread out developments, as in the U.S., became overwhelmingly dependent on automobiles, and even, in some cases, on private toll roads that allowed the wealthy to get to work more quickly.[7] These patterns have been observed across the Americas, especially in Argentina, Chile, Mexico, and Brazil.[8]

Two trends are notable in the shifting structure of the Latin American periphery in the twenty-first century. First, gated communities and fenced suburbs are now spreading into zones that were previously occupied by only squatter communities. The new gated suburbs in Latin America are called *barrios privados* (private communities) in Argentina, *condominios* in Chile, *conjuntos* or *urbanizaciones cerradas* in Ecuador, *condominios fechados* (closed condominiums) in Brazil, and *fraccionamiento cerrados* in Mexico. In Buenos Aires, middle and upper class suburban enclaves have been built; they are now surrounded by illegal settlements and garbage dumps. In general, on the Latin American periphery we are now seeing luxury residential quarters served by freeways juxtaposed against squatter communities, literally "islands of wealth in an ocean of poverty."[9] This trend alludes to a dramatic shift in the scale of segregation. In the twentieth century, large scale segregation was the hallmark of urban form, with rich and poor profoundly separated in space. Today we are seeing what one scholar terms "small-scale segregation," in which wealthy and upper middle class enclaves are spread across the metropolitan region. The enclaves are fortified with fences and walls, but localized on plots that become available depending on topography, land markets, and other factors. And now these enclaves are typically adjacent to squatter neighborhoods.[10]

The second recent trend in the Latin American periphery lies in the tendency to build "mega-projects" that are not merely gated communities, but, rather, "gated cities," giant developments of 30,000 and more inhabitants—in Chile, Brazil, Mexico, and elsewhere. The original mega-suburb was probably Alphaville, on the edge of São Paulo, Brazil, where construction was begun in 1974. Many scholars point out that Alphaville and other projects in São Paulo were influenced by North American ideas about suburbs and marketing.[11] From Mexico to Brazil, we find evidence of either direct foreign investment in mega-projects or the influence of foreign design and marketing strategies in building those projects.[12] This is a good reason to consider these "global" mega-projects.

Both of these early twenty-first century trends in the Latin American periphery underscore the overwhelming role of exclusion as the emerging structuring force in the social and geographical construction of urban space in Latin America. This exclusion is observed not only in the formation of gated elite and upper middle class residential zones, but also in the rise of highly protected, often fortified privatized business centers, schools, leisure and recreation spaces, and the ever ubiquitous shopping malls. Exclusion, isolation, and fragmentation also hint at a corresponding loss of community and public life, which once again speaks to a familiar lament in U.S. "fast" suburbs. As one scholarly report points out: "If modernity . . . meant urban and community life, social interaction and a common responsibility, then the contemporary or post-modern Latin American city seems to loosen these urban qualities."[13]

The New Suburbs of Mexico City

There is a well known saying one hears in Mexico and along the border. It encapsulates both Mexico's historic pride and its ambivalence toward the U.S.: "Poor Mexico. So far from God, and so close to the United States."[14] Despite its geographic proximity to the United States, when it comes to architecture and city-building, during much of the twentieth century Mexico prided itself on being independent of its giant and powerful northern neighbor. More generally, it is known that the loss of the northern territories of the southwestern U.S. following the U.S.–Mexican War of 1846–8 led to more than a century of tension between the two nations. Scholars acknowledge that this tension has created, at the very least, Mexican ambivalence toward the U.S. Mexicans may feel admiration for American consumer culture and wealth, but resentful of both the nineteenth century loss of territory and the U.S. position of economic, cultural, and political power.[15] This has led to a tendency for a "masked" and sometimes seemingly contradictory national psyche.[16]

Mexico has carved its own place in history, very distinct from its northern neighbor. It prides itself on the 1910 Mexican revolution and its various legacies, including promotion of the national cultural identity and preservation of the nation's history, especially its "cultural patrimony"—from indigenous archaeological sites and historic colonial districts to modern works of architecture.[17] Mexico has had a very different urban experience than the United States, beginning with the extensive indigenous city-building period highlighted by the ceremonial stone architecture of the Nahuatl, Aztec, and Mayan cultures, among others, followed by the three hundred plus years of colonial urban design. No less significant have been the unique efforts to build modern cities, influenced by European modernists like Le Corbusier. Also, post-revolutionary Mexico institutionalized the construction of contemporary monuments and physical representations of the nation's rich historic past.[18]

Still, despite Mexico's ambivalence toward the U.S., the painful memory of lost colonial territory, and a nationalist desire to cling to culturally unique city-building ideas and traditions, American influence on architecture and urban development could not help but slip south across the international border. For more than one hundred and fifty years, millions of immigrants have flowed north into the United States, creating a gargantuan cross-border family exchange network, unsurpassed anywhere on the planet. The two nations exchange billions of dollars through international trade; in 1992 they formalized this reality through the North American Free Trade Agreement (NAFTA), which also included Canada. In 2011, as an example, the total size of U.S.–Mexico trade was 500 billion dollars.[19] These global social (immigration) and economic (trade) interdependencies inevitably become embedded in vast interchanges of culture and media, in film, television, radio, print, and the internet, which have generated a massive U.S.–Mexican cross-border flow of information, consumption, and artistic and creative collaboration.

Thus it should not be surprising that the phenomenon of the American suburb and its sprawl crossed south of the border into Mexico. The first experiments with suburban developments occurred, not surprisingly, in the national capital, Mexico City. Many important cultural projects begin in Mexico City, the nation's epicenter for cultural expression, economic power, and political decision-making. The first two experiments with the American style suburb unfolded just after World War II—one in the northwestern part of the capital, in a development called Ciudad Satelite, the other in the southern part of the city, in the project known as Jardines de Pedregal. Because both were built in the 1940s and 1950s, one could argue that if they did not outright physically copy the U.S. suburban model from that era (which was just then taking form to the north), they did embody the "suburban American imaginary," the narrative of the American suburb, of a place where you could escape the density of the city to a neighborhood closer to nature, and where you could own your house and travel around with the modern convenience of the automobile.[20]

Jardines de Pedregal was planned and developed in the mid-to-late 1940s, on the Pedregal lava fields south of downtown where a volcano had erupted in 5000 B.C. The site was adjacent to an important pre-Columbian settlement called Cuicuilco, which was the largest city in the Valley of Mexico in 300 B.C. Luis Barragan, one of Mexico's most important modernist architects, proposed to develop the new suburb. His idea was to promote harmony between architecture and the landscape. He designed and built two initial works in 1949—the Plaza de Las Fuentes, a semi-public gateway that included a sculpture set into lava rocks, and Lote Muestra, a demonstration house and garden, surrounded by walls made from volcanic stone.

The Jardines de Pedregal development was advertised as a new town filled with modernist homes on a lava rock landscape with natural vegetation from the region. Unfortunately this utopian suburb was never completed in the form Barragan had hoped for, and was ultimately overwhelmed by large scale urbanization projects that encroached on it as the city boomed after 1960. The Plaza de Las Fuentes was engulfed by giant glass and concrete office buildings. The original Lote Muestra gardens were subdivided and sold off for houses after the 1950s, while many of the original houses were converted to condominiums or schools or replaced by higher density structures. Not surprisingly, Barragan was disappointed by the destruction of the original Pedregal plan.

To the north of downtown Mexico City, Ciudad Satelite (literally translated as "Satellite City") has its own story, one that echoes the experience to the south. Satelite was made possible by the development of major highways, especially the ring road, or *periférico*, which linked it to the wealthy districts in the west (Lomas Chapultepec, Santa Fe) and south, and the *viaducto*, which linked it to downtown and the airport. The growth of this area may have responded to political pressures. It is common knowledge that President Miguel Aleman owned land on the site of Ciudad Satelite, and supported the modernization of cities.[21]

Like the Jardines de Pedregal, Ciudad Satelite was planned as a utopian suburb by architects Mario Pani and Luis Barragan. Pani utilized the English garden city model adapted in early U.S. utopian suburban designs in places like Radburn, New Jersey, and Columbia, Maryland. It included residential super-blocks with cul-de-sac designs that separated pedestrian flows from automobiles and preserved huge swaths of green space. Pani employed a street layout system of wide oval circuits or *circuitos*, each named for different professional careers—Scientists, Engineers, Architects, Sculptors, Economists, and Novelists. The plan was approved in 1948 and built over the next decade. Its status as a symbolic and functional center of the new modern Mexico was symbolized by the completion in 1958 of one of Mexico's iconic public art projects, the Torres de Satelite (Satelite Towers), designed by Luis Barragan and Mathias Goerritz. These colorful high rise stone towers were metaphors for modern Mexico, a nation of high rises and technology, though somewhat ironically they were located at the entrance to a mainly low rise garden suburb!

Ciudad Satelite's status as a symbol of the future of Mexico was sealed by the building of the city's first large scale, luxury shopping mall, the Plaza Satelite, opened in 1971. At the opening ceremony, developers, according to one Mexican author, proudly claimed that the Satelite

Figure 4.1 Towers of Satelite: Public Sculpture at Entrance to Mexico City's First Suburb
Source: Photo by Lawrence A. Herzog

district was now "distinguished by its culture of consumption, its social status and its appearance as an American suburb."[22]

Marketing was a critical part of the success of early American style suburbs in Mexico City. There were three important elements to marketing these homes. First, there was the dream of having your own home, and especially of owning a detached or individual house, as opposed to living in a more collective one. A typical ad back in the 1960s, from the newspaper *Excelsior*, reads: "the whole family will be happier if you own your house; don't think it's a dream to make this longing a reality: buy a house."[23] A second element was the desire for a connection with nature. This is clearly linked to advertising campaigns in the U.S. which emphasized the idea of suburban housing as "living in the countryside," using names in the developments (gardens, meadows, rolling hills, and farms) that evoke the feeling of nature. This idea was attractive in Mexico because it overlapped with the cultural importance of the family—and the idea that babies would sleep in quiet, peaceful surroundings, children could play in green areas, and the family would have its own garden.[24]

In the cases of both Jardines de Pedregal and Ciudad Satelite, the maps used in advertisements usually distorted the distances between the new developments and the central city, making them look much closer. This helped mollify concerns about the lengthy commute to jobs back in downtown, a ploy frequently used by American suburb developers as well. A third marketing element in the Satelite suburb was the actual reference to life in the United States in Mexican advertisements, such as one that advertised a project where the housing would be "built using the most modern American design."[25] There was also frequent allusion to the convenience of travel by automobile attached to these new suburbs, and in the 1960s a drive-in movie theater (similar to those built in U.S. suburbs during this period) was built in the Ciudad Satelite district of Mexico City.

Mexican architects and urbanists might debate whether suburbs like Jardines de Pedregal and Ciudad Satelite were Americanized or not. Certainly, in terms of their initial designs, there was much about them that was uniquely Mexican—the emphasis on Mexican modernity, for example, which combined pre-Columbian ideas about the use of stone and nature with modernist building techniques. However, the cultural narrative, and the psychological and symbolic meanings embedded in these suburbs, were strongly influenced by the imagined idea of the American suburb. As local experts put it, "Ciudad Satelite is seen, in general and by its own inhabitants, as an American suburb with American ways of life."[26]

As in Jardines de Pedregal, however, the continued growth of Mexico City around and inside the original utopian suburb of Ciudad Satelite led to the eclipse of the original design plan. For example, a green belt around the zone was eventually destroyed by property speculation and development. As the neighborhood grew, lots were bought up and changed, the result of which brought smaller houses, multifamily blocks, and development that compromised the original flow of streets. The Mexican architect Mario Pani was so disappointed with the changes to Satelite that he later claimed it had turned into a "Tinacolandia," a Mexican version of Levittown, with ticky-tack houses massed in a sprawling, car-oriented suburb with no sense of place or identity.[27]

Ciudad Satelite also became increasingly congested as the number of automobiles and commuters increased, to the point that it has become one of the many zones with serious gridlock and air pollution in the Mexico City region today, a textbook example of the negative aspects of urban sprawl. Development grew out of control in and around Satelite. One important scandal is illustrative: an outdoor shopping mall was built here, but later abandoned. The irony is that it was called "Acropolis"—it never became popular (precisely because the polluted air does not lend itself to an outdoor mall in Mexico City's north zone). It remains in ruins to this day, a living example of the flawed attempt to copy American suburbia in a very different Mexican context. Quite a few squatter settlements and *colonias* have also oozed into the spaces between and around suburban developments, mostly just south of Ciudad Satellite.

While utopian suburbs were being built in the 1950s, another important trend facing Mexico City was the boom in informal development of *colonias* and squatter neighborhoods on the periphery of Mexico City, mainly to the east and northeast but also in some locations in the south and west.[28] The magnitude of this peripheral urbanization was enormous and included people living in illegal subdivisions on the dried up lakes to the east and on the slopes of volcanoes in the southwest. The Mexican government has been extracting water from underground aquifers created by the original lake. Unfortunately, the government is taking water out more than twice as fast as it is replenished. This renders the surface of land on the periphery into a spongy clay that is gradually drying up, and in some cases sinking.

Many of these outer communities suffer extreme ecological dysfunction—from polluted air and lack of water to toxic industrial waste spills. This massive explosion of *colonias populares* (popular colonies) in some parts of the Mexico City metropolitan area added to the overall polarization between rich and poor, and led to the increasing search for neighborhoods that would allow upper and upper middle class citizens to escape the perceived ills of what was becoming the largest metropolitan region in the Americas, and one of the largest in the world. It would also lead to the acceleration of new ways for the government to provide some kind of alternative to the chaotic illegal occupation of the city's periphery.

Mega-projects and the New Global Suburbs

Some observers believe the 1982 economic crisis in Mexico, and the social instability it created, contributed to a new era in which Mexican real estate interests sought to move up to building high end gated communities and "mega-projects." The signature example of such a mega-project is Santa Fe, a high profile corporate and residential development planned and built in the 1980s and 1990s. Ten miles to the west of the historic center, Santa Fe was originally a toxic garbage dump where about 2,000 poor people lived in illegal cardboard shacks and earned a small wage recycling garbage. The squatters were eventually removed from here and later from areas around this part of Mexico City to make way for "mega-project" building, including giant corporate, residential, and commercial complexes such as those in Santa Fe.[29]

The idea was to turn Santa Fe into the new center of an emerging more global Mexico City economy, more oriented toward service than industry. Up until the 1990s, Mexico City's wealth was generated mainly by industry, especially import substitution, a strategy dating to the first half of the twentieth century, but one that had become obsolete. Also, too many industries were heavy polluters in a city already suffering from toxic air pollution problems. Santa Fe would now house the free trade (NAFTA) companies that would be doing business in a globalizing Mexico by the twenty-first century, as well as all the high tech, financial, computer, and other emerging post-industrial sectors. Planned and built in the 1980s and 1990s, Santa Fe became an enclave of multinational corporate headquarters, the new center for global finance in Mexico.

Santa Fe was both symbolically and functionally the place where Mexico announced that it sought to become a player in the global economy for the new century. It is said that the developers of Santa Fe were the same investors and developers who built global resort destinations like Cancun or Cabo San Lucas.[30] Among the transnational companies with headquarters here are Hewlett Packard, General Electric, IBM, Goodyear, Pepsi, Federal Express, and Kraft. Mexican corporate giants have also moved their headquarters here—Banamex, Televisa, Bimbo, and two tequila companies, Cuervo and Sauza. There are five hotels with four- and five-star ratings, forty restaurants, and seven schools here, including two universities. One of the city's largest and most lavish shopping malls, Centro Comercial Santa Fe, was built in the 1990s; it is the third largest mall in Latin America, with 300 stores and fourteen movie theaters.

Santa Fe was designed to imitate new high rise business districts like La Défense, outside Paris, places that are autonomous and help decentralize and take pressure off the city center.[31] As in other elite suburbs, famous architects like Ricardo Legorreta were brought in to do the master plan, while others, such as Teodoro Gonzalez de Leon and Abraham Zabludovsky, were contracted to design key buildings. But rather than create an ecologically progressive new town center outside the urbanized core, the Mexican government actually built an elite suburb for a small number of very wealthy residents—about 20,000 by most estimates. Meanwhile nearly a quarter million poor people would end up adjacent to the new mega-gated suburb living in dilapidated squatter housing.[32] Santa Fe quickly became an environmental problem for the Mexico City region. Designed entirely for automobiles, Santa Fe is now one of the more congested places in the metropolitan zone. With only a few roads leading into and out of Santa Fe, and limited public transit, it is a traffic planner's worst nightmare come to life.

Inside the district, one finds urban planning problems that mirror those found in U.S. sunbelt suburban areas like Phoenix and Las Vegas. For example, there are virtually no parks, gardens, streets, or other vibrant public spaces to walk in. Even within Santa Fe, most destinations can only be reached by car; few people walk from one location to another within the community. The residential spaces are largely high rise, luxury condominium complexes. Most of the wealthy residential zones are gated. They market their exclusivity, as in this sample advertisement for one of the gated complexes, Bosque Santa Fe: "City Santa Fe: Welcome to Civilization. Exclusivity in the Best Location."[33] This kind of isolation and polarization has not impressed visiting designers. In the words of a well known Spanish urbanist: "Lacking public space, Santa Fe is like a walled city for exclusive use of its residents, owners and

Figure 4.2 View of Office Building in the Elite Mega-suburb of Santa Fe, Mexico City
Source: Photo by Lawrence A. Herzog

cowards. It's good business for the municipal government, but a poor urban design model for the private sector."[34]

Santa Fe is symptomatic of the new globalized, elite suburbs that appeared on the outskirts of cities throughout Latin America after the 1980s and 1990s, a kind of barometer of the fast pace of globalization, and the way in which it is producing a new type of urban region. It mirrors the qualities of "fortified enclaves"[35] in cities across the Americas—the emphasis on spatial segregation of the wealthy and upper middle class, the heightened obsession with security, increasing privatization, and the development of spaces of consumption (shopping malls) as central to the identity of these suburban places.

Santa Fe is just one of many "mega-projects" found in the emerging elite suburbs of Mexican cities. These mega-projects are argued to be attempts to create new centers away from the aging, decaying downtowns and outmoded industrial zones of cities like Monterrey, Tijuana, Puebla, and Mexico City. Globalization, it is argued, is feeding the creation of these new places. For example, outside Puebla, Mexico's fourth largest city, developers built a mega-suburb called Angelopolis. It has middle and upper income gated residential developments, five star hotels, two private universities, three giant shopping malls, a business park, and a government complex. What it does not have is people walking or bicycling slowly from home to work, or from home to commercial destinations. Ethnographic observations of these spaces make it clear there is a great deal of U.S. cultural influence, for example young people living the "fast urbanist lifestyle," and who are described as "texting furiously and drinking Frappuccinos" in cafes inside malls. Observers report feeling that the spaces are designed to imitate iconic global places like Miami, Milan, or London.[36] More critically, however, there is a sense of social fragmentation and escalating polarization brought on by these mega-projects. In the words of one study, "the mega-projects fragment the city, disembedding spaces from a wider urbanism."[37]

While giant shopping malls in the new mega-projects appear to be elitist and even discriminatory toward the urban poor, one cannot assume these new globalized shopping malls are routinely rejected by the underprivileged classes. It's been shown, for example, that shopping is often seen as not merely a transaction, but also a place for the pursuit of ideals like "beauty, truth and perfection."[38] Malls can have a transcendent or theatrical quality for the poor, who have few other comfortable public spaces within which to dwell.[39]

The social ecology of elite suburbs and giant shopping malls raises larger issues about globalization, politics, and consumerism. This is clearly illustrated by the example of the "Walmartization of Mexico." Walmart owns nearly 1,000 businesses for its franchise in Mexico, not only Walmart super-stores but also several other national supermarket franchises (Bodegas Aurrerá, Superamas, Suburbias) as well as the popular Vips restaurant chain. Nearly a third of all their businesses are in the Mexico City region. Overall national sales among Walmart owned establishments in Mexico are estimated to be around $20 billion/year, with some 150,000 people employed. This makes Walmart Mexico's largest private employer. As one of the largest corporations in the world, Walmart's gross earnings of $250 billion/year[40] make it an important actor, though not the only one, in the globalization debate.

Walmart has an especially huge impact on small and medium towns, such as those in the suburbs of mega-cities like Mexico City. While Walmart frequently advertises its commitment to "social responsibility," its track record on social and environmental issues is mixed. For one, Walmart employees are essentially prohibited from collective bargaining or the formation of unions. Secondly, the mega-stores and giant supermarkets often wipe out other retailers, thus consolidating power in the hands of a foreign-owned corporation, leaving towns, cities, and regions vulnerable to their corporate policies.[41]

Walmart super-centers are one of the driving forces that perpetuate urban sprawl by creating one single giant destination that requires large numbers of automobile trips, while often causing neighborhood scale commercial enterprises to go out of business. This requires more net families to drive further, since they are shopping at the super-centers rather than in local stores. One estimate suggests that Walmart's share of the extra miles driven in the U.S. is resulting in more than 5 million metric tons of CO_2 emissions each year. Walmart's imprint on our landscape, in the words of Kaid Benfield, director of the Sustainable Communities and Smart Growth program at the Natural Resources Defense Council, is "their most serious legacy for the environment. In terms of global warming, it's a huge issue. Our per person emissions are much higher in sprawl locations than they are in more walkable locations."[42]

In Mexico, Walmart's ascendancy as a major player in the expansion of urban regions since 1990 has happened so quickly, in a nation that has only just begun to build environmental preservation institutions, that it has not really been given much attention. Citizens in Mexico generally like the availability of consumer goods at lower prices. As one author describes, "suddenly in an air conditioned, fluorescent-lit warehouse, pushing their children in wide-body metal cars, Teotihuacán's citizens are confronted with more options than they have ever imagined: umpteen brands of diapers, breakfast cereals, soda pop."[43] Yet the same writer goes on to say: "Still, I wondered how many people who live in the town could actually afford to fill a grocery cart and pay for the merchandise."[44]

The debate about Walmart's environmental impact in Mexico came to a head in 2004, when the company decided to develop the Bodega Aurrerá super-store on the edge of the UNESCO World Heritage Site at Teotihuacán, the archaeological zone known for its giant ancient pre-Columbian pyramids. It lies in the suburban municipality of San Juan Teotihuacán, on the outskirts of Mexico City, about thirty miles northwest of the city center. Law suits were filed against Walmart by the left wing Partido de la Revolucion Democratica (PRD) party, while Frente Civico, a coalition of artists, writers, intellectuals, and others, campaigned vigorously in the national and global media to stop the development. The project was eventually approved by the pro-development government of then president Vicente Fox. It rationalized that Teotihuacán was already growing in a chaotic manner, and that its residents needed the many jobs created by the new store.

Many local residents in San Juan Teotihuacán were not opposed to the Walmart-owned super-store. But they already depend on tourism employment from the pyramids and the surrounding archaeological site, and one could surmise that anything that potentially threatens the cultural importance of that site should be kept away by the government. In fact, Mexican law under the agency INAH (National Institute of History and Anthropology) prohibits all construction inside the immediate archaeological site itself, and in two surrounding zones. But in the outer perimeter of the surrounding zones (what is called "Perimeter C") the regulations are more vague. They state that "new constructions will be allowed that do not negatively impact the preservation or integrity of the zone of archaeological monuments."[45] One would think that building a giant mega-store so near archaeological ruins would be deemed to have a negative impact. However, as observers studying the controversy suggest, the new, pro-business Mexican president, swept into power in the national election of 2000, appointed an INAH director sympathetic to allowing Walmart to build on the site.[46] The government approved the construction permit and the super-store was built and opened in 2004.

An ironic cartoon appeared in Mexico City soon after, in the national newspaper *La Jornada*. It showed the President of Mexico, Vicente Fox, standing next to the pyramids at Teotihuacán saying: "If the conquistadors built churches on top of the pyramids, why not let those from Wal-Mart build a superstore on top of them"? This biting cartoon alludes to the idea of global capital as a new kind of "conquest," the potential destruction or trivialization of the past by overdevelopment, and the degree to which the pro-development philosophy in Mexico may be environmentally and culturally destructive, following a similar path to that of the United States.

In fact, labor statistics show that, for every two jobs created by Walmart in Mexico, three jobs are lost from other sectors.[47] It was also later shown that the pro-development INAH director appointed by President Fox may have colluded with Walmart officials to find ways to avoid INAH's own laws prohibiting this kind of development. After the inauguration of the Walmart store in 2004, historic artifacts were uncovered on the site. Rumor had it that INAH may have known about these artifacts. The director of INAH resigned shortly thereafter.[48] More recently, records and interviews show that Walmart de Mexico arranged to bribe an official to change the zoning map in the municipality before it was sent to the newspaper. The zoning map would not become law until it was published in a government newspaper. Once the bribe had been paid, the map was published, and the zoning on land that had prohibited commercial development was redrawn to allow Walmart's store.[49]

New Suburbs for the Working Class

As Mexico urbanized in the 1950s and 1960s, millions of migrants arrived in its large cities from small and medium sized towns, and from the countryside. At first, these mainly poor migrants tried finding rental housing in older neighborhoods on the edge of the central city, districts which later became known as *vecindades*. Migrants lived in small one- or two-room units inside apartment blocks. But as the scale of immigration became too large for *vecindades* to absorb them, millions of migrants shifted toward a "self-help" solution by building their own makeshift homes on land they often invaded or occupied either illegally or with questionable ownership status. Typically these self-help neighborhoods were located in the growing periphery of cities.

By the 1970s, having long opposed these settlements, local governments gradually accepted these self-help communities, which were called *colonias* or *colonias populares*. Over time, faced with its own inability to provide formal public housing for this massive wave of new urban dwellers, governments often helped "regularize" these districts. This included bringing in electricity, piped water, roads, and schools, though often not every *colonia* received the full package of services. Further, many residents did not necessarily receive title to their land. This led to the evolution of a national urban popular movement to protect these residents from the loss of their homes and neighborhoods, and to defend their need for services. It is estimated that, during the decades of the 1970s and 1980s, self-help housing solutions represented the main form of housing production in large Mexican cities, some two-thirds of all housing.[50]

In Mexico City, *colonias* developed in the north and east of the metropolitan region. To the east, the government eventually permitted spontaneous construction on the former lake bed in an area called Nezahualcóyotl, or "Neza," which had 1.2 million residents by the year 2000. In the 1980s, Neza was the largest self-help *colonia* district in the nation, a massive city of squatter shacks that lacked basic services and was dominated by substandard, irregular housing. Over the next three decades, local government gradually incorporated infrastructure, provided services, and helped improve housing conditions.

The federal government also tried building subsidized housing for the poor, mainly through agencies like the National Housing Fund (FOVI) and the National Institute for the Development of Workers' Housing (INFONAVIT). FOVI built over 800,000 units nationally from 1970 to 1992, while INFONAVIT built around one million units during the same time period. Those houses were built in a modernist style—low, medium, and sometimes high rise buildings with very basic amenities, in fairly high density locations, often close to downtown. While these numbers are impressive, they were not enough to address the massive demand (in the millions) for urban housing during this period of urban expansion in Mexico. Also, these housing units were mainly available to either salaried government employees or middle income city dwellers. Meanwhile, the housing needs of the poor and the working class remained unmet.

In the 1990s, the Mexican government shifted its housing policy strategy. The most important change was to switch INFONAVIT from a producer of housing to a financial institution. INFONAVIT is financed by a 5 percent salary contribution by employers on behalf of all full time private sector workers, and thus it has quite a bit of funding. The new policy approach would be market driven, allowing those eligible to purchase homes with financing through INFONAVIT. Around the same time as this policy shift, the Mexican government also changed the laws associated with *ejidos* (communal lands), for the first time allowing *ejido* lands to be sold in the free market. This freed up millions of acres of valuable land on the urban periphery for suburban residential development. It also made possible a new era of large scale development in the periphery with stable financing. These conditions opened the door to rampant sprawl.

What has unfolded in Mexico over the last two decades is unprecedented in the nation's history—a massive construction boom of master planned, suburban housing developments, many of which are low and medium density and aimed toward the middle and working class sectors of the nation, and even toward the lower classes in some cases. As one study observed, "a majority of new houses are now built in large, speculative suburban developments by formal private sector companies . . . these developments of tract housing are being built at a rapid rate, sprouting like fields of corn."[51]

This is quite different from the first waves of suburbs in the 1950s and 1960s, which were built only for the wealthy, and also different from the gated, high end suburbs built in the 1980s and 1990s (like the elite development of Santa Fe outside Mexico city or Angelopolis in Puebla). These new suburbs consist of poorly designed homes in subdivisions that are often quite distant from shopping areas, schools, or other urban services. The houses tend to be absolutely homogeneous—every single one is the same. The developments are on the scale of Levittown, with projects of 5,000 homes or more. They range in price from a low of $13,000 U.S. to a high of $100,000.[52] For the first time, large masses of working and low income Mexicans are being offered an alternative to self-help housing, with its uncertain ownership and poor access to electricity, piped water, and paved roads. But this opportunity is creating the same deadly environmental damages of the urban sprawl north of the border in Phoenix, Las Vegas, San Diego, and other western U.S. cities.

Most of these suburban housing developments sprawling on the edges of large cities like Mexico City, Guadalajara, Monterrey, Ciudad Juarez, Mexicali, and Tijuana are being built by a handful of mega-home builders who have taken advantage of the change in government policy. They market these giant subdivisions by appealing to working class desire for security, and a better lifestyle. One observer comments on the mega-home builders' marketing strategy: "Their sales marketing is also reminiscent of U.S. suburban developments, with an emphasis on lifestyle packages and living closer to nature." It has also been pointed out that young people in Mexico seek this kind of housing because they desire freedom and independence from their parents, since traditionally children have remained with their parents even after they began to have their own families.[53]

Some of the new developments are gated communities, while others are semi-closed. Yet, the vast majority of these developments lack well planned roads, or any connection to public transit or other public services. One study in the mid 2000s was highly critical of this kind of new suburban housing outside Mexico City, noting the poor quality of the houses themselves, as well as the lack of a sense of community in the new districts, and the poor access to public transit. The study concluded that the main impact of these projects has been to enrich a small number of mega-construction companies. Those mega-building companies are also the largest landowners in Mexico, in many cases. They include companies like Casas GEO, Urbi, Homex, Sare, and Hogar. Further, the new developments tend to segregate income groups, while their lack of integration to the larger city is excluding these new suburban dwellers from urban life, creating a kind of "ruralization" of the city.[54]

Critiques of these suburban projects have grown both louder and more detailed. One report from the Guadalajara metropolitan area offers a scathing inside look at the kind of developments low income families have bought into, and later come to regret. The study claims that, between 2006 and 2009, of all the housing financed by INFONAVIT in new suburbs across Mexico, a shocking 25.9 percent is unoccupied or abandoned. This includes locations as far ranging as the states of Veracruz, Michoacán, Nuevo León, Guanajuato, Puebla, and Morelos, as well as the state of Mexico. This amounts to some 356,000 homes nationally. Of that total, almost half of the homes have been abandoned. In Guadalajara, the same study suggests, in one municipality on the edge of the city, called Tlajomulco de Zuñiga, out of 251 subdivisions built in the new suburbs, and over 57,000 homes, nearly 33 percent are uninhabited.[55]

Since these drastic conditions represent only what INFONAVIT has reported and is willing to admit, one can imagine the crisis of poorly designed and abandoned new working class suburbs in Mexico may be even worse. What is striking in these reports is the detail one learns about why people are abandoning homes they bought and paid for with life savings, only to discover the homes and the sprawling neighborhoods they were built in were deeply dysfunctional. One of the biggest complaints among residents of these new suburbs is that the builders promised scenarios they never delivered upon. For example, the homes were advertised as being safe, with walls around them, but many of the developers never actually construct the walls. Common areas, parks, better roads, and commercial centers were presented as part of the communities buyers believed they were getting; most of these amenities were never delivered. In the case of Tlajomulco outside Guadalajara, commentators note that the size of the subdivisions is so large and spread out (developments of 20,000 homes in one section and 15,000 in another) that building a wall around the entire sprawling development would have been almost impossible from both a financial and an engineering perspective.[56]

A second critical point is that these developments are geographically distant from the city center, and isolated from services desperately needed on a daily basis—such as shopping, schools, or health care clinics and hospitals. There is often only one road leading to these distant ruralized suburbs, and little or no public transit. For people of limited economic means, buying a car is not so easy, yet it ends up becoming absolutely necessary for survival in these far-flung subdivisions. Meanwhile, even those who have cars find the process of living in distant suburbs difficult.

A *New York Times* report in the late 1990s carried a headline familiar to Americans: "Mexico City Spawns Distant Suburbs." In it, it was reported that middle and working class suburbs were being built in cities and towns far from Mexico City for families whose owners were commuting back into Mexico City each day. The commutes were two hours or more in each direction. "A half century after Americans began to abandon cities for suburbs, thousands of Mexicans are for the first time making a similar choice, fleeing the pollution and clamor of Mexico City in search of quiet houses, well-clipped lawns and safer streets in cities and towns hours away."[57]

In the end, the problem with these suburbs, as the *New York Times* article pointed out, is that they are being built before any real planning is done. They are giant islands of housing floating in distant, rural towns, with no real connection to the city. "They are fragments," says one architect from the Guadalajara region. "There is a socio-territorial fragmentation because these isolated enclaves are not built within any kind of social context or any planned spatial structure. They end up as marginal 'colonias' built institutionally by the formal real estate market."[58]

Sadly, where the Mexican government sought to end the self-help housing dynamic by building social interest housing for the masses, they may have created an even more frightening outcome—sprawling, distant, low density housing subdivisions that many no longer want to live in, dystopic suburban ghost towns. In the words of one disgruntled resident: "We would like to be able to return the house. It was a lot of money for what it is. No one would pay to live in this place."[59]

Now, the Federal government is beginning to admit that perhaps the model of sprawling, isolated suburban developments, consisting of tens of thousands of tiny, box-like houses of between 200 and 400 square feet in the middle of nowhere, might not be a good model for the future. "I think that, yes, the model for the future should look for a development that is less horizontal and with more density," says one official.[60]

Mexican Border Suburbs

During the boom period of the 1990s, when asked about the future of Tijuana, Mexican promoters and politicians usually pointed to the same symbols of success—high tech *maquilas* (global factories), or sleek, glass high rise office buildings erected during the NAFTA boom of the 1990s in the *Zona del Rio* (River Zone), where executives in three-piece suits talk with their brokers on cell phones. "Tijuana is the new global city," they would say. "Tijuana is the next Hong Kong."

The globalization of Tijuana was one of the main reasons more than a million migrants came to the border. Once they landed here, many ended up staying, as the city's economy took off and it became part of the global manufacturing boom. Tijuana was one of several northern border cities that became the focal points of Mexico's *maquiladora* (assembly plant) industrial development strategy, where foreign corporations relocated their assembly operations to low cost labor enclaves in different parts of the world. Mexico became a key player, through the "twin plant" program with the U.S.

In 1970, there were 160 *maquiladoras* in Mexico, employing around 20,000 workers. Some twenty-five years later, there were an estimated 2,400 assembly plants in Mexico, employing nearly three-quarter million workers, with a value-added estimated at roughly three billion dollars. The vast majority of these plants are foreign owned, from the U.S., Japan, South Korea, Canada, and Germany. Tijuana was one of the major centers for global factory location. *Maquilas* created an alternative labor source for millions of Mexican immigrants heading north. Their multiplier effects in generating linked employment clusters in services further expanded urban growth. The sheer numbers of workers amplified pressure on cities like Tijuana to find housing for new migrants.

If Tijuana's future partly hinged on its global factories, it was also embodied in the many remote *colonias* scattered across its suburbs. The *colonias* house both the global factory workers and those employed in some of the other jobs created by the overall economic surge. One such *colonia* was Maclovio Rojas, a collection of semi-rural, self-built homes in the eastern hills of the city, along the Tijuana–Tecate highway. At first glance, this modest neighborhood of the poor, with its spontaneous homes built from scrap wood, concrete, or recycled metal sheets, looks like any of dozens of similar *colonias* that sprawl over the hills and canyons of Tijuana. But look again. This community typifies the essence of Mexican border cities like Tijuana, where for nearly a half century migrants from the interior came either to seek work across the border or to find a better life closer to the U.S. economy.

Maclovio Rojas is a typical peripheral *colonia*, a place migrants moved to during the rapid urbanization of the period from the 1960s to 1990s. *Colonias* on the outskirts of cities are common across all of Mexico. But this particular *colonia*'s location in the path of the construction of the new "global suburbs" of a border city like Tijuana, where middle class employees of foreign-owned assembly plants or NAFTA-inspired businesses might own a house, put it in harm's way. Its subsequent poor treatment by the Mexican government was extensively reported on by the U.S. media machine, which in the wake of the North American Free Trade Agreement (NAFTA) became more sensitized to what was happening along the border. The apparent violation of this community's right to legal neighborhood status exposed the dark side of a government that is still willing to bend the rules to appease corporate powers, even at the risk of jeopardizing the well-being of nearly 10,000 people.

Maclovio Rojas was formed in 1988 by twenty-five families. Most of the founding families are ex-farmers from the rural Mexico state of Oaxaca. They say they paid former *ejido* (rural land cooperative) officials for the land. But today, more than two decades later, they are witnessing their dream of ownership fade away into a twilight zone of government bureaucracy and political posturing.

Most poor *colonias* in Tijuana eventually morph into working class and then middle class communities. But Maclovio Rojas has the misfortune of being located on prime real estate along the Tijuana–Tecate highway. It lies in the path of industrial development, between the highway and the rail line to Mexicali. Just ten miles down the road is a huge new Toyota plant. Hyundai owns adjacent land it uses for giant container storage. There are new sprawling suburban housing subdivisions nearby, and plans for more.

Some 2,000 families, or about 10,000 residents, now reside in this *colonia*, which they have transformed into a viable community. Two new buildings anchor the neighborhood—a school and community social services center. On their own, residents constructed water lines that feed off official piped water systems run by the state and federal government. They are willing to pay for their water. The community did, in fact, petition the government to permanently certify its public school, officially install water meters in all the homes, and recognize land ownership. The government response was mute. While some initial efforts were made to send water technicians into the community, that action was mysteriously aborted in the early 2000s. Meanwhile, the local school was not able to achieve permanent recognition by state education officials, despite earlier promises that this could be possible.

What held back the government? In a word, globalization. That is, fast urbanism, North American style—malls, single family subdivisions, office parks, clean, strategically profitable global factories, all served by highways—spread further and further from the original center. Build for consumers, and build to heighten the value of land. And worry about planning for the environmental impacts later. Land values around Maclovio Rojas, near the highway to Tecate, and in the area of eastern Tijuana with the most vacant space for suburban and industrial development had taken off by the 1990s. It was becoming a global investment target. This once innocent *colonia* suddenly found itself smack in the middle of the hottest industrial and residential real estate in town.

Public officials suddenly began to waffle and back-pedal on promises made to the *colonia*. Worse still, in 2001, police came into the neighborhood at night to arrest and jail the three main community leaders. The charge was illegal theft of water, a strange charge since the community openly offered to pay for its water services, and the municipal water agency never came back to install meters. One woman was arrested; she was in jail for over a year. The other two leaders managed to escape. They went into hiding.

Maclovio Rojas had the misfortune of being in the path of corporate investment land deals that needed to find a way, in the name of profit, to make thousands of residents disappear. But, its location on the border also meant that its plight did not go unnoticed by the U.S. media. San Diego-based filmmaker Beth Bird directed and produced *Everyone Their Grain of Sand*, which narrates the story of Maclovio Rojas' battle for basic human rights such as water and education.[61] This powerful 2005 documentary was shown in cities in Europe and the United States, bringing global attention to Mexico.

Among Mexico's fastest growing cities during the last four decades, Tijuana's periphery became increasingly important; it was the only place where global investors could find vacant land. The lure of employment in the U.S. and the subsequent attraction of living near the post-NAFTA southern California economy brought thousands of migrants from the poorest regions of Mexico. These sending regions included the western states of Jalisco, Sinaloa, Michoacán, and Sonora, where, like elsewhere in Mexico, the rural economy could no longer sustain millions of farmers and people who lived in small and medium sized towns. Between 1960 and 2000, Tijuana's population increased from 165,690 to 1.8 million.[62]

As in other fast growing urban regions, the Mexican government was incapable of building or subsidizing housing for the arrivals. This meant that, of the more than one million people who moved to the urban region over four decades, it is estimated that more than half the population ended up living in spontaneous irregular settlements, mostly in the hills and canyons in the southern and eastern zones of the city, where more land was available.[63]

The urbanization of Tijuana's periphery moved in three waves. From the 1960s through the 1980s, spontaneous migrant *colonias* formed either in undesirable flood-prone canyons and river beds (some of which were eventually expelled by the government) or, as mentioned, in distant peripheral lands to the south and east far from downtown. Beginning in the 1980s, a second wave of peripheral expansion began—the building of gated communities for the upper and upper middle classes. Most of these gated suburbs were located in Playas de Tijuana, along the Pacific Ocean, or further south along the Tijuana–Rosarito highway, also taking advantage of pristine ocean views. In addition, some new high end housing was built in the central urban zone, close to the River Zone.

The third and largest wave of suburban development was a completely new trend in Tijuana, but one mirrored in other cities in Mexico—the building of gated developments for the working class and urban poor starting in the 1990s. These master planned developments were made possible, once again, by financial backing from INFONAVIT, and the participation of some of Mexico's giant corporate housing developers like Urbi, Casas Geo, and Ara. Seen as a way to replace self-help housing, large tracts of land were bulldozed, and new subdivisions built in the eastern suburbs. Over 30,000 residential units were erected by the larger developers, including 21,000 units by Urbi, 7,500 units by Ara, and 4,700 units by Geo.[64] Most of these homes were marketed to working and poor migrants. The advertisements, in the words of one study, "emphasize a vision of community values; of the exclusivity, privacy and security of the complex; and even of the happiness, success, well-being and physical beauty that supposedly can be achieved within gated community life."[65]

With shining examples of American suburbs situated just a few miles north of the border, and almost within sight, it is not surprising that these marketing techniques would bear fruit in a border city like Tijuana. What is troubling, however, is the way in which these images were adopted by public officials, and used as rhetoric to shield them from criticism when the severe problems with these gated, planned communities began to come to light: "Local authorities, we found, are prone to reproduce this discourse (marketing), ignoring or erasing the urban and social problems that result from privatization of urban services."[66]

Crisis in the New Suburbs

In Tijuana and other Mexican border cities, mega-builders and developers, backed by the national mortgage program under INFONAVIT, built new communities, spread out in far flung suburbs that are poorly designed from an urban planning perspective. In legal terms, community space (streets) inside these new developments is considered private. This removes government and results in poor delivery of what would normally be public services, such as garbage collection, street lighting, and police. The developers also typically leave out such amenities as parks and plazas. Roads leading in and out of these master planned communities are not always paved, or are very narrow and difficult to drive along. Other infrastructure, like sewerage and drainage, reportedly doesn't always work. In short, the privatization of working class suburbs ends up creating communities without basic public services.

Tijuana's municipal planning department studied these communities and found serious problems, including crowded spaces, lack of urban services and infrastructure, substandard road networks, higher cost of services, and social tension.[67] Local architects are troubled by the larger implications of these developments:

> All these tract communities, what they sell is surveillance, safety, supposedly hygiene. People fall in love with this idea of getting away from the chaotic center . . . every house is detached, and there is a beautiful backyard and front yard, and everything is nice and dandy, but what they are selling ultimately is boredom, you just have to realize that under that beautiful, picturesque village there is a huge monster developing, of violence and alienation and isolation.[68]

A second problem with these new suburbs is that developers are creating spaces far too small for a typical Mexican family. Although smaller houses might be considered more sustainable, there is a limited acceptable size from a public health perspective, as defined by international standards. The average house size in most of these developments is about 27 square meters (290 square feet) on the lower end, and 59 square meters (635 square feet) on the upper end. This falls far below the 72 square meter (775 square feet) minimum standard recommended by the United Nations. The way builders in Tijuana get around government guidelines is that they privatize the streets within their developments, thus allowing them to create their own building code standards, rather than having to follow city or state codes. One architect who worked for these building companies admitted the houses they were building were unacceptably limited:

> what's been going on here in Mexico, the house we make, instead of welcoming the inhabitant, expels him. It's a centrifugal house, isn't it? It's like you were expelled, pushed out because the spaces are so small, so reduced, that it pushes you out to the street.[69]

Builders defend the small house size in Tijuana in economic terms. They argue that the high price of land and real property elevates housing costs to the point that the only way to keep costs down for the poor is to build very small homes. The result is that builders are creating a double crisis: constructing absurdly cramped, unlivable spaces, and then locating them in distant, isolated subdivisions that are generally not served by mass transit, lack schools, community centers, shopping and other neighborhood facilities. In short, Mexican developers have invented new forms of urban sprawl, copying some of the worst elements of the U.S. suburb and exporting them to their urban peripheries.

In Tijuana, as in other parts of Mexico, builders are crafting exaggerated versions of the American suburban model—and, in the process, magnifying all of its flaws: the lack of accessibility to transit, the over-reliance on the automobile, and the misleading idea that a gate or wall means less crime will be committed. There has been a failure to create village-like designs where people can walk to a center with commerce, services, and public spaces. Instead, developers are producing place-less suburbs, over-homogenization, and feelings of alienation. Local

Figure 4.3 New Mass Produced Suburbs in Tijuana: Villa Fontana
Source: Photo by Rene Peralta, Woodbury University, San Diego, California

observers are disappointed with both the condition of Tijuana's gated suburbs and their mimicry of the U.S.:

> Is this the image of the future? You know if this is the image of the future, it's sad. It's incredibly depressing . . . the first image is that of a cemetery, these small mausoleums. This is not that different from San Diego, in that sense. Yes, we can find in those master planned communities a more manicured and more beautiful landscape, but ultimately, in terms of alienation and isolation, and the kind of erasure of social relations, of complexity, of diversity, a lot of those things, notions that might seem very trivial, but they are what life is about.[70]

The source of Mexican imitation of U.S. suburbs is clear. With the construction of *maquila* parks across the outskirts of Mexico's booming northern border region cities during the 1980s and 1990s, Mexico also imported the U.S. model for building its new "global suburbs." Mexico embraced the commodified spaces and low density, suburban landscapes of its northern neighbors. Only four decades ago, nationalist and proud Mexico rejected most U.S. commercial enterprises within its borders— from McDonald's and Burger King to 7–11's or The Gap. But once the ink was dry on the signing of NAFTA in 1993, Mexico opened its doors to U.S. and foreign business. Today, hundreds of U.S. chain stores and hotels have swept across the Mexican landscape—from Blockbuster Video, Office Depot, and Sears to Direct TV, Costco, and Walmart. Most of the global hotel chains—including Hilton, Hyatt, and Sheraton—have also exploded onto the Mexican scene.

Along the international border, the ascendance of U.S. consumerist values has been particularly intense. In the early 1990s, the invasion of fast food outlets in border cities like Tijuana occurred virtually overnight. In the span of just a few years, iconic American food outlets—McDonald's, Carl's Jr., Burger King, or Domino's Pizza—burst onto the urban landscape. Around the same time, small, medium and large strip shopping centers and malls began appearing along commercial boulevards and highways in the exurban fringe. In Tijuana, these mini-malls served to interrupt the pedestrian scale of the downtown, since buildings were set back from the sidewalk, while parking lots stood in front. U.S. style suburban, mega-shopping malls also sprouted along the border—Tijuana has two regional sized shopping malls.

As for advertising, most Mexicans living in border cities can tap into satellite TV from the U.S. markets. Mexican border city dwellers use satellite television to receive programming from southern California, or further away. An enormous, captive Mexican audience can be reached by advertisers on California TV and radio channels, and more recently through social media and the internet. Mexican consumers learn how to consume, partly by watching American television and film. As a result, Latinos living along the border have proven to be highly motivated customers on the U.S. side. Studies have shown that Mexican consumers have similar, if not better, information and a slightly better understanding than California residents of locations and qualities of stores and products in the San Diego region.[71]

Once the NAFTA boom hit, U.S. style condominiums and suburban housing developments for Mexicans spread across Tijuana. Mexican consumers are familiar with U.S. housing, both from crossing the border, or through the print and visual media. Global advertising has altered their taste in housing. Wealthy consumers want condominiums with jacuzzis, sunken bathtubs, and satellite television. Even poor migrants aspire to U.S. house types. A former border architect speaks of his frustration with people who, despite incredibly limited incomes, refuse to live in houses that could be technically designed to fit their budgets.

> My clients don't want to live in a house designed with recycled metal or junk parts, even if it is excellently constructed. They want a California tract house, with a picture window and a garage. A lot of people can't afford to buy a house in the United States, but they buy the magazines, and then they find a photograph of a house they like. They bring it to the architect in Tijuana, and they say "I want a house like this." But they forget that in Mexico our lot sizes are smaller and narrower. We don't have the space to design with ideal lighting and ventilation. To meet their needs, we end up designing caricatures of American-style houses in miniature.[72]

As the crescendo of studies showing the profound flaws of these new gated suburbs in all Mexican cities grew, the federal government was pressured to begin to come up with alternatives. In a landmark study of sustainable housing recently put together by INFONAVIT, with the Mexican Treasury department (SHP) and the National Housing Commission (CONAVI), the government advocated, for the first time, various new policies for its future suburbs: these include a "Green Mortgage" program that will help poor and working class families purchase a house with sustainable energy, as well as the Sustainable Integrated Urban Development (DUIS) strategy, which will seek to build more sustainable communities with mixed land uses. This new approach will include 40 percent funding for lower income families under the "This Is Your House" (*Esta Es Su Casa*) program, which provides economic assistance for home purchases. The government expects to be able to build DUIS developments for over a million people between 2008 and 2012, according to its latest study.[73]

In Tijuana, this strategy would be welcome, since the population of the region is expected to double by 2030, and will require over 400,000 new housing units.[74] The city is hoping to build three sustainable communities—or DUIS's, to use the current popular acronym—in the south and east. The largest is the Valle de San Pedro project, about twelve miles south of the border, where the municipality envisions a new city of one million people emerging around 2030. It would include a "new town" being designed by Urbi, as well as similar sustainable and ecologically driven developments by other large developers including Homex and GEO. The promotional literature on these new developments looks very much like proposals for master planned communities in San Diego, Orange, and Riverside counties just to the north. The plan is to construct "outdoor living spaces around residential avenues, paseos and small parks that will extend the home's livable space to outdoor areas and streets."[75]

In the Urbi project, Valle de San Pedro, 160,000 units will be built in three phases. Promotional information shows a town center with mixed use, a university, bicycle corridors along green spaces, a river/park in the second phase, with residential developments of mainly single family housing at fifteen dwelling units per acre on average. An industrial park is planned, and efforts are being made to attract various manufacturers in the "life sciences" field (companies that produce medical devices or solutions to diseases such as obesity and diabetes), with the idea of partnering with the bio-medical sector across the border in San Diego. A visionary plan like this suffers from the uncertainty that projected jobs for the new population center won't meet the demands of a booming younger demographic that has become the norm in cities like Tijuana.[76]

Two other major new suburban centers are projected. "Los Nogales" will be a master planned community near the El Florido section of Tijuana. The proposal is to build 35,000 housing units for a population of 160,000, also in three phases. It projects attracting forty-seven medium and large manufacturing firms that will bring an estimated 25,000 jobs to the zone. Its land use plan shows mixed uses with retail, hotels, a university, high school, clinics, hospitals, and a central civic area. Housing and industrial districts are arrayed around the center. Another project proposed to the south of Los Nogales is called "Natura," and it seeks to build 56,380 units for some 200,000 new residents. Its master plan, like the other two mentioned here, is driven by a smart growth approach—with residential developments surrounded by parks, a bikeway, shopping in central nodes, industry, and education.

All of these projects look good on paper. But whether they will live up to their promises remains unclear. The previous wave of developments— giant gated suburbs for the working class—had similar advertisements, but few of the public spaces—schools, town centers, and other promised amenities—were ever built. These projects, as mentioned, provide housing for urban workers and lower income families, but without the neighborhood amenities (schools, activity centers, parks) residents need. This has produced a new kind of Mexican dysfunctional sprawl.

Based on current maps, the new developments lie ten or fifteen miles from the core of Tijuana. Notwithstanding the rhetoric of "smart growth" employed in presentations by city officials and economic development promoters of these new mega-projects, their remoteness, combined with a weak track record for building alternative transit along the northern border, lead one to believe the problem of automobile dependent sprawl will continue here. While drawings show a single bus line to serve the Valle de San Pedro, for example, no one seems to know exactly when and if Tijuana will get the capital to invest in a rapid transit system.

Mexico has made great strides to modernize its economy and become a major economic player for the twenty-first century. It has the second largest economy (after Brazil) in Latin America. Like Brazil, its economic boom in the late twentieth century largely took place in cities. Mexico's urban explosion was concentrated on the outskirts of its cities, where previously the urban poor had constructed shantytowns. Armed with new technology in the fields of architecture and urban planning, one would have hoped that Mexico would find a sustainable model for building on the periphery. Instead our southern neighbor has largely copied American urban sprawl, whether in the form of gated communities, mega-malls, and global suburbs for the rich, or in more recent low density, isolated working class subdivisions exploding across the nation's urban periphery. Along the border with the U.S., this unsustainable model has sometimes led to conflicts between poor squatter communities already in place and global investors trying to usurp their land for more profitable use. Amidst the clamor for change, there is much uncertainty about the future of global suburbs along this border. Meanwhile, as we shall see in the next chapter, this problem has spread further south.

Notes

1 In contrast with the original post-World War II urban design prototype—a low density, mainly single family residential subdivision on the outskirts of a city that evolved in the United States in the 1950s and 1960s, and offered homeowners the values of privacy, exclusivity, and security—Latin American "suburbs" evolved differently. In Mexico, before the 1960s, most people thought of "suburbs" as peripheral zones where poor migrants built makeshift homes in squatter neighborhoods. See, for example, Guernola Capron and Martha de Alba, "Creating the Middle Class Suburban Dream in Mexico City," *Culturales* (UABC), Enero-Junio, 2010, 161. Equally, as we shall see in the next chapter, in Brazil the term "*subúrbio*" also has a very different meaning. It is associated with lower income, peripheral neighborhoods.

2 See Mike Davis, *Planet of Slums.* New York: Verso, 2006.

3 Richard Ballard and Gareth A. Jones, "Natural Neighbors: Indigenous Landscapes and Eco-estates in Durban, South Africa. Annals," *Association of American Geographers*, 101 (1), 2011, 131–48.

4 See Anthony King, *Spaces of Global Cultures.* New York: Routledge, 2004.

5 For an overview of Spanish city building history in Latin America, see for example Lawrence Herzog, *From Aztec to High Tech.* Baltimore, MD: Johns Hopkins University Press, 1999, chapter 2, and Daniel Arreola and James Curtis, *The Mexican Border Cities.* Tucson: University of Arizona Press, 1993. For an excellent description of the importance of the historic center in Latin American cities, see also Joseph Scarpaci, *Plazas and Barrios.* Tucson: University of Arizona Press.

6 Ernst Griffin and Larry Ford, "A Model of Latin American City Structure," *Geographical Review*, 70, 1980, 397–422; Alex Borsdorf, Rodrigo Hidalgo, and Rafael Sanchez, "A New Model of Urban Development in Latin America: The Gated Communities and Fenced Cities in the Metropolitan Areas of Santiago and Valparaiso, Chile," *Cities*, 24 (5), 2007, 365–78.

7 Borsdorf et al., 2007.

8 Ibid.; Rodrigo Salcedo and Alvaro Torres, "Gated Communities in Santiago: Wall or Frontier," *International Journal of Urban and Regional Research*, 28 (1), 27–44; Martin Coy and Martin Pohler, "Gated Communities in the Latin American Megacities," *Environment and Planning B: Planning and Design*, 29, 2002, 355–70; Gareth Jones and Maria Moreno-Carranco, "Mega-projects: Beneath the Pavement, Excess," *City*, 11 (2), July, 2007, 144–64.

9 Borsdorf et al., 2007.

10 Francisco Sabatini, Gonzalo Caceres, and Jorge Cerda, "Residential Segregation in Major Cities in Chile," *EURE*, 27 (82), December, 2001, 21–42.

11 Martin Coy, "Gated Communities and Urban Fragmentation in Latin America: The Brazilian Experience," *Geojournal*, 66, 2006, 121–32.
12 The best example, discussed below, is the elite suburb of Santa Fe, on the western outskirts of Mexico City. Santa Fe's development involved U.S. and other international investors, as well as the building of foreign-owned commercial, industrial, and office developments.
13 Borsdorf et al., 2007, 377.
14 This quote is often attributed to late nineteenth century Mexican president Porfirio Diaz, although some Mexican historians say its origins are unclear.
15 Peter Ward, *Mexico City*. New York: John Wiley and Sons, 1998, 237.
16 Ibid. and see also Octavio Paz, *The Labyrinth of Solitude*. New York: Grove Press, 1961.
17 The importance of cultural patrimony in Mexican city-building is discussed in Jerome Monnet, *Usos e imagines del centro historico de La Ciudad de Mexico*. Mexico City: Departamento del Distrito Federal, 1995, and Ward, 1998.
18 An overview of Mexican memory in the urban built environment can be found in Herzog, 1999.
19 The U.S. exported $223 billion and imported $277 billion from Mexico in 2011. See Office of the U.S. Trade Representative, http://www.ustr.gov/countries-regions/americas/mexico.
20 Capron and Alba, 2010.
21 Ibid. He was not the only Mexican president to benefit from this kind of land deal, however; it is well known that Mexican presidents become wealthy, sometimes through acquisition or investment in land development, during and after their service.
22 Sergio Flores Peña, "Are First Generation Suburbs of Mexico City Shrinking? The Case of Naucalpan," in I. Audirac and J. Arroyo Alejandre, eds. *Shrinking Cities South/ North*. Mexico, D.F.: Juan Pablos Editorial, 2010, 113–47.
23 *Excelsior*, January 15, 1961, cited in Capron and Alba, 2010, 171.
24 Capron and Alba, 2010.
25 Ibid.
26 Ibid.
27 "Tinacolandia" was a veiled reference to the "tinacos" or water tanks on the roofs of working class and lower class homes across the city
28 For a description of the growth of squatter zones in Mexico City, an excellent source is Ward, 1998.
29 The term "mega-project" is used by Jones and Moreno-Carranco, 2007, to describe the scale and style of these new developments. See also Alfonso Valenzuela, "Santa Fe: Megaproyectos para una ciudad dividida," *Cuadernos Geograficos*, 40 (2007), 53–66.
30 Valenzuela, 2007.
31 That has not turned out to be the case for Santa Fe. For one, it is not autonomous, in the sense that many who work here commute from other parts of the city. Second, unlike La Défense in Paris, there is no alternative mass transit (bus rapid, subway) that serves Santa Fe, so it is mostly an auto-centric place.
32 See David Lida, *First Stop in the New World*. New York: Riverhead Books, 2008.
33 Jones and Moreno-Carranco, 2007, 152.
34 Jordi Borja, cited in Valenzuela, 2007, 65.
35 See, for example, Teresa Caldeira, "Fortified Enclaves: The New Urban Separation," *Public Culture*, 8, 1996, 303–28.
36 Jones and Moreno-Carranco, 2007, 153.
37 Ibid., 161.

38 Sharon Zukin, *Point of Change: How Shopping Changed American Culture*. New York: Routledge, 2003. In a recent ethnography of consumerism and culture in Puerto Rico, an anthropologist cautions about making generalizations about consumers in malls. In Puerto Rico, she argues, women are stereotyped by real estate speculators as being impulsive and wasteful shoppers. Field research suggests a far more complex pattern. Shopping malls are used in different ways and for different activities in various locales. Senior residents come to exercise or socialize, while young women display highly developed knowledge, bargaining skills, and an ability to calculate and consume carefully. See Arlene Davila, *Culture Works*. New York: NYU Press, 2012, 47.

39 The idea of shopping malls as theater is mentioned in the work of Australian feminist Meaghan Morris, who views malls as spaces for action and transformation for women, not just places of consumption. See Meaghan Morris, "Things to Do with Shopping Centers," in Simon During, ed. *The Cultural Studies Reader*. New York: Routledge, 1993, 391–409.

40 See Margath Walker, David Walker, and Yanga Villagomez Velasquez, "The Wal-Martification of Teotihuacan: Issues of Resistance and Cultural Heritage," in Stanley D. Brunn, ed. *Wal-Mart World*. New York: Routledge, 2006, 213–24.

41 Ibid.

42 Stacy Mitchell, "Can You Say 'Sprawl'? Walmart's Biggest Climate Impact Goes Ignored," http://grist.org/business-technology/2011–11–29-can-you-say-sprawl-walmarts-biggest-climate-impact-goes-ignored/.

43 Lida, 2008.

44 Lida, 2008, 96.

45 Walker et al., 2006.

46 Ibid.

47 Organization for Economic Cooperation and Development (OECD) study of Mexico, cited in Walker et al., 2006.

48 Walker et al., 2006.

49 David Barstow and Alejandra Xanic Von Bertrab, "The Bribery Aisle: How Walmart Got Its Way in Mexico," *New York Times*, December 17, 2012, http://www.nytimes.com/2012/12/18/business/walmart-bribes-teotihuacan.html?pagewanted = all&_r = 0.

50 The popular movement was coordinated nationally by CONAMUP, the National Coordinating Committee of Urban Popular Movements. See Joe Foweraker and Ann L. Craig, eds. *Popular Movements and Political Change in Mexico*. London and Boulder, CO: Lynne Rienner, 1990. On self-help housing, see Jan Bredenoord and Otto Verkoren, "Between Self-Help and Institutional Housing: A Bird's Eye View of Mexico's Housing Production for Low and Lower Middle Income Groups," *Habitat International*, 34, 2010, 359–65.

51 Paavo Monkkonen, "The Housing Transition in Mexico: Local Impacts on National Policy," *Working Paper* D09–001, 2009, University of California, Berkeley.

52 Paavo Monkkonen, "Do Mexican Cities Sprawl?" *Urban Geography*, 32 (3), 2011, 406–23.

53 Daniel Hiernaux and Alicia Lindon, "Modos de vida y utopias urbanas," *Ciudades*, 53, enero-marzo, 2002, 26–32.

54 Beatriz Garcia Peralta and Andreas Hofer, "Housing for the Working Class: A New Version of Gated Communities in Mexico," *Social Justice*, 33 (3), 2006, 129–41.

55 Diego Mendiburu, "Vivir en en gueto," *Emeequis*, July 11, 2011, 29—36, http://www.m-x.com.mx/2011-07-10/vivir-en-un-gueto/.

56 Ibid., 30.

57 Sam Dillon, "Mexico City Spawns Distant Suburbs," *New York Times*, December 18, 1999.
58 Architect Alejandro Mendo, quoted in Mendiburu, 2011, 31.
59 Mendiburu, 2011, 36.
60 Ibid., 36.
61 *Everyone Their Grain of Sand*, a film by Beth Bird, Tijuana, 2005.
62 Mexican census data, and estimates from the Office of the Governor, State of Baja California, cited in Lawrence Herzog, *Where North Meets South: Cities, Space and Politics on the U.S.–Mexico Border*. Austin: University of Texas Press/CMAS, 1990, 107.
63 Ibid. Because coastal land remained valuable for tourist development, or upper end residential development, Tijuana's lower and working class *colonias* sprang up in the less desirable non-coastal periphery. Only the outlying beachfront zone saw higher end residential development.
64 Brisa Violeta Carrasco Gallegos, "Tijuana: Border, Migration and Gated Communities," *Journal of the Southwest*, 51 (4), Winter, 2009, 457–75.
65 Ibid., 469.
66 Ibid., 469.
67 Instituto Municipal de Planeación de Tijuana (IMPLAN), *Plan de desarrollo urban centro de población Tijuana*, B.C., 2002–2005, Periódico Official, Sept. 13, 2003.
68 Teddy Cruz, in the documentary film *Mixed Feelings: San Diego/Tijuana*, 2002.
69 Representative of GEO, quoted in Carrasco Gallegos, 2009, 472.
70 Ibid.
71 See Lawrence Herzog, 1999.
72 Jorge Ozorno, cited in Herzog, 1999, 206.
73 CONAVI (National Housing Confederation), *Sustainable Housing in Mexico*. D.F.: SEMARNAT (Secretaria de Medio Ambiente y Recursos Naturales)/INFONAVIT/ SHP/, 2012, http://www.conavi.gob.mx/documentos/publicaciones/2a_Sustainable_ Housing_in_Mexico.pdf.
74 David Mayagoitia, "New Community Developments in Tijuana," presentation to Urban Land Institute, San Diego, June 7, 2012.
75 John Suarez, "Building Better in Latin America," *Urban Land*, September, 2008, 173.
76 Interview, David Mayagoitia, President of DEITAC, a private economic development agency in Tijuana, June 27, 2012.

5

A GLOBAL SUBURB IN
RIO DE JANEIRO, BRAZIL

Much the same as they did in Mexico, investors and developers farther
south in Latin America discovered there was a growing market in their
countries for U.S. style suburbs. They built the kind of suburban enclaves
that were spreading from San Diego to Mexico City: sprawling settlements with secluded residential subdivisions for the elite, and even for
the middle class. In the final decades of the twentieth century, Latin
American cities mobilized to build scores of secluded, high end subdivisions where residents could escape from the inner city, and enjoy greater
privacy and a sense of security. This chapter explores the emergence of
such developments in cities in Brazil, focusing on an illuminating case
study of one global suburb in Rio de Janeiro.

Brazil is a timely case. For several decades, it has been fashionable to
write about the United States' cultural impact on Latin America—and
frequently Mexico, America's closest neighbor, has received the bulk of
attention on this question. But Brazil is just as important. First, it is
the largest and wealthiest nation in Latin America. Its population of
180 million is the highest in Latin America; its 2010 GDP of about two
trillion dollars makes it the seventh largest economy in the world.[1] By
comparison, Mexico's population is 108 million, and its GDP about one
trillion dollars. Brazil, of late, has also been the most potent economic

giant of the Americas, with a GDP growth rate of 5.1 percent in 2011, compared with 3.9 percent in Mexico.[2]

Brazil is one of the fastest urbanizing nations in the world, and certainly in the Americas, and also one of the so called "BRIC" (Brazil, Russia, India, and China) group—fast changing nations of the newly industrializing world, who are considered to be increasingly important in global geopolitics. Its fifteen major metropolitan areas hold some 32 percent of the total population of the country, or 55 million out of the 180 million.[3] It houses two of the largest metropolitan areas of the world—São Paulo, with nearly twenty million inhabitants (third largest city in the world) and Rio de Janeiro with over 11 million. World attention turned to Rio de Janeiro late in 2009, when the International Olympic Committee awarded Rio the Summer Games of 2016, which will be the first time a South American city has hosted the event. Brazil will also host the 2014 FIFA World Cup for soccer, with twelve of the nation's largest cities holding the matches.[4]

Brazil burst further into the global media spotlight in 2013, when regional street demonstrations escalated into a national wave of protests that brought millions onto the streets in major cities across the nation. In early June of 2013, a protest in São Paulo over the cost of transport went national when the government announced a twenty-centavo (nine cent) increase in bus fares across the nation. This was nearly a 10 percent increase for the working class and poor who are dependent on buses to travel to work, to shop, and simply to live in large cities. The São Paulo protests, and later those in Rio and other large cities, were quickly met with brutal police responses, including the firing of tear gas, stun bombs, and rubber bullets into crowds. Protesters were chased, harassed, and even jailed, while journalists were injured and innocent bystanders sometimes arrested.

This caused the protests to escalate. By late June, over one million were on the streets in a series of planned demonstrations, and President Dilma Rousseff's administration was under pressure.[5] The government quickly dropped the bus fare increase proposal, but by then the street protests had turned into a national movement aimed beyond the question of transport costs. Citizens' groups were now protesting inflation, escalating prices, high taxes, poor schools and hospitals, low wages, long workweeks, and teachers' rights.[6] The governments' ill timed bus fare increase was seen as an attempt to pile out-of-control spending on the backs of the working people. As one group of church leaders noted: "the protests show all of us that we cannot live in a country with so much inequality."[7]

The inequality that galvanized these national street protests manifests itself in cities, and most of all in the two largest, Rio de Janeiro and São Paulo. It speaks to the way in which governments disproportionately spend and use public monies on infrastructure that reinforces wealth in some parts of the city, while ignoring poverty in others. In the largest Brazilian cities, that inequality is becoming more pronounced as government funded infrastructure fortifies the new, gated suburbs, on the one hand, while mostly ignoring the problems of the poor in *favelas*, on the other.[8]

In Rio de Janeiro, the protests soon focused on specific sites of inequality. For example, thousands poured into the streets in front of the Maracanã Stadium, to criticize nearly a half billion public dollars spent on renovating the stadium for the 2014 World Cup, and the 2016 Summer Olympics. These monies were dispersed precisely at the moment when *favela* residents in the hills nearby were being evicted to make way for Olympic sports facilities or Bus Rapid Transit lines that will move tourists from the airport to Olympic sites. Many of the multi-million dollar Olympic facilities are located in the wealthy new suburbs to the south and west of the city. The 2013 protests, in effect, are precisely about urban inequality; citizens became aware of the inequity of paying higher taxes for improvements that they will not personally benefit from.

The Vertical Suburbs of São Paulo

The crowning model of suburban growth in Brazil, the place that sets the tone for the rest of the country, is the São Paulo metropolis. São Paulo is one of the largest metropolitan regions on the planet, with nearly 20 million inhabitants. Along with Mexico City, New York, and Los Angeles, it is a primary center for global corporate headquarters, and thus one of the key financial mega-cities of the Americas. Its phenomenal expansion in the last half of the twentieth century inspired a style of peripheral growth perhaps never seen in the Americas. In every sense, São Paulo represents a template for globalization and urban growth in Brazil, if not the rest of the world.

São Paulo's geographic advantages historically included higher elevation and abundant rainfall, which facilitated the evolution of a lucrative coffee growing economy in the pre-industrial era. Railroad infrastructure built with British capital in the nineteenth century further elevated its potential for growth. Unlimited physical space for expansion and massive immigration into the region provided critical European labor power (especially from Italy), which allowed a regional entrepreneurial elite to build a manufacturing economy in the early twentieth century, especially around the food and textile sectors.

By the late twentieth century, São Paulo had become the "business capital of MercoSur," with some of the top manufacturing, finance, and service firms migrating into the region from other parts of Brazil (especially Rio de Janeiro). It quickly became the preferred headquarters for national and multinational corporations—with twenty-five of the Fortune Top 100 corporations in the world. São Paulo also was ranked eleventh in the world for housing multinational headquarters.[9] It was ranked tenth globally based on the size of its advertising markets. [10] In short, by the end of the twentieth century, a former coffee growing market town had evolved into Brazil's most important global city.

The São Paulo region's population mushroomed from 4.7 million inhabitants in 1960 to 12.5 million in 1980, and to nearly 20 million by 2005. As in Mexico, from the 1940s through the 1970s, migrant workers from the countryside streamed into the city and began moving to squatter communities on the periphery. Meanwhile, luxury high rise apartment complexes and single family homes were concentrated in enclaves for the rich, closer to the center. Since the 1980s urban space has become more and more "walled off," with the middle and upper income classes increasingly residing in what have been termed "fortified enclaves," while the poor remain either in slum apartments (*cortiços*) or *favelas*, the generic term in Brazil for the poorest squatter settlement zones. For the wealthy, fear of crime led to the building of thousands of high rise "closed condominiums," a Brazilian version of the "gated community."[11]

Perhaps growth is the most important influence on the shape and scale of São Paulo. The rapid pace of growth and a period of violent crimes led to São Paulo developing giant masses of very tall buildings spread over an enormous region. It became more than a skyscraper city; it evolved into a skyscraper *region*. It has become a metropolis defined by high density and by high rise towers packed in and around the downtown, and proliferating as far as the eye can see across the landscape over several hundred square miles, in every direction. The greater São Paulo region is about three thousand square miles in size, with nearly half of that covered in high density urbanization. So densely packed are São Paulo's skyscrapers that they run up along the edges of the older airport at Congonhas. Seen from the air as you fly in only eight miles from the downtown central business district, this verticality is striking.

The vertical cityscape extends to the periphery of the city. The suburbs of São Paulo, unlike those in the United States, almost entirely consist of high rise towers. This verticality contrasts with the more low rise sprawl we observed in Mexico in the last chapter. Indeed, São Paulo is a city of luxury apartment tower suburbs, elite gated compounds that are spread across the periphery of wealthy enclaves, especially in the south and southwest parts of the city. These compounds were inspired by the British garden city concept, though, unlike the original garden cities, the São Paulo versions are entirely automobile-oriented. The primary gathering spaces are shopping malls, of which there are more in São Paulo than anywhere else in Brazil.[12]

São Paulo has seen a shift among the wealthy from low rise "mansions" to islands of suburban towers that have been referred to as a "forest of high rises."[13] In Morumbi, one of the early elite suburbs, built in 1976, the Portal de Morumbi project consisted of sixteen separate twenty-five-story tower blocks. As São Paulo grew in the 1970s and 1980s, a large class of underemployed residents turned to violence as a source of survival. As a response to the violence, uncertainty, and fear, middle and upper class residents became alienated from the public world of the street and its unpredictability, shifting instead toward the safer interior

Figure 5.1 Endless Skyscrapers Define the Landscape of the São Paulo Mega-region
Source: Photo by Lawrence A. Herzog

world of high rise privacy and security. They not only moved inside tall towers; they closed them off with fences, walls, and security gates, and then installed video cameras, television monitors, computerized alarms, or hired security companies to maintain twenty-four hour surveillance.

One of the signature elite suburbs in São Paulo is Alphaville-Tamboré, a gated community built in the early 1970s about fifteen miles southwest of downtown São Paulo. It has been compared with the scale and style of Irvine, the giant suburb in Orange County, California. The community grew to some thirty-three gated developments, mostly high rise condominiums with a few low rise, single family gated areas. It has more than 22,000 residential units, with a population estimated at about 90,000, making it one of Brazil's largest elite suburbs.[14] This Brazilian mega-suburb has eleven schools, universities, shopping malls, and office complexes. Some 150,000 people travel in and out of Alphaville each day, which eventually led the developer company and local government to build a toll freeway for affluent commuters. The Alphaville project was so celebrated, the developer—Alphaville Urbanismo, S.A.—successfully proceeded to market it to many cities in Brazil, including Salvador, Fortaleza, Belo Horizonte, Manaus, Natal, and Rio de Janeiro.

Urban life for most residents in São Paulo suburbs has been characterized as "a relationship of rupture and denial with the rest of the city."[15] Indeed, one of the striking characteristics of São Paulo's suburbs is their distinct lack of public places and walkable space. Public life is increasingly marked by suspicion and restriction. People prefer to remain either inside their "fortified enclaves" or in the privacy of their cars. They only emerge to walk in highly secluded and guarded shopping malls. The cultural obsession with privacy and security has permeated São Paulo culture for some time. As one Paulista who had lived in both São Paulo and Rio de Janeiro told me: "Rio is a more gregarious and public city than São Paulo. In Rio, public space is part of the character of the city—you have the beaches, the Aterro park, the downtown streets, the Lagoa—you have many places for people to walk and see each other. São Paulo, on the other hand, does not have that tradition of meeting in public places. Paulistas are more private."[16]

At some point, the closed condominiums, isolated tower block settlements, and lust for privacy in São Paulo find a parallel with the American experience, where Americans long ago fled the inner city to find an escape from its perceived ills. "For the first time, something like the American suburb became popular among the elite," notes one of the city's observers.[17] Further, many of these communities are notable because they lack a sense of place and exist in denial of their surroundings, with more emphasis on security than on forging a connection between the home and the surrounding neighborhood. They are gated, fenced, or closed off more than 90 percent of the time, far more even than in the U.S., where only about 20 percent of our suburban communities are actually physically gated.

The predominance of high rise living adds to the feeling of being disconnected from the adjacent streets. Residents reportedly prefer remaining aloof from their neighborhoods, or, as one expert puts it, "residents seem to deeply reject this idea of community"; their objective is intense privacy and anonymity and all the security it brings.[18]

There is also a sense of being disconnected from nature, although the building industry has sought to market the suburbs as being closer to it. In this sense, the move to the suburbs is as much a psychological phenomenon as it is a cultural and behavioral one. Developers and investors employ an array of marketing strategies in their advertising regimes. Promotional material on suburban condominiums in São Paulo builds on the idea of a separate world, one that is secure, closer to nature, healthier, and above all safe. Most of this is achieved by elevating people high above the street, with views to green belts in the distance, despite the soaring high rises that surround them. By building walls and fences around these luxury towers, and using strategic placement of trees, flowers, plantings, a feeling of nature is created, even in relatively high density suburbs.

Figure 5.2 Panamby: A Typical São Paulo Global Suburb in the *Zona Sul*
Source: Photo by Lawrence A. Herzog

São Paulo's vertical suburbs have much in common with the horizontal suburbs of the United States; both represent places of escape from the perceived ills of crowded city life—crime, noise, discomfort. Both also display a tendency toward homogenization. In São Paulo's suburbs, the site plans and floor plans are uniform, and the larger cityscape seems predictable.[19] Copying the United States has been a conscious part of the marketing strategy of Brazilian developers. At one point in the 1980s and 1990s, developers tried to sell the "edge city" concept in Brazil. They invited a U.S. journalist, Joel Garreau, who had written a 1991 book on "edge cities,"[20] to speak to community groups about their advantages. Garreau's book argued that "edge cities" represented a new kind of medium density, automobile-oriented agglomeration of retail, office, and entertainment activities that was the next frontier of urban growth on the planet. His book cited places like Tyson's Corner, outside Washington, D.C., and Century City on the west side of Los Angeles as economically prosperous emerging exurban centers that epitomized this "new frontier." This idea coincided nicely with Garreau's lecture in Brazil, since his arguments about new suburban centers delivered a degree of legitimacy to existing residents and future home buyers in the new suburbs of São Paulo.[21]

But, São Paulo's suburbs sometimes appear as exaggerated versions of U.S. developments. For example, some residential complexes were created with quirky identities and Disneyland-like fakeness, giving them a "theme park" quality. In one case, a residential enclave called Place des Vosges sought to copy the Parisian square, but placed it inside of a private walled complex patrolled by an army of private security guards. In other cases, gated condominiums were connected to shopping malls and office complexes in an attempt to mimic the "new urbanism" that had become popular as an innovative suburban model in the U.S. New urbanism is built around the idea of creating walkable, village-like centers on the outskirts, instead of car-oriented subdivisions.

The disdain for public life in these new elite suburbs is illustrated by one author's comment on the wealthy high rise enclave of Morumbi. "To walk in Morumbi is a stigma," she writes; "the pedestrian is poor and suspicious."[22] The spacing of buildings and the construction of walls in the fortified enclave districts of São Paulo make walking unpleasant and out of proportion to the scale of the human form. Street life is less desired. There is little sense of public interaction. Those who do choose to live closer to the street cover their doors and windows with iron bars, and build high walls and fences around the perimeter, not only to be protected from crime but also to symbolically close themselves off from the public life of the city. Lost are the traditional urban rituals of walking on streets, town squares, or in parks, a public life that hardly exists anywhere in São Paulo. "The oases of intensive and mixed use are very few and only a few places in the city have vital public life."[23]

São Paulo is the quintessential mega-city of high rises, a true "vertical city." The idea of a vertical cityscape is itself premised on a twentieth century modernist idea in the world of architecture and city planning—the single tower isolated on a lot, and with open spaces around it. This product of the CIAM (International Congress of Modern Architecture) emerged in Europe after the Swiss architect Le Corbusier formed the CIAM in 1928. These ideas about modern architecture have permeated Brazil's modern city-building to this day. They were critical to the thinking of Brazil's greatest architects of that era, including Lucio Costa and Oscar Neimeyer, the head urban planner/architect team for Brasília. The approach was adapted on a grand scale for the design and building of Brasília, the first planned national capital, with its stand alone residential towers and high rise ministries along the Monumental Axis. But the idea of the single tower isolated on a lot was also a reaction to what was viewed as the failure of chaotic high rise development. One frequently cited example of poor high rise urbanism was older neighborhoods like Copacabana, in Rio, where critics bemoaned the fact that buildings were allowed to be sited too close, blocking ventilation and sunlight, and eliminating open space.[24]

In an attempt to prevent "more Copacabanas," local and state governments imposed stricter regulations on high rise development, spacing, zoning, and setbacks. In a market society, government regulations are often negotiated between powerful interest groups, and in Brazil developers and investors also had a great deal of say. Thus, the new high rise suburbs represented a compromise reached between modernist architects and the government. One contradiction, however, was that modernist architecture in its original form espoused egalitarianism, yet the new high rise, modernist suburbs were mainly for the privileged, those who could afford to live in the new vertical tower compounds with their lush landscaping and heavy security.[25]

If the vertical tower is a ubiquitous element in the modern São Paulo landscape, so too is the shopping mall, which has exploded onto the São Paulo region. The first mall—Iguatemi—was built in 1966. Ten years later, there were eight malls. A decade after that, there were thirty-four. By 2004, the region had an astonishing 579 malls. In fact, the state of São Paulo has 35 percent of all the shopping malls in Brazil. They have become the new streets of São Paulo, passageways from one high rise complex to another.[26]

The Evolution of Rio de Janeiro

While São Paulo may offer an extreme example of a U.S.-influenced model of suburban growth, the case of Rio de Janeiro, Brazil's most globally recognized city, is equally striking. It is, in some senses, a counterpart to São Paulo, not driven by finance and manufacturing but by culture, entertainment, tourism, and services. Recently, offshore oil production has injected further vitality into the city's economy, as well as global mega-sport venues, including the 2014 World Cup and the 2016 Summer Olympics. Rio also has been one of the fastest growing metropolitan areas in Brazil, and, like São Paulo, its peripheral growth has been shaped by U.S. suburban values. From San Diego along the southern border of the United States to Rio, this model of fast urbanism and sprawl poses huge ecological risks.

In the nineteenth century, Rio de Janeiro was Brazil's most important city, its national capital, and a port that served as an outlet for exporting mining wealth in the interior. Its physical beauty (mountains, bay, coastline) made it a haven for government officials and export business. Its colonial importance brought a mix of cultures, both from other parts of Brazil and from Europe (Portugal, England, France, Germany). In 1872, its population was 274,972, far overshadowing its modern rival São Paulo, which had only 31,385 at that time. One hundred years later, Rio would have about eight million, and so would São Paulo, but after that the cities began switching places. São Paulo became the demographic and economic giant of the nation, while Rio fell into second place.

Rio would remain as capital of Brazil for almost two centuries—from 1763 to 1822, while it was a Portuguese colony, and from 1822 to 1960 as an independent nation. It was the *de facto* capital of the Portuguese Empire from 1808 to 1821. By 1900, Rio was still a compact city, its urban development confined within the topographic limitations of a region with steep mountains flowing toward the sea, wide bays, and flat surfaces along the beaches and waterfront. In particular the wall of mountains west of the downtown core pushed the colonial city into the hills north of downtown; later, the wealthy classes, politicians, and developers would move to the south along the coast, in what is today called the *Zona Sul* (south zone). Meanwhile, in the north zone (*Zona Norte*), in the late nineteenth and early twentieth centuries, working class neighborhoods, or *suburbios*, formed along the rail lines and near factories there. The proximity of the industrializing port zone further stimulated workers to live in the north zone. As poor immigrants arrived in Rio in the twentieth century, they began to build *favelas* in the hills and valleys of the *Zona Norte*. Today nearly half of the city's population lives in this densely populated subregion.

Early twentieth century mayor Francisco Pereira Passos strongly subscribed to the French urban design strategies of nineteenth century Parisian planner Baron Haussmann, who rebuilt Paris around a network of diagonal boulevards. Pereira Passos sought to reinvent Rio as a "tropical Paris."[27] He put in place three projects: the Avenida Central, which became the commercial and financial spine of the city; transfer of the port to Guanabara Bay; and the construction of a seaside boulevard—Avenida Beira Mar—to connect downtown with Botafogo bay. By the 1920s, the first large scale slum clearance (the first of many) was an earth moving venture to allow Rio to expand up into the nearby hills and mountains. Another influence of French planning came in the form of French town planner Alfred Agache, who was invited to Rio to advise the city on a new urban design plan. He recommended leveling Castelo hill and building toward the southeast. Mayor Pereira Passos also was the first local politician to push for a more international image for Rio. He recognized the competition for tourism and foreign business in this part of South America from rival Buenos Aires. Public sanitation and *favela* clearance were included in the mayor's strategy for improving Rio's image to outsiders.[28]

Thus a cosmopolitan Rio emerged. The new French urban design influence allowed the city to grow beyond its colonial shell. New avenues, like the Avenida Central, created a modern transport axis through the heart of the urban core. This was followed by adding other important arteries over the next two decades, including Avenida Presidente Vargas. Lower income residences were pushed toward the new *favelas* in the hills; this polarized landscape became a dominant part of Rio's identity for the next century.[29]

The 1950s brought economic modernization and dramatic changes in Brazilian cities. Rio was in the forefront of this trend. One important mega-urban development project of the era was the design and construction of the Aterro do Flamengo—a landfill that opened space for a giant public park, promenade, and beach along the waterfront from Flamengo to the Bay of Gloria. The park created a huge public space along the beach for the masses. Construction of the Leme tunnel opened the way for a new highway, connecting downtown with the newer suburbs of Urca and Copacabana. A second tunnel beyond that allowed roads to reach further south to Ipanema and Leblon. This paved the way for the growth of the south zone's iconic high rise beachfront landscape, which later became the model for most of Brazil's high end coastal development in other beach cities like Natal, Recife, and Salvador.

The Globalization of Rio

In the second half of the twentieth century, Rio continued to grow. By 2012, according to the World Bank, the larger metropolitan region had a population of 11,838,752.[30] The primary direction of growth was now toward the south and west, since the mountains hemmed in the city in all other directions. On the one hand, it would appear Rio's growth is profoundly shaped by its physical geography. On the other hand, global forces also became central to the metropolitan region's destiny in the last decades of the twentieth century.

The new global Rio evolved into a world-city on the back of its culture. Its global image, celebrated in the media, is driven by the region's physical beauty, music, food, people, the annual "Carnaval" celebration, and its globally recognized landmarks—Sugar Loaf, Corcovado, Maracanã stadium (soccer),[31] Ipanema beach. People around the world who know anything about Brazil usually know it because of Rio. As wealthy and successful as São Paulo may be, there are few iconic images of Brazil that connect outsiders to São Paulo. Rio remains the gateway to Brazil, and thus an important place both symbolically and concretely.

Rio may be the most globally recognized city in all of Latin America.[32] Rio advertises itself to people across the planet in a variety of ways. For one, the city's nickname—"cidade maravilhosa" (marvelous city)—evokes its various attractions to outsiders: natural beauty (mountains, ocean, jungle), beachfront iconic splendor (Ipanema), Carnaval

Figure 5.3 Rio's Physical Beauty Defines Its Global Image
Source: Photo by Lawrence A. Herzog

celebrations, and music (bossa nova, samba, chorinho, jazz, and rock). It is a city that the world identifies with a culture of leisure, something that has become critical to global economies in the twenty-first century.[33] Beaches like Copacabana and Ipanema became household words by the middle of the twentieth century. "Copacabana" was the title of a hit 1978 song by American singer Barry Manilow.[34] Ipanema entered the global imagination through the song that launched the samba/jazz inspired hybrid music form called bossa nova; the song was "The Girl from Ipanema" (Garota de Ipanema) by Antonio Carlos "Tom" Jobim and Vinícius de Morais, two musical icons in Brazil.[35] That song was reproduced in a 1962 album by Stan Getz and Charlie Byrd, and later on a 1965 album that popularized it across the U.S.[36]

Even Rio's lower income neighborhoods—especially the mountainside *favelas* with their drug dealers, crime, and poverty—are legendary throughout the world, partly because of contemporary Brazilian films like *City of God* (*Cidade de Deus*, 2002) and *Elite Squad I* and *II* (*Tropa de Elite*, 2007, 2010). Moreover, Rio is such a photogenic and compelling city that it has been chosen as a site for popular films on many occasions. Examples include the James Bond movie *Moonraker* (1979), the popular hit *Blame It on Rio* (1984), and, more recently, the film *Fast Five* (2011). An earlier film with Rio as the star was the classic *Black Orpheus* (*Orfeu Negro*).[37] Rio's global association with Brazilian music, as mentioned, also enhances the city's image.[38] Films have brought samba, bossa nova, chorinho, and other Brazilian music to a world stage. Equally, of course, great architecture is a trademark of Brazil, and its two most famous figures—Oscar Neimeyer and Lucio Costa[39]—were either born in Rio or lived there most of their lives.

More recently, adding to its distinguished cultural history, Rio was selected for two global mega-events—the 2016 Summer Olympic Games, and it is one of twelve cities that will host soccer matches for the 2014 World Cup.[40] Many cities around the world have sought to use Olympic Games to enhance their cultural branding.

Barcelona used the 1992 Summer Olympics to construct its image as a global landmark, and to market itself as a tourism and investment destination.[41] Rio is taking advantage of the global media attention on the Olympics to build international interest to expand markets for businesses ranging from fashion, cosmetics, furniture, and tourism to oil, chemicals, steel, food, and pharmaceutical products.[42]

The globalization of Rio has led to the emergence of elite suburbs on the outskirts of the city. During the 1960s and 1970s, as Brazil modernized, its relationship with the United States grew closer. Brazilian developers and consumers were aware of the growth of modern suburbs in the United States, and, just as in Mexico City and Tijuana, this model became an attractive lifestyle prototype that influenced the emergence of Brazil's new elite suburbs during that era.

Barra da Tijuca, Rio's Global Suburb

A towering example of a globally inspired "mega-suburb" was born on the outskirts of Rio de Janeiro. Barra da Tijuca is a large suburban corridor with more than one-quarter million people, and still expanding. The story of its formation and its evolving impact on Brazil's second largest global metropolis is a poignant example of how what began as a well-intentioned urban design plan for a modernist "new town," in the spirit of Brasília, ended up being absorbed by private landowners and turned into an elite, U.S.-influenced suburb.

Before the 1960s, the region of Barra da Tijuca and its inland area of the Baixada de Jacarepaguá (Jacarepaguá Basin) were isolated from Rio by a set of geographic barriers—mountains, lakes, marshes, and sand dunes. It therefore remained largely undeveloped, except for some farms and small residential dwellings. But as Rio went through a growth boom in the 1950s and 1960s, a number of factors contributed to an interest in developing this space, and led to a coalition of government, large developers, and real estate interests, partly influenced by the U.S. model of suburbia, that would dramatically transform this part of the metropolitan region over the next four decades.

Within Rio, a growing upper middle class and elite were rapidly consuming land and space in the south zone neighborhoods, from Copacabana to Ipanema, Leblon, Jardim Botánico, and Gavea. Real estate values skyrocketed in these zones, and residential space was quickly becoming saturated. Meanwhile, people who lived in the northern suburbs wanted to move either south or west. The demand for coastal property and a lifestyle away from the hustle-bustle of the city among newly upper middle and upper class residents would eventually mean that Barra da Tijuca would become the largest suburban land development in all of Brazil.

In the 1960s and 1970s, a tidal wave of global factors kicked in to strongly influence the direction and style of urban development that would unfold in Barra da Tijuca. The first global factor was Brazil's economic boom, which was significantly enhanced by courting foreign investment, especially from the United States. U.S. companies like Ford and General Motors opened plants in Brazil in the 1950s and 1960s; U.S. pharmaceutical and chemical companies soon followed. Before 1960 (when the capital was moved to Brasília), Rio was still the capital, and it benefited directly from these international investment schemes.

Shortly after being elected president in 1955, Juscelino Kubitschek visited the United States in search of foreign capital to exploit Brazil's natural resources. In a *Time Magazine* interview in 1956, the Brazilian president stated: "No matter how busy I may be, any foreign investor who comes to Brazil will find my door open."[43] Later that year the U.S. Export-Import Bank gave Brazil a thirty-five million dollar loan for its steel industry. This unleashed an unprecedented flow of hundreds of millions of investment dollars into Brazil, which subsequently leveraged state-sponsored construction of infrastructure and development projects, including the Trans-Amazonian highway, the Itaipu hydroelectric dam, nuclear power plants, bridges, railways, telephone systems, subways, airports, port improvements, urban redevelopment, and industrial expansion. The emphasis was on grandiose projects that advertised the new resources of a growing nation-state.

Politically, Brazil had been closely aligned with the United States, beginning in the post-World War II era, when it defined itself as part of the capitalist bloc in the face of global factional splits between socialism, communism, and capitalism. Yet, Brazil was also building an independent political position as early as 1961, when its new military government sought to promote stronger nationalism and protectionism.[44] Still, soon after he was elected, President John F. Kennedy proudly announced a new ten-year "Alliance for Progress" plan, which sought to increase per capita income, education, and economic growth in Latin America. It was signed in Punta del Este, Uruguay, a short hop across the border from Brazil. The U.S. guaranteed $20 billion in aid, with Latin America to supply $80 billion. This project served to enhance the friendly relations between the U.S. and Brazil which grew during the 1960s.

Not surprisingly, the 1960s bridge between the U.S. and Brazil coincided with the rising popularity of Brazilian culture in the U.S.—especially music. U.S. tourism visits to Brazil, and especially to Rio de Janeiro, began to accelerate during this period. At the same moment, U.S. foreign policy toward Brazil was intensified to stem the flow of communism in different parts of the world. The flow of loans from the U.S. into Brazil continued, even during the 1968–74 period, when a hard-line military tribunal was in power in Brazil. This is the context for understanding the creation of a new mega-suburb beyond Rio's south zone along the coastline.

The Creation of a Pilot Plan for Barra

If any one infrastructure project epitomized Brazil's modernization program of the 1950s and 1960s, it would have to be the construction of the city of Brasília as the nation's new capital, to replace Rio. Completed in 1960, but still a decades-long work in progress during the decade of the 1960s, Brasília symbolized to the world everything the Brazilian government wanted to promote about itself—an economically dynamic nation on the move, capable of creating grandiose public works and reinventing itself as a modern industrial nation, not a poor underdeveloped one. The shadow of Brasília would lie in the background of every great public works project in Brazil during this period. Yet it was matched by the importance of one of the nation's largest suburbanization master plan projects only a little more than a decade later—the urban development of Rio's new coastal territory of Barra da Tijuca and the Baixada de Jacarepaguá.

Brasília was built from 1957 to 1960, the first planned modern national capital on the planet. It was a tribute to the new paradigm of modern architecture and city-building. Lucio Costa, born in France, was the chief city planner. Despite all the criticism of Brasília by some architecture critics,[45] the fact is that its completion was an epic achievement—the first truly planned national capital of its scale in the world, and in a developing nation at that. Applying the principles of modern architecture to a great building was one thing—that was being done successfully in cities around the world such as Paris, London, and New York—but applying the principles of modern architecture to the building of an entire city—a brand new national capital—was something else.

If Brasília was an example of the possibilities of modern architecture, the planning of the first great mega-suburb of Barra da Tijuca, outside Rio, was an example of its limitations. Brasília's head planner Lucio Costa was selected to create a Pilot Plan for Rio's southern coastal development project at Barra da Tijuca. However, although Costa's touch would be infused with the same modernist and rationalist spirit of the national capital, the development of Barra would turn out to be far more influenced by privatization, private developer capital, and U.S. suburban values. Where Brasília's development remained under close

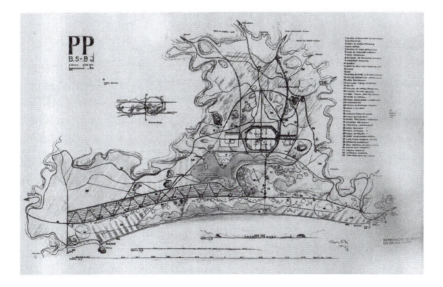

Figure 5.4 Lucio Costa's Pilot Plan for Barra da Tijuca, New Coastal Suburb outside Rio de Janeiro

Source: Photo by permission of Alfredo Sirkis, Rio de Janeiro, Brazil

government supervision, Barra da Tijuca's development was taken over by major landholders and private investors. Brasília, the national capital, was under constant public scrutiny, since the image of the nation was at stake. Barra, a private suburban enclave, quietly unfolded with very little public scrutiny.

Lucio Costa's Pilot Plan for Barra displayed much of the same thinking he had employed in Brasília—but a number of things had changed by the late 1960s and 1970s, both in Brazil and in Rio, and thus the way that Barra subsequently evolved was quite different. Brasília was much more a public sector driven plan with a great deal of emphasis on civic and national pride. Its design gave priority to monumental and ceremonial spaces. Barra da Tijuca emphasized residential space, private commercial shopping malls, and security. It became a giant seaside enclave for the affluent, a Brazilianized form of the American sprawl that has produced so many public health and environmental problems in the United States.

Costa's plan for Barra carried much of his thinking about Brasília, and much of the optimism of the era, though it was applied in a very different context. It is important to note, from the outset, that he saw Barra as a separate city, and not necessarily as a place connected to the existing tissue of Rio. He also viewed it as a new city that would be intimately tied to the natural landscapes already there—ocean, lagoons, lakes, and waterways. He writes in the Pilot Plan: "What most attracts one in this region is the ocean air, the openness, the scale, the beaches and dunes seem without end, and that rare sensation of being in a pristine, untouched world."[46] He also frequently refers to Barra as a separate city, one that would be "a mais bela cidade oceânica do mundo" (the most beautiful oceanic city in the world).[47]

In the physical design of the city, the parallels with Brasília are noteworthy. They include the creation of a cross-like design, much the same as the airplane shaped morphology of Brasília. As he had done in Brasília, Costa emphasized in Barra the modernist principle of single use zones, specialized sectors for housing, commerce, offices, and public buildings. He organized the entire new city along two main axes: a horizontal axis called Avenida de Las Americas and a perpendicular axis,

Avenida Ayrton Senna, which ran from the ocean toward the secondary center at Jacarepaguá. A secondary axis, Avenida Sernambetiba, ran parallel to Avenida de Las Américas along the ocean, following the natural contour of the coastline. He proposed three centers within the cross-like form: one at the original eastern end of Avenida Sernambetiba, in Jardim Oceánico, which was already urbanized; a second at the intersection of the two monumental axes; and a third on the northern end of Avenida Ayrton Senna, which would serve as the future center of the inland district of Jacarepaguá. The civic center at the intersection of the two highway axes was proposed to have the same monumental scale as the center of Brasília. Along the main axes, his Pilot Plan spaces buildings apart in the same Corbusian style as Brasília—high rise towers surrounded by open spaces. The plan also had a monumental formality and a sense of abstraction typical of Costa's style.

Viewed in hindsight, the plan for Barra shares the modernist rationality of Brasília, giving priority to machines (cars) over humans (pedestrians), and emphasizing rows of high rise towers isolated in space, with no public spaces connecting them. This stems from following the American "single use" land use planning approach, which carved out separate zones that were detached in space and only reachable by car. The Costa plan, from the beginning, severely curtailed the kind of "walkability" needed to create human scale communities. One critic succinctly captures the dilemma of designing a place like Barra on the edge of a city (Rio) so rich in public space experiences: "Barra is the only neighborhood in Rio that does not have a celebrated *botequim* (neighborhood bar), mainly because there are no street corners where one could build a botequim."[48] Indeed, the absence of street corners for people in Barra can be traced to the simple fact that its streets were designed for cars and not for people. As a social plan, there is also a sense of exclusion in the Barra Pilot Plan, a sense that this new city is for the upper middle and upper classes, especially in the zones along and close to the ocean.[49] As it turned out, Costa's plan provided a blueprint for the coming of gated condominiums that are even more exclusionary than the Brasília *superquadras*. This can be seen by the increasing segregation of the wealthy in Barra da Tijuca, far more than what one saw in Brasília.

As in Brasília, despite the language of the Barra Pilot Plan, the commitment to community life and social well-being was inconsistent. In Brasília, Costa presented the *superquadra* or super-block as a socially egalitarian, harmonically conceived environment that would foster collectivity and integration.[50] Indeed, many of Brasília's super-blocks have some of the design elements that would support such an idea—parks, gardens, schools, churches, and commercial spaces that offer, at least in theory, nodes or gathering points that could connect residents in time and space. Also, Brasília's *superquadras* are, for the most part, accessible to the public.

Figure 5.5 Barra da Tijuca, Aerial Photo, a Planned, Elite High Rise Suburb
Source: Photo by permission of Alfredo Sirkis, Rio de Janeiro, Brazil

In Barra a very different kind of residential community emerged. While Costa's plan generated a template for bringing in a certain type of modernist high rise community, most of those communities, with some exceptions, quickly became closed, gated condominiums, with no public space and few options that allowed outsiders to come inside. Like many exclusive gated suburbs around the world, Barra was a patchwork of isolated, enclosed complexes, offering no public spaces or meeting places for residents to interact.

The first two large scale condo-residential complexes built in Barra were called (not without some irony) Nova Ipanema and Novo Leblon, thus creating the illusion that newly rich migrants, mainly from Rio's north zone, were moving to a place like the south zone's iconic and much celebrated beach communities of Ipanema and Leblon. In fact, they were notably different—Ipanema and Leblon are pedestrian scale neighborhoods with cafes, restaurants, and street-friendly residential buildings, but the two new Barra communities consisted of individual high rise buildings surrounded by unused green space. Nova Ipanema, built in 1977, was a privatized version of the Brasília *superquadra*. Later some single family housing was built nearby, schools were added, and even shopping malls appended along the primary auto axis. Novo Leblon, built in 1980, featured: "Towers spaced across a platform of leisure space, with swimming pools and recreational infrastructure, all apart from cars."[51]

Apparently, many politicians and prominent officials wanted Barra to be different from Copacabana. Copacabana, for many modernists in Brazil, came to symbolize what they thought was wrong in Rio by the 1960s and 1970s. Lucio Costa himself once described Copacabana this way: "concrete barriers built right against the sea, blocking the view and preventing proper ventilation of residents."[52] But there may be a more nuanced social interpretation of why they disliked the famous beach community. Copacabana was a high density, spontaneous, noisy place, a slice of New York City. Modernists wanted calm, efficiency, and order. They preferred Barra to offer social exclusion, where Copacabana represented diversity—in its spread of uses, activities, social groups, and spatial form. As one critic of Barra wrote: "it would become an imitation of a city, where what is fundamental about urban life—mixture, confrontation, creative disorder, is always exorcised in the name of 'ethical principles' (moral exclusion and security) and aesthetics."[53]

Not surprisingly, advertisements for homes in Barra emphasized that Barra is *not* Copacabana, i.e. that it is not about spontaneity, chaos, or density, but about open space, tranquility, and the feeling of creating something perfect, a touch of Midas. A brochure advertising Barra spoke of "fuga do caos urbano e a busca da natureza" (an escape from urban chaos toward a closer connection to nature).[54] Barra's objective was to create a space of capital where real estate investors could more freely operate than in other parts of Rio.[55]

Privatization, Social Exclusion

Once the Pilot Plan for Barra was completed in 1970, local and state governments quickly stepped in to provide supporting infrastructure. In the early 1970s, transit links were built, including the Elevado das Bandeiras (an elevated highway) and tunnels through the mountains at Dos Irmãos and Pedro da Gavea. This created a direct highway connection from Rio's south zone to Barra da Tijuca. Meanwhile, no mass transit links of any kind were constructed to link Barra to the urban core of Rio.[56] It was clear that automobiles were going to be the mode of transit for this new global suburb.

From the beginning, Lucio Costa and other government planners and officials allowed Barra's development to be controlled by large scale developers. Indeed, in the 1970s, much of the land was controlled by a small group of mega-developers, including ETSA, S.A., Grupo Desenvolvimento, Sr, Pasquale Maura, and Carvalho Hoska, S.A. The land was divided into mega-estates, and their dominance of the land market meant that smaller scale developers had to pay a high price to acquire land that was held by only a few sources. This drove up the price of Barra land, thus ensuring that it would mainly house upper middle class and wealthy landowners.[57]

From 1976 to 1985, during the first big wave of land development, records show that it was overwhelmingly dominated by large scale projects. These produced high rise luxury apartment and condominium

Figure 5.6 Privatized Luxury High Rise Mega-housing Dominates Barra da Tijuca
Source: Photo by Lawrence A. Herzog

towers, or groupings of towers around a central nucleus, and a smattering of single family homes, generally inside the luxury tower developments. One analysis of real estate agents during this period found that, out of thirty-one key agents operating in Barra, nineteen, or 61 percent of the total, were handling either mega, very large, or large deals, and only seven were in the medium to small category.[58]

By the early 2000s, Barra had become a sprawling, privileged zone of newly rich residents, many of whom had fled the north zone, which had become increasingly poor, surrounded by more and more *favela* communities, and subject to a higher incidence of violent crime and gang battles. Developers sold these upwardly mobile migrants the idea of a "suburban paradise," away from the problems in other parts of the city. They offered the safety of gated luxury high rise buildings, upscale shopping malls (there are dozens in Barra, more than in any other neighborhood in Rio), giant supermarkets (including Walmart, Bon Marche, Carrefour, Extra, and Makro), and other amenities like an airport, a Formula One Grand Prix racetrack, two theme parks (Rio Waterplanet and Terra Encantada), a sports complex, used in the Pan American Games of 2007, and the largest music performance complex in Brazil, the "City of Music" (Cidade da Musica) designed by well known French architect Christian de Portzamparc.[59]

All of these features pointed to a degree of social inequality even greater than in other Brazilian cities. In Brasília, observers chronicled that modernist architects like Costa used the technique of "shock" to transform the social nature of capitalism, giving the public sector greater power over how the city is designed and managed, and thus remaking the city for those in power and those they are aligned with. It was further argued that, in Brasília, government planners and those in power tried to blur the distinction between public and private, making the private world more public and the public world more private. This created a "strange" environment, where the government could achieve a "hidden agenda" with a subversive character, one with socialist leanings that created communal spaces—*superquadras*—which pretended to be egalitarian but, like Soviet politics, were really more elitist.[60]

In Barra, by contrast, there was no hidden agenda; it became exactly what it set out to be—a highly exclusive gated condominium beach suburb. This did not go entirely unnoticed. During the 1980s, Rio's community leaders realized what Barra was becoming. One day, there was a rallying cry to do something about Barra's growing exclusivity. Finally, under political pressure, the more liberal municipal government agreed to hold a public workshop in 1986, which they called "Seminario Barra '86." Its advertised purpose was to review the Pilot Plan and seek to make Barra accessible to all social groups. In one ad for the seminar, it was announced that "Ha que democratizar o Plan Piloto" (it is necessary to democratize the Pilot Plan).

The timing of the seminar is not surprising. Only two years earlier, Brazil had finally returned to a civilian government, after sixteen years of hard-line military rule. The incoming president, Jose Sarney, was in the process of drafting a new constitution. Politicians were sensitive in that moment to the question of social equality, and, in particular, to the critique that Brasília had ended up as a kind of "socialist purification" plan, where the poor were systematically moved to satellite cities, while the privileged classes lived in the newly designed Pilot Plan core area.

In Barra, some observers found even more elitism than in Brasília. In the words of one: "Ja não existen mais superquadras como em Brasília, aqui são condomínios exclusives" (There are no more super-blocks like in Brasília, here in Barra only exclusive condominiums).[61] Lucio Costa was known to have remarked in designing the super-blocks of Brasília that "neighborhoods are not waterproof, they leak."[62] He was aware that Brasília was criticized as being rigid and brutalist, and so he tried to design Barra with an emphasis on nature. But, in the end, his designs were no match for real estate interests that reinforced the exclusivity and segregation that came to define Barra.

This dilemma was the underlying theme when the seminar of 1986 unfolded. The first thing that happened there was that critics blasted public officials for allowing Barra to become an elitist settlement zone. Community leaders argued that people of lesser means were being excluded. Over the course of the seminar, a set of policy changes was proposed: make housing more available and affordable to diverse social groups, and mandate more environmental controls. When the seminar ended, the response of private landowners, banks, the real estate industry, and private developers was immediate and dramatic. In the words of one observer of that period: "The sectors of mega-capital and real estate development had a different conception of the expansion of Barra da Tijuca, one that was diametrically opposed to the decisions expressed by the Seminar."[63] The large property owners, financial interests, and their representatives immediately began to explore their political options in the wake of a seminar whose results worried them, and threatened their financial objectives.

Finally, in 1988, private developers and their colleagues announced a formal proposal to separate Barra da Tijuca from Rio, merge it with the Baixada de Jacarepaguá, and create an independent city with its own government. This would free them from what they now considered the shackles of Rio city politics, which in that moment had moved to the left and appeared to be trying to mollify the demands of residential associations from the poor and working class communities, and other groups who wanted to make Barra more socially diverse.

Seceding from the troubled city comes straight from the pages of U.S. history. For much of the twentieth century, American suburbs had found that the best way to escape responsibility for the social ills of the larger city was to cut their political ties with the city that had historically evolved, incorporate, and form their own suburban government. Thus, the new global suburb of Barra was borrowing from its global partner to the north. However, it should also be noted that Brazil does not have the same tradition of incorporated, separate suburbs. In 1990, the petition to separate Barra was reviewed, debated, and finally denied by the state government of Rio. Everyone agreed to keep the Pilot Plan of Lucio Costa as the governing instrument, and not to change the political process in any way.

While the developers and landowners may not have gotten their way on the matter of political separation, the pace of growth accelerated in the 1990s, and the pattern of exclusivity hardly changed. If anything, Barra became even more expensive and more of a wealthy suburban enclave. From a population of 45,000 in 1980, Barra grew to nearly 250,000 by 2010; combined with the growth of the basin of Jacarepaguá, a much more middle and working class zone, the subregion had over one-half million people and was the fastest growing part of Rio.

In Barra, the form of growth had become even more privatized and exclusionary—this was observed by various city planners and writers who tracked urban development in the south and west zones. In one study, it was noted that development became more and more restricted inside gated complexes.[64] Shopping malls began to add security and put up other real and psychological barriers to public entry. In general, in the 1990s and early 2000s, public spaces were appropriated by private interests. This was buttressed by an urban plan which allowed large real estate interests to dominate the land market, further driving up prices at a time when housing was becoming more expensive. Government housing policy, meanwhile, made housing more difficult to build for those of limited means, and allowed overvaluing of homes for the elite.[65]

Sprawl and the Coastal Ecosystem

The building of a sprawling mega-suburb in a coastal zone like the Barra da Tijuca region has been profoundly damaging to the beach ecosystem. As a nation, Brazil has one of the longest coastlines in the world, some 4,600 miles (or 7,500 kilometers); its coastal ecosystems contain an array of unique but fragile elements—coral reefs, cliffs, sand dunes, estuaries, lagoons, and salt marshes.[66] The Barra de Tijuca zone is called a "double barrier lagoon coast," due to its long narrow barrier island that sits in front of a system of lagoons and waterways. This geographic formation of lowland lagoons, canals, and marshes is highly vulnerable to climate change. Storms and heavy rainfall cause strong tidal flows and shifts in waves which result in floods and the blocking of channels. This then causes "overwash," where waters back up into lagoons and flood adjacent lands. Since global climate change is now understood to be raising sea levels across the planet, lowland coastal zones like Barra da Tijuca are even more endangered by this phenomenon.[67]

Urban sprawl in this kind of fragile ecological setting is problematic. Among other things, sprawl encourages fragmented development, which impedes managing coastal bioregions. The Brazilian government passed legislation in 1988 to define its coastal region as a "national patrimony" that needed special management. The National Coastal Management Plan (Law 7661) created in 1988 was supposed to designate "permanent preservation areas" along the coast and restrict use; these included mangrove zones and sand dunes (*restingas*), vulnerable natural resources native to regions like Barra da Tijuca.

Unfortunately, many of these designated zones have not been well managed or are compromised by interest groups with different objectives—from oil and gas extraction or fish production, to tourism and real estate. On the pristine beaches of the state of São Paulo, for example, one study showed that only 4 percent of residential homes had proper sanitary sewage disposal services, and that "fundamental policies are simply not obeyed on coastal enterprises."[68] This is exacerbated by the reality that economic interests along the coast (fishing, shrimp farming, shipyards, the petrochemical industry, chemicals, and other minerals) account for 73 percent of the gross national product of Brazil.[69] The government ends up treading carefully when managing coastal ecology in the face of its largest economic sectors.

This problem is especially acute in what one study calls the "fast urbanization of Barra da Tijuca."[70] The rapid urban expansion of the

Jacarepaguá lowland basin involved the arrival of an estimated 650,000 inhabitants over a mere three decades. Barra da Tijuca (the coastal portion of the larger basin) increased in size from around just 5,000 inhabitants in 1970 to over 175,000 in 2000. This explosive growth spread in sprawl-like fashion across the basin, invading the edges of canals, lagoons, and bays, encroaching on wildlife, and interrupting the natural flows of water. Since urbanization, the extent of flooding, landslides, beach erosion, and blocked waterways has exponentially increased.

Population growth has not been matched by environmental stewardship. Indeed, for almost forty years there was no regional sewage sanitation system; instead government required developers to install small, local sewage treatment facilities for their developments. But these were reportedly not carefully monitored; thus many facilities functioned only sporadically. Ironically, while developers were lax in maintaining sewage treatment systems, they were using the natural beauty of the basin (beaches, lagoons, and mountains) to market their condominium projects. So, the sewage they were not treating would end up destroying the very ecosystems they relied on to sell their luxury condos.

Finally, in 2001, the state sewage company (CEDAE) began construction of a regional sewage treatment system; it took another decade to complete. But, reportedly, the system is still not serving the entire region. Individual sewage treatment plants inside condominium projects (required by the government before giving permits to developers) are frequently not operating, due to the high costs of maintenance and of disposing of sewage in sanitary landfills. So instead, many of these condos simply discharge directly into the lagoons and canals.[71]

All of this contamination from urban sprawl and unregulated, piecemeal urbanization has been damaging to the ecosystem. The *restinga* (sand dune/marsh ecosystem) of this part of the Brazilian coast is considered one of the world's biodiversity "hotspots," due to its diverse flora and fauna.[72] But that ecosystem is in trouble. Illegal occupation of the fragile edges of lagoons, rivers, and canals, as well as improper land grading and embankments, have led to flooding and to contamination of the lowland basin waters. Direct dumping of effluent from residential and industrial sites is the main source of pollution. Residential sewage comes from unregulated closed condominium complexes as well as from *favelas* in the lowland region. There is also an additional problem of garbage flowing into the watershed. The result is high levels of pathogenic microorganisms in the water, including coliforms and e-coli, all of which pose significant public health dangers.[73]

Municipal government considered building larger sewage treatment systems in the most polluted sites, but opted to begin dredging the lagoons and canals in an effort to remove accumulated sludge from the bottom, and thus open a circulation stream that would allow flows from the lagoons to the sea. The state government concentrated on completing the larger sanitation sewage facility; it took over a decade, and finally opened in the early 2010s. However, that system is incomplete, with numerous areas of the basin still without sewerage. This allows the destructive nature of Barra's urban sprawl to continue. One of the biggest problems is that, by not planning for the larger region, the government simply allowed scattered and fragmented growth of condominium projects. In fact, it gave the luxury condominium complexes independent responsibility to regulate and dispose of their sewage on their own. There was minimal oversight from public agencies, and no attempt to create a regional planning approach to the management of this watershed.

As a result, the loss of pristine ecological resources continues. There were originally 260 square kilometers of mangroves here, which has been reduced to only about 80 square kilometers today. Only half the original *restinga* (sand dune) ecosystem remains. The heavy rains, flooding, and uncontrolled toxic waters have not gone away. At the same time, the mega-sport developments, such as the 2016 Olympics, and the real estate boom in Barra da Tijuca will put even more pressure on local and state government to relax zoning and environmental regulations here, so as not to be seen as impeding corporate investment and the profits to be had from these global economic activities.[74]

Barra: a U.S. Suburb in Brazil?

During the decades of the 1960s and 1970s, *cariocas* (residents of Rio) came to look upon the United States favorably. Rio was going through a fervent era of growth, modernization, and change. While the construction of Brasília infused nationalist pride, in Rio the importance of foreign tourism and the growing popularity of Brazilian music, food, and Carnaval celebrations to the American market led to a gradual increase in Rio's cultural, political, and economic ties to the U.S. As the former Director of the City of Rio's Department of Urbanism (2001–6) noted, reflecting on his childhood: "We lived in Flamengo. My dad had an American car, a Mercury. He worshipped that auto, and he prayed that the tramways would be eliminated, since they interrupted the flow of cars at that time."[75]

The admiration for U.S. culture and lifestyles in Brazil's cities is highlighted by what some referred to as the "Miami effect." Barra da Tijuca has periodically been called a "Brazilian Miami." Many Brazilians, mainly affluent Brazilians, frequently travel to Miami for business, tourism, or to make consumer purchases. It is often the first city Brazilians see in the U.S., and thus, in a sense, it is a gateway city and a cultural symbol of the United States. It is also viewed as a "success story," a prosperous city, with Latino culture, located in the U.S. It has skyscrapers along the coast, so it looks and feels familiar to Brazilians.

The Miami effect accelerated during the 1980s and 1990s. According to one expert on Barra:

> During the 1980s, many investors and developers wanted to recreate Miami in Barra. Miami was a place many Brazilians visited to shop or be tourists. It was a symbol of many things Rio's north zone residents (the ones who moved to Barra) wanted— security, shopping, consumer goods, the whole package.[76]

Ironically, as others pointed out, Miami was not necessarily the American city that Barra most resembled. "In terms of its scale, automobile orientation and its playful shopping mall architecture, Barra is more like Las Vegas than Miami,"[77] states one source. "Barra is not really Miami. It's worse. Miami has high density and a sense of place. Barra is an American freeway in the middle of nowhere. It's isolated condos and shopping malls. As an urban design experience, I hate it," said another.[78]

If reference to Miami was meant to copy the sense of well-being and consumer success connected with North America, it is also true that developers and real estate agents wanted to sell Barra as a safe place to live, like a quiet U.S. suburb. Given all the violence in Rio, and especially in the north zone, this became as important in Barra as in other large cities like São Paulo. The murder in the 1990s of the son of a supermarket owner on the streets of Barra, and the kidnapping of a businessman in a condominium in Novo Leblon, suddenly meant that the pristine image of the new suburb was threatened. Public officials quickly swung into action to counter this—they installed special gates on all main roads leading into and out of Barra. This meant that police could cordon off the city in the event of a kidnapping or an assault.[79]

Privacy and security would increasingly dominate the culture of Barra. One local writer jokingly described a fictional residential project in Barra:

> The Barra 2000 project, conceived as an Iron Curtain, will install automatic controls for road access into and out of the zone ... the project will add to the autonomy and independence, will be fenced and fortified. Passports will be requested of all foreigners ... all administered by armed militia and commanded by a computer named Hal.[80]

Even shopping malls in Barra emphasize security and privacy. They are enclosed, protected from the streets, and generally only entered by automobile with guards in kiosks inspecting each entering vehicle. Armed security guards can be seen throughout the malls. Many are enclosed, air conditioned, and evoke an atmosphere of privacy and security.

Advertisements by developers and real estate agents for Barra also emphasized security, privacy, and exclusion. Often one sees the use of phrases like "a new lifestyle" or "a new paradise." By the early 2000s, most of Barra consisted of enclosed, privatized tower blocks, privatized shopping malls, or high security office buildings. At the same time, civic and public spaces were scarce. There is only one walkable commercial street in Barra, and it lies in the first neighborhood built (called Jardim

Oceánico), while the Pilot Plan of Lucio Costa was being completed. Jardim Oceánico is an anomaly in Barra. It preceded the explosion of closed condominiums after the 1980s, which came to define the region's identity. There are very few other walking corridors, gardens, or commercial centers that residents can reach on foot. The vast majority of residential spaces in Barra consist of isolated high rises with no sense of community and no destinations within walking distance. Most of the shopping malls are located along the Avenida das Americas, which is a fast moving car-oriented corridor that cannot really be reached on foot from the residences. Like in many suburbs in North America, one does not see many people walking on the streets of Barra.

Barra's expansion in the 1980s and 1990s came at a time when Brazil was moving away from its state-centric approach to city building. That is, the era of Brasília and state mega-planning was long gone. So even though Lucio Costa was hired to design the master plan for Barra, the development that unfolded was much more U.S. style and private sector

Figure 5.7 American Themes Abound in the "Citta America" Shopping Mall in Barra de Tijuca
Source: Photo by Lawrence A. Herzog

driven. Almost every major study of Barra's development since the 1970s emphasizes the dominance of mega-property owners, high end luxury residential development and commerce. The only brief pause was the 1986 seminar to "democratize Barra." But, in the end, that project did not lead to any long-term changes, and the quality of development remained in the hands of developers and the private sector. It's also been suggested that Barra's planning process was left too much in the hands of one person (Lucio Costa), and that that one person depended mainly on a somewhat secretive group of advisers who made most of the key decisions with Costa.[81]

Visually, Bara is dominated by two realities—high rise luxury condos and shopping malls. The proliferation of shopping malls is very much adapted from the U.S. In Barra, they are spread along the Avenida das Americas, virtually defining that road as a "shopping mall highway." While Lucio Costa's original plan called for concentrating commerce in three distinct nodes—the older part of Barra's Jardim Oceánico, the future downtown of Baixada de Jacarepaguá, and the intersection of the two main transit axes (Avenida Americas and Ayrton Senna)—in fact, shopping malls run the entire length of Barra, from the entrance on the east all the way to the next elite suburb of Recreio dos Bandeirantes.

The themes and architecture of the malls borrow heavily from the American experience.[82] First, the naming of the malls themselves is frequently in English, and with heavy references to the U.S. and its culture. Examples include "New York City," "Downtown," "Midtown," "Barra Garden Shopping," "Open Mall Shopping," "Barra World Shopping," and "Citta America." The malls also tend to try to create a theme park-like, fake world, an escape from the outside into a space that allows people to imagine themselves somewhere else, and then to consume. Perhaps the most extreme example is Barra World Shopping, which feebly copies Disney's Epcot Center in Orlando, a theme park that simulates different world cultures. In Barra World Shopping, the mall is divided into themed spaces with references to various world regions— Japan, Italy, France, Holland, or the Arabian region. Giant sculptures evoke images of those places within the mall—a two-story Eiffel Tower, a fake Leaning Tower of Pisa, a copy of the Sphinx. These fake stage

Figure 5.8 Fake Eiffel Tower in the "Barra World Shopping" Mall
Source: Photo by Lawrence A. Herzog

sets copy the trend of post-modern fake themed malls and festival market spaces that became popular in the U.S. in the 1980s and 1990s. They
are epitomized perhaps by places like the Universal Studios "City Walk,"
a mall designed by a theme park company to look like a city street but
filled with fake scenography, and no public seating.

A culture of consumerism within artificial spaces dominates the
quality of life in Barra. It, in effect, replaces the experience of living
and walking in real neighborhoods that fill most of the rest of Rio. It
replaces older urban neighborhoods and their strong sense of place with
spaces that advertise leisure, safety, comfort, privacy, and exclusivity,
which, increasingly, many residents of Barra want. Like the U.S. suburban model, the shopping mall amidst a sanitized Barra lifestyle allows
people the fantasy of leaving the city even while still living in its reach.
This idea was polished in the U.S. and then exported through the media
and global tourism.

Brazilian critics question the suburban culture of leisure and consumerism in Rio's exurb enclaves. Some observers note that in Barra an entire generation of children are growing up without ever living outside a gated world. As one set of critics describe, there are kids who have been to Disneyland in Florida but not to downtown Rio, kids who have flown in airplanes or ridden in a Mercedes Benz, but have no idea how to ride a city bus or take the metro.[83] Adults in Rio worry about these questions. As in the United States, they worry about social isolation. In the late 1990s, during the first attempt to form inter-condominium dialogue through a series of community meetings in Barra, residents demanded that community associations contract with psychologists and social workers to help children and adolescents growing up alienated and isolated in these fake cities.[84]

Notes

1 World Bank, World Development Indicators database, July, 2011. Gross domestic product (2010).
2 Ibid. Mexico's per capita GDP in 2010 was $10,604, while Brazil's per capita GDP was $12,574.
3 Instituto Brasileiro de Geografia e Estadistica, www.ibge.gov.br.
4 The host cities include São Paulo, Rio de Janeiro, and national capital Brasília, plus most of the large coastal cities of the north—Natal, Fortaleza, Recife, and Salvador—as well as the southern cities of Porto Alegre and Curitiba, and the inland cities of Belo Horizonte, Cuiabá, and Manaus.
5 Marca Sibaja, Jenny Barchfield, and Bradley Brooks, "One Million Brazilians Hit the Streets," *Huffington Post*, June 21, 2013, http://www.huffingtonpost.com/2013/06/21/brazil-protests-2013_n_3478101.html, retrieved 10/29/13.
6 See "Protests in Brazil: Taking to the Streets," *Economist*, June 22, 2013, http://www.economist.com/news/americas/21579857-bubbling-anger-about-high-prices-corruption-and-poor-public-services-boils-over; and Dom Phillips, "Thousands on Streets in Brazil Protests," *Guardian*, July 11, 2013, http://www.theguardian.com/world/2013/jul/12/thousands-streets-brazil-protests, retrieved 10/29/13.
7 Sibaja et al., 2013.
8 Arguably, one exception in Rio de Janeiro is the UPP program, or pacification of *favelas*, in which local and state police and the army have occupied *favelas* and driven out the drug smugglers and local violence. Not everyone believes this is an acceptable long-term solution.
9 Brian J. Godfrey, "Revisiting Rio de Janeiro and Sao Paulo," *Geographical Review*, 89 (1), January, 1999, 94–121. By comparison with São Paulo, Rio de Janeiro has only ten of the top Fortune 100 corporate sites.
10 John Rennie Short and Yeong-Hyun Kim, *Globalization and the City*. New York: Prentice Hall, 1999, 34.
11 See Teresa Caldeira, *City of Walls: Crime, Segregation and Citizenship in Sao Paulo*. Berkeley: University of California Press, 2000.

12 See Gilda Collet Bruna and Heliane Comin Vargas, "The Shopping Centers Shaping the Brazilian City," in V. del Rio and W. Siembieda, eds. *Contemporary Urbanism in Brazil: Beyond Brasilia*. Gainesville: University Press of Florida, 2009, 104–19.
13 Ibid.
14 Peter Gotsch, "NeoTowns—Prototypes of Corporate Urbanism," Ph.D. dissertation, Karlsruhe Institute of Technology, Germany, 2009.
15 Caldeira, 2000.
16 Marcelo Marques, interview, São Paulo, Brazil, March, 2008.
17 Caldeira, 2000.
18 Ibid., 261.
19 One possible contrast with the U.S. is that some residents reportedly want to avoid uniformity and homogeneity; thus, developers have sought to give each apartment tower a different exterior architectural style. See Caldeira, 2000.
20 Joel Garreau, *Edge City*. New York: Doubleday, 1991.
21 Garreau's lectures also served his own interests since he left his position as a journalist with the *Washington Post* and formed a consulting firm called the Garreau Group, which specialized in delivering lectures or doing "scenario planning" on demographic, geographic, and socio-economic change for clients ranging from cities to corporations. See http://www.garreau.com/, retrieved 1/14/14.
22 Ibid.
23 Ibid., 320.
24 Copacabana, however, has a thriving street life, a greater sense of place, and a more engaging streetscape. This points again to one of the critical flaws in the modernist vision, its rejection of the virtues of diversity and spontaneity in crowded, street-oriented urban neighborhoods.
25 The fragmentation and isolation of elite suburbs in São Paulo are even worse than anything one finds in the modernist *superquadras* of Brasília, which were heavily criticized when the city was finally completed. Anthropologist James Holston, for example, devotes an entire chapter in his book to elegantly critiquing the modernist vision of urban design, which he sees as "the death of the street." He argues that Brasília's formal design impeded the possibility of street life. See James Holston, *The Modernist City*. Chicago, IL: University of Chicago Press, 1989. Holston, however, could not have predicted the ways in which residents would later create organic public spaces within the Pilot Plan district. These include spontaneous kiosks along the Monumental Axis, weekly outdoor markets, and cafes and pocket parks in and near the commercial areas (*entrequadras*) between the super-blocks. One does not find such organic public spaces across the urban region of São Paulo.
26 Collet Bruna and Comin Vargas, 2009.
27 Brian J. Godfrey, "Modernizing the Brazilian City," *Geographical Review*, 81 (1), January, 1991, 18–34.
28 Vicente del Rio and Denise de Alcantara, "The Cultural Corridor Project: Revitalization and Preservation in Downtown Rio de Janeiro," in del Rio and Siembieda, eds., 2009, 125–43.
29 The origin of the term *favela* appears to date back to the early 1900s. Soldiers returning to Rio de Janeiro from having fought in a civil war in the Bahia region settled in the hills above Rio. They came from a region called Caatinga, well known for a plant called "Favela." They named their new community in Rio "Morro da Favela" (hill of the *favela*) as a reminder of the plant that grew in the region where they had achieved victory. The term *favela* ultimately was adopted in Brazil as a generic term for the poorest settlement zones in cities. See Licia Valladares, "Social Science Representations

of Favelas in Rio de Janeiro: An Historical Perspective," Lanic Resource Papers, University of Texas, Austin, n.d., http://www1.lanic.utexas.edu/project/etext/llilas/vrp/valladares.pdf.

30 World Bank, *Creating More Livable Cities: The Case of Rio de Janeiro.* Washington, D.C.: World Bank Latin American and Caribbean region (LAC), No. 172, December, 2011.

31 Brazil has been consistently ranked as the number one national soccer team in the world over the last four decades. It has won more World Cups than any other nation—five. Maracanã is considered the largest soccer stadium in the world, is a tourism site, and symbolizes Brazil's global status in football.

32 Though one could argue that Mexico City in the north and Buenos Aires in the south also have a powerful pull in the global media.

33 Leisure has been important to the image of exotic vacation destinations like Hawaii or the French Riviera for more than a century.

34 "Copacabana (At the Copa)," words and music by Barry Manilow, Bruce Sussman, and J. Feldman.

35 "Garota de Ipanema," by Vinícius de Moraes, Norman Gimbel, and Antonio Carlos "Tom" Jobim.

36 See Juliana Barbassa, "At Fifty, 'The Girl from Ipanema' Still Making Heads Turn," Associated Press essay, *San Diego Union Tribune,* July 29, 2012, E-3.

37 *Black Orpheus* was a 1959 film made in Brazil by French director Marcel Camus. It is based on the play *Orfeu da Conceição* by Vinícius de Moraes, which is an adaptation of the Greek legend of Orpheus and Eurydice, setting it in the modern context of Rio de Janeiro during the Carnaval. The film was an international co-production between production companies in Brazil, France, and Italy. It featured the bossa nova soundtrack by legend Antonio Carlos Jobim, with two songs—"Manhã de Carnaval" (written by Luiz Bonfá) and "A felicidade" that both became bossa nova classics. *Black Orpheus* won the Palme d'Or at the 1959 Cannes Film Festival as well as the 1960 Academy Award for Best Foreign Language Film and the 1960 Golden Globe for Best Foreign Film. Meanwhile, a vibrant Brazilian film industry has also turned out popular films that highlight Rio. *City of God* is one; other films include *Pixote* (1981), *Central de Brazil* (1998), and *Tropa de Elite* (2007).

38 Some of Brazil's best known musicians are "Cariocas" (people from Rio)—they include Tom Jobim, Chico Buarque, Milton Nascimento, Paulino da Viola, Vinicius de Moraes, and Pixinguinhe.

39 Lucio Costa was the urban planner and Oscar Neimeyer the architect for the monumental project to build, from the beginning, the first planned city of the world, Brasília. It remains as the single greatest achievement of modern architecture, the building of a national capital and functioning city of some two million people, which includes stunning designs by Neimeyer and a city shaped like an airplane. Brasília became a UNESCO World Heritage Site in 1987.

40 In fact, the Final match of the World Cup will be played in Rio's Maracanã Stadium.

41 Barcelona's successful global marketing of its Olympic redevelopment project is discussed in my book. See Lawrence A. Herzog, *Return to the Center.* Austin: University of Texas Press, 2006, chapter 4, "City of Architects," 91–114. More generally, writers and scholars have acknowledged that culture and spectacle are critical elements in the globalization of a city. See, for example, Short and Kim, 1999. Scholars also speak of this as part of the growing "symbolic economy." See Sharon Zukin, *The Culture of Cities.* New York: Wiley/ Blackwell, 1996.

42 See, for example, Forbes.com article on Brazil, http://www.forbescustom.com/EconomicDevelopmentPgs/BrazilCreativelyComingOutAheadP1.html, retrieved 10/23/13.

43 *Time Magazine*, February 20, 1956.
44 This increasing autonomy indicates that Brazil was not entirely caught up in an interdependent relationship with the United States.
45 See, for example, Robert Hughes, *The Shock of the New*. New York: McGraw Hill, 1991, 209–11; James Holston, *The Modernist City*. Chicago, IL: University of Chicago Press, 1989.
46 Lucio Costa, *Plan Piloto para urbanizacão da baixada compreendida entre a Barra da Tijuca, O Pontal de Sernambetiba e Jacarepaguá*. Agencia Jornalistica Image, Rio de Janeiro, 1969.
47 Cited in Ana Cristina Gomes and Vicente del Rio, "A Outra Urbanidade: A Construcao da Cidade Pos Moderna e o Caso de Barra de Tijuca," in Vicente del Rio, ed. *Arquitectura: Pesquisa y Projeto*. Rio de Janeiro: Universidade Federal do Rio de Janeiro, 1998, 108.
48 Eduardo Paes, cited in Gomes and del Rio, ed., 1998, 111.
49 The idea that Costa's urban design ended up being socially exclusive was a key critique of his design plan for Brasília. See Holston, 1989.
50 For a detailed analysis of the planning of Brasília, see Holston, 1989.
51 Gomes and del Rio, 1998.
52 Cited in Gomes and del Rio, 1998.
53 Geronimo Leitão, *A Construcao do el Dorado Urbano: O Plan Piloto de Barra de Tijuca e Baixada de Jacarepaguá 1970–88*. Niteroi: Editorial da Universidade Federal Fluminense, 1999, 8.
54 See Gomes and del Rio, 1998; see also Adauto Lucio Cardoso, *O Espaco do Capital: A Barra de Tijuca e a Grande Promocao Imobilaria*. Rio de Janeiro: Instituto de Pesquisa e Planejamento Urbano e Regional, IPURR/UFRJ, 1990.
55 Ibid.
56 The Brazilian government is planning to install a Bus Rapid Transit (BRT) line that will link Barra to downtown through the existing metro underground system. This Transoeste BRT line is expected to be up and running by the time of the 2014 World Cup and the 2016 Olympic Games. See Christopher Gaffney, "The BRT's of Rio de Janeiro," presentation at the Congress of Latin American Studies Association, May, 2012, San Francisco.
57 Cardoso, 1990.
58 Ibid.
59 The City of Music will include a Philharmonic Concert Hall (1,800 seats convertible into a 1,300 seat Opera House), a Chamber Music Hall (500 seats), an electro acoustic hall (180 seats), headquarters of the Brazilian Symphonic Orchestra, a music school, rehearsal rooms, media library, two small movie theaters (150 seats each), another larger cinema theater (300 seats), a restaurant, shops, administration offices, equipment rooms, and a parking garage.
60 This is essentially the argument made in Holston, 1989.
61 Leitao, 1999, 80.
62 Ibid.
63 Ibid., 116.
64 Annie G. Eppinghaus, Marcia Poppe, and Vera Tangari, "A Barra de Tijuca e a Apropriacão dos Espacios Publicos e Semi-Publicos, Quatros Estudios de Caso," unpublished essay, 2007.
65 Cardoso, 1990. It should be noted that as early as the 1960s the Brazilian government built some limited public housing for the poor in the adjacent suburbs, in the Jacarapaguá area near Barra da Tijuca; the purpose of those public housing projects was

to relocate residents from *favelas* in the wealthy south zone that were being removed. However, these developments were farther inland and isolated from the coast, and from Barra. The most famous public housing project was in Cidade de Deus (City of God), which was the setting for an internationally acclaimed 2002 film.

66 An excellent overview of Brazil's coastal environments is found in Dieter Muehe, "Brazilian Coastal Vulnerability to Climate Change," *Pan-American Journal of Aquatic Sciences*, 5 (2), 2010, 173–83.

67 Muehe points out that floods will have the biggest impact on coastal instability in the future. Ibid.

68 Silvio Jablonski and Martinus Filet, "Coastal Management in Brazil: A Political Riddle," *Ocean and Coastal Management*, 51, 2008, 541.

69 Ibid., 536.

70 Gabriela da Costa, "Environmental Impacts on Lagoon Tijuca and Lagoon Camorim: Barra da Tijuca, Rio de Janeiro, Brazil," International Planning History Society Conference, Barcelona, Spain, 2004.

71 Gabriela da Costa Silva, "Urban Watershed Management Decision-Making in Jacarepaguá Lowland Watershed, Rio de Janeiro, Brazil." International Planning History Society Conference, Chicago, IL, 2008.

72 Cecilia Herzog and Ricardo Finotti, "Local Assessment of Rio de Janeiro: Two Case Studies of Urbanization Trends and Ecological Impacts," in T. Elmqvist et al., eds. *Urbanization, Biodiversity and Ecosystem Services: A Global Assessment*. Dordrecht: Springer, 2013.

73 See D.M. Zee and C.M. Sabio, "Temporal Evaluation of the Contaminated Plume Dispersion at Barra da Tijuca Beach, Rio de Janeiro, Brazil," *Journal of Coastal Research*, 39, 2006, 531–6.

74 It should be noted that government has tried to create a number of ecological protected parks, but many have been privatized, and some have even been relocated inside the closed condominium developments, thus cutting off public access and public control. See Marcos Cohen and Jorge Ferreira da Silva, "Evaluation of Collaborative Strategies for Ecotourism and Recreation Activities in Natural Parks of Rio de Janeiro," *Revista de Administração Pública*, 44 (5), September/October, 2010, 1097–1123.

75 Interview, Alfredo Sirkis, Rio de Janeiro, May, 2008.

76 Interview, Geronimo Leitão, May, 2008

77 Interview, Ana Luisa Nobre, May, 2008.

78 Sirkis interview, 2008.

79 Gomes and del Rio, 1998.

80 Ibid.

81 Nobre interview, 2008; Leitão interview, 2008.

82 This point is argued in Vera Rezende and Geronimo Leitão, *O Plan Piloto para a Barra de Tijuca e Baixada de Jacarepaguá*. Rio de Janeiro: CREA-RJ, 2004.

83 Gomes and del Rio, 1998.

84 Ibid.

6

BEYOND URBAN SPRAWL IN A GLOBALIZING WORLD

How do we move beyond the pattern of urban sprawl that has become so dominant in North and South America? I've suggested in this book that, while we've been busy searching for urban design alternatives to the U.S. suburban prototype, sprawl has diffused beyond our southern borders and is now shaping urban peripheries across the Americas, from Mexico to Brazil. Meanwhile, despite the best attempts to alter urban development over the last decade and a half, America continues to remain a "suburban nation."

We need to begin to sketch out what a different urbanism will look like. The current "state of the art" alternative to sprawl is embodied by the overlapping strategies of "smart growth" and "new urbanism," which seek to move beyond dispersed, auto-centric, single use zoning templates in favor of higher density, mixed use, pedestrian scale, and neighborhood-oriented cities. To quote the website of the "new urbanism" movement, this involves "the creation and restoration of diverse, walkable, compact, vibrant, mixed use communities composed of the same components as conventional development, but assembled in a more integrated fashion, in the form of complete communities."[1]

Smart growth and new urbanism correctly advocate the proper *form* that will lead to less sprawl and "slower" urbanism. But too much burden is placed on city planners, architects, and local design officials. The shift away from urban sprawl demands a broader societal transformation beyond physical design or land use to what I am calling "slow urbanism." We need a metamorphosis that extends from politicians and educators to communities and social institutions, including conventional and social media. Cultural values, behaviors, and lifestyles that contribute to our urban form will need to evolve, if cities are going to become more compact and sustainable. Even as we legislate to create "smarter" designs, the future of our cities is also going to demand "smarter" citizens.

With this in mind, in this final chapter I synthesize a set of critical thinking points that must be addressed if we are truly going to embrace a "slow urban design" paradigm. I argue that we must rethink urban development at four scales, moving from the macro to the micro: the bioregion, the slow city, the revitalized (and slow) neighborhood, and the slow self. At each level, changes will resonate at both the local and global scale. New approaches will not only be adaptable across all parts of the globe; they will borrow from best practices in other cultures, from the wisdom of Eastern philosophy to organic neighborhood movements in Brazil and Mexico, to the Slow Food and *Cittaslow* (Slow City) movement that has diffused from Italy across Europe and beyond.

The crux of my argument is that the practice of "slowing down," at each successive scale, is about enhancing city dwellers' engagement with their surrounding environment—its natural elements, its history, its sense of place, and the people who are connected to it. We have become disengaged by the many factors I've written about—technology, work, cars, consumerism, a culture of speed. We need to find a way to slow ourselves down. We need to produce and consume locally grown food. Indeed, the Slow Food movement has already achieved some credibility in the wider world, bringing together First World "foodies" and Third World farmers. We must reconnect with our existing neighborhoods, or reinvent community where it is weak. Slow urbanism, I would agree, is a complex idea, and not easily reduced to measurable scientific principles. Yet, the same might be said of important objectives like "sense of place" or "neighborhood preservation," and we are, nevertheless, not about to abandon those worthy values.

Personal responsibility is also a delicate subject to write about. I can imagine some readers may either roll their eyes or simply reject the logic of a link between urban planning and Buddhism. But, I will take the risk in suggesting it, nonetheless. The Slow Food movement demonstrates that the Buddhist principle of mindfulness and the practice of urban design need not be polar opposites. They can be reconciled as aesthetics and politics, pleasure and rationality. Deep ecologists, in fact, argued for a link between ecology and spirit two decades ago, but I fear those ideas fell mostly on deaf ears, outside of a limited circle of writers and thinkers. Their basic argument remains sound: citizens should be the stewards of their own environmental condition. And perhaps a first step in that direction will need to come from a national movement that emphasizes urban design "mindfulness," or, again, what I am calling "slow urbanism."

From Planning Regions to Bioregionalism

The pattern of urban sprawl I have written about in this book is exacerbated in the U.S. by the fact that most developers of master planned communities are able to locate their projects in politically separate suburban jurisdictions. Each development plan is reviewed within independent suburban governments, with little or no legal control outside local boundaries, and often with no oversight of their broader regional implications. Over time, the cumulative impact has been to create urbanized areas that are fragmented into archipelagos of peripheral development, waves of suburban and exurban development that disperse further and further out, giving form to what have become our twenty-first century mega-regions.

Despite calls for a regional approach to urban growth among early utopian thinkers like Patrick Geddes in Scotland or Ebenezer Howard in the United Kingdom, regional management of urban expansion never fully caught hold in the U.S. It was famously promoted by the Regional Planning Association, formed in 1922 by leading urbanist thinkers including Lewis Mumford and Clarence Stein. Only a few experimental communities were ever built,[2] and by the 1950s the boom in peripheral growth was mostly generated by large scale private builder-investors like Levitt and Sons, who were backed by mortgage guarantees through two federal agencies—the Veteran's Administration and the Federal Housing Association (FHA). By the 1950s, the movements toward suburban autonomy had carved out our metropolitan political geographies in the form of a central city surrounded by a constellation of independent suburban governments. This reinforced the pattern of locally managed—rather than regionally unified—housing construction in the suburbs.

Regional planning evolved as an advisory activity in the United States, and took the form of what were called "metropolitan planning organizations" (MPOs). MPOs coordinated transport funding and planning decisions, but they did not have binding legal jurisdiction over how individual governments planned their physical growth, or whether they even chose to participate in a regional planning process. Single purpose regional entities also evolved to manage specific functional needs like air quality, water, open space, or port districts. Yet, none of these entities was tied together into a single regional governance mechanism with political teeth. Meanwhile, in academia the study of regions, beginning in the 1940s, was dominated by a field called "regional science," which viewed regions as zones of economic activity, applying scientific modeling and mathematics to measure them. Physical design and the earlier sustainable objectives of the Regional Planning Association were forgotten. This, as some have noted, produced an approach that generally did not address "real places."[3]

By the 1970s and 1980s, a resurgence of interest in more holistic (or, we might say, "slower") approaches to regional planning emerged, as cities realized that watersheds, air quality, land use, open space, transport, and urban design were intertwined and needed a regional governance approach. Portland, Oregon, created an Urban Growth Boundary (UGB) in the 1970s and then crafted a regional government entity called Metro to enforce the region's decision to control urban sprawl and protect farmland. By the 1990s, the Portland metropolitan area had become a leading example of a regional approach to sustainable urbanism, compact growth, preservation of open space, and alternative transit. Salt Lake City, Utah, also sought to create a citizen-based regional approach called Envision Utah, which emphasized transit-oriented development growth nodes for the future. The Seattle, Washington, region took steps to try to manage the problems of rampant growth and traffic congestion by crafting a Vision 2020 Plan to contain urban sprawl and protect open space.[4]

More recently, a force that has galvanized regional movements is what is called bioregionalism, or the emerging recognition of the connection between human culture and nature. One of the critical elements of bioregionalism is the goal of reintegrating human settlements within their regional ecosystem. Citizens are beginning to come together to address watersheds, air quality, and other natural elements that must be managed on a unified basis, incorporating bioregionalism, which one writer defines as "a social movement and action oriented field . . . focusing on enabling human communities to live, work, eat and play sustainably within earth's dynamic web of life."[5] What is critical is that a bioregional approach bridges physical geography and the consciousness of citizens; inhabitants become re-engaged with their ecological conditions. It also reinforces "localization," citizens and community retaking control of the places/regions they inhabit. This kind of local empowerment of citizens over their ecological setting is an idea that cuts across other scales (city, neighborhood, etc.) and was voiced early on by planning scholars like John Friedmann, who has long called for planning to be more community-oriented, where knowledge and information are linked to action.[6] However, bioregionalism can only work if a form of regional governance with legal backing is put in place.

Wildfire Bioregions in Southern California

An applied example of bioregional thinking lies in the ecology of wildfires in the San Diego/southern California region, a case study that was highlighted in Chapter 3. There I showed, using the border city of San Diego as an example, that California's suburbs have evolved with relatively little attention being given by local officials to the regional ecology of wildfires. The glaring fact is that many cities along the southwest border region of the U.S., from San Diego, Tucson, and Phoenix, to Las Vegas and El Paso, do not have comprehensive wildfire strategies in place that utilize the tools of bioregional planning for fire ecology and land management. If wildfire management is to become part of an urban design strategy for inland suburbs in places like San Diego, local and regional governments will have to recognize that wildfires are a permanent fixture of their biological setting, and create zoning and planning policies that reflect this.

A critical first step will be to recognize the location of primary wildfire target zones, and designate them as separate regional ecological management districts—in this case, what might be termed "fire plains,"[7] which would then be subject to specific planning rules about the nature and scale of development.[8] In the first decade of the 2000s, as it became clear that mega-wildfires were becoming more routine, the state of California initiated guidelines for landowners, builders, and residents in these zones. Indeed, in 2008, CALFIRE (the state agency that regulates wildfires) formally announced the creation of "Fire Hazard Severity Zones." Maps were drawn, and new subregions designated, where updated standards of construction and site design would be established for fire protection. These new standards included one hundred foot defensive space clearings around buildings, road width minimums, water supply and signage regulations, and real estate industry requirements for disclosure of natural hazards. However, when the Fire Hazard Severity Zone maps were finally completed, CALFIRE announced that those maps would "be *considered* in city and county general plans."[9] The use of the word "considered" is troubling, since it demonstrates that adherence to the regional fire zones by local governments remains voluntary and is not legally binding.

This will not suffice. Wildfire ecology must become a permanent element in the bioregional planning process for arid ecosystems like those in the southwestern United States–Mexico borderlands. Wildfire planning should be incorporated into each level of regional management—environmental reviews, General Plan, Specific Plans, subdivision mapping and permits, as well as building codes. By law, hazards and mitigation measures are identified in General Plans, normally under the Safety element. Because General Plans are legally binding, they represent a critical mechanism for legislating specific regulations that would force developers and builders to create sustainable and less fire-prone communities. This would also be the case for Specific Plans used in California for large scale projects inside municipalities. Further, special building codes and regulations for fire zone management should be part of the process of granting permits; in California this falls under the Subdivision Maps Act. Lot size, location, site design, setbacks, and local infrastructure would all come under review in subdivision maps for new developments. If General Plan provisions were set up to require developers to respect the fire hazard element in their housing designs and subdivision plans, city and county governments might begin to gain control over the severity of wildfire incidents. A regional government would represent the best administrative scale to oversee this approach.

A bioregional toolkit for wildfire ecosystem planning would include both site planning and zoning to enhance ecological protection in the master planned suburbs of the wildland urban interface (WUI) where so many fires have burned. If regional General Plan guidelines for fire hazard zones were standardized, specific site planning policy guidelines could be introduced. For example, site plans could incorporate fire danger

Figure 6.1 Home Damaged by 2007 Wildfire, Rancho Sante Fe Suburb of San Diego
Source: Photo by Lawrence A. Herzog

into the design of open spaces—plans should require fire break plantings along the edges of developments, especially those facing into canyons, where wind funnel effects tend to spread wildfire. Another design strategy might be the regulation of setbacks from steep slopes and fire-prone corridors and canyons. Sprinkler system infrastructure could be required at strategic locations where wildfire vulnerability is deemed greatest.

Zoning will be a powerful regional and local tool for creating an ecologically based fire management in metropolitan areas like San Diego. Zoning could raise and lower densities where appropriate. Zoning could help preserve agricultural areas, wilderness zones, and open space buffers. It should also regulate the rate and scale of suburban development in the name of sustainability. Many California counties have hesitated to use zoning to rein in subdivisions in former rural estates; in doing so, they are endangering local agriculture and creating suburban lot designs that are difficult to defend.[10] U.S. Senator Diane Feinstein (D-California) alluded to this when she spoke in southern California after the 2007 fires: "Local governments have to begin to look at their zoning and siting of large subdivisions in the path of Santa Ana winds in parched, dry areas of the state."[11]

From Slow Food to Slow Cities

Across the planet, citizens have taken note of the whiplash effects of our hyped up urban lifestyle, and many are beginning to respond at the city level. In Italy, the Slow Food movement began in 1986; it was started by Carlo Petrini as a way to challenge the globalization of fast food. When McDonald's planned to build a franchise outlet near the Piazza di Spagna in Rome in 1986, Petrini organized a demonstration in which he and his followers brandished bowls of penne as weapons of protest. The demonstration led to the founding of the International Slow Food movement which seeks to counter fast food, fast life, non-sustainable food production, and the eroding of local economies. Petrini and others drafted a "Slow Food manifesto," which stated that:

> We are enslaved by speed and have all succumbed to the same insidious virus: Fast Life, which disrupts our habits, pervades

the privacy of our homes and forces us to eat Fast Foods, which diminish opportunities for conversation, communion, quiet reflection and sensuous pleasure, thus shortchanging the hungers of the soul. In the name of productivity, Fast Life has changed our way of being and threatens our environment and our landscapes. Our defense should begin at the table with Slow Food. Let us rediscover the flavors and savors of regional cooking.[12]

The Slow Food movement emphasizes a set of cooking and eating behaviors that resurrect a more deliberate savoring of food, and an emphasis on local and regional products. It speaks of "taste education," the promotion of eco-regions, local food products, regional culture and cuisine, organic farming, ethical buying in locally owned marketplaces, and preventing the risks of monoculture. During the 1990s, Slow Food grew and began developing a political agenda—lobbying the European Union (EU) on trade and agricultural policy and working to save endangered foods. The organization expanded from 20,000 to 65,000 members in forty-two countries in Europe, the U.S., and Latin America within a decade; by 2013, its membership was over 100,000 in 153 countries.[13]

Following the Slow Food example, the Slow City movement, or *Cittaslow*, was also born in Italy. It held its first meeting in Orvieto, Italy, in 1999. About thirty towns sent representatives. The coordinator was Paolo Saturnini, the mayor of Greve, a small town in the Chianti province of Italy. The meeting produced a charter which pointed to globalization as a phenomenon that wipes out uniqueness and generates mediocrity. The charter went on to propose that cities with under 50,000 inhabitants could join the association, and use its logo, as long as they would agree to follow the fifty-five guiding principles. Among the key principles required of prospective members of the Slow City movement are: cutting noise pollution, decreasing traffic, encouraging alternative transit such as bicycling, increasing green spaces and pedestrian zones, backing farmers who produce local products and the shops and restaurants that market them, supporting organic farming and organic products, and preserving local aesthetic and design traditions (architecture, historic places).[14]

As some observers have noted, the Slow Food movement is largely about protecting "territory" or local culture.[15] The idea is to preserve both local ecology (agriculture, vegetation, grown in local soil, water, etc.) and human tradition (cultural practices), both of which allow diverse parts of the planet to generate their own unique foods, styles of consumption, and ways of life. This is seen as an inherently positive thing, and a pattern that must be preserved. It is thus a movement which connects ecology, human behavior, and regional culture.

Slow City simply takes the principles of the Slow Food movement and seeks to apply them to the larger setting of cities themselves. The preservation of local ecology and culture, the argument goes, must become central to the economy of a city, its physical form and its governance. A relatively young organization, within ten years the *Cittaslow* movement had over fifty cities as members by 2009, mainly from Italy, Germany, Norway, Portugal, Poland, and the U.K. By 2013, the membership had reached 176 cities in twenty-seven nations, and included cities in Australia, South Korea, Turkey, Japan, China, and the U.S.[16] To become members, cities have to initiate a program with Slow City principles, based on sustainable development. They must also make a commitment to heritage preservation and promoting local identity and sense of place. For example, candidates for membership in the *Cittaslow*/Slow City group must demonstrate support not only from the traditional local arts and crafts, but also from local industries whose products lend distinctiveness and identity to a region. They must also commit to conservation, creating green spaces, walkability, making public spaces more appealing, improved public transit, and eco-friendly design.[17] In short, the Slow City movement represents a formalization of North American ideas like smart growth and new urbanism into the process of governance, as well as a commitment to expand these principles across nations and borders.

Revitalizing Slow Neighborhoods

The neighborhood is a critical scale to implement the slowing down of urban life. Yet, as I've argued in this book, a huge obstacle to creating anything at the neighborhood or community scale is whether people actually feel that they are part of that neighborhood or community, and whether the neighborhood has political meaning. I've made reference to the fact that nearly two-thirds of Americans who live in cities now live in "suburban sprawl" communities. Studies demonstrate that these suburbs are lacking the very structural elements needed to foster a sense of neighborliness—a walkable scale, gathering spaces to meet neighbors, and an architecture/urban design style that enhances community identity. Many suburbs in the U.S. lack the "sense of place" that can physically make people feel like they are part of a community. Suburb critic James Howard Kunstler has written that sprawling suburbs represent "the greatest misallocation of resources in the history of the world . . . these are places that are not worth caring about."[18] Further, as I pointed out in Chapter 3, automobile-dependent suburbs accentuate a lifestyle that emphasizes values—privatization and consumerism—that don't always mesh with building civic conscience and a sense of community. Thus, the first step in thinking about slow neighborhoods is to acknowledge the huge obstacles that exist in the average suburban community in the United States.

There has been a consensus among writers and social scientists that community identity suffered a general decline in post-industrial American urban life. That decline is thought to have been hastened by technological changes—automobiles, smartphones, and computers all loosen citizen connection to neighborhoods. Automobiles literally diminish the amount of time city dwellers spend walking, biking, or otherwise experiencing their community firsthand. Meanwhile, the places where people do walk have tended to be shopping malls and other private, commercial spaces, thus fostering a shift from public to private life. This has led to the documented pattern of a less civic-oriented society, and confusion about the role of citizenship and collective embrace of the "public good" at the neighborhood scale.[19] When citizens become distracted by consumerism in private spaces, their neighborhood consciousness can lapse. This is then exacerbated by technologies like smart phones, iPads, laptops, and the social media, which tend to focus on the individual, who may be connected in cyber space but not in the real space of his or her community.

It should also be pointed out that American cities are still highly segregated and unequal. While many Americans may live in the cocoons of comfortable suburban life, other less fortunate city dwellers reside either in inner-city slums or in decaying old suburbs that suffer from run-down schools, poor quality public transit services, high unemployment, and greater exposure to environmental pollution. Slow urban design practices in these communities will face the obstacles of needing to be couched in a larger strategy of equitable economic development.

Yet another obstacle facing the slow urbanism movement at the community level is the overall historic weakness of community planning as a political tool in the U.S. While urban planning began at the state level, the "police powers" to plan were eventually passed on to cities in the early decades of the twentieth century. But when nearly all land is privately owned, the government's ability to plan is limited to negotiation. Moreover, most communities lack the political power to shape local planning and zoning decisions. Using the example of the state of California, the formal instruments of city planning—the General Plan, zoning, and environmental regulation (through CEQA, the California Environmental Quality Act)—all empower city or regional governments, while only limited legal authority has passed on from the city level to the community. Community groups have mainly asserted their power through grassroots citizen movements and locally based oversight of the city government role in planning.

In the San Diego region, the history of community planning illustrates how, as early as the 1960s, community groups never had access to planning decisions unless they fought for it. When the city first started to grow at that time, it created a city planning department. However, historians point out that local business and conservative elements tried to get rid of the planning department in its early years; they were convinced that "city planning" was a form of communism, and that zoning and general plans were anti-American. This, however, unleashed a grassroots campaign to save the planning department and, later, to fight a number of battles over urban growth, including controls on ugly billboards along freeways, opposition to overdevelopment of canyons and valleys, and support for downtown redevelopment at a time when developers were looking toward shopping centers and suburban growth.[20]

In San Diego, a grassroots organization evolved as the main form of citizen oversight of city planning issues. It was called "Citizens Coordinate for Century 3" (later C-3) and composed of architects, writers, professors, landscape designers, and other citizens. Their success and other citizen movements eventually led the city government to formally recognize community planning by establishing local "planning committees." In 1966, the city of San Diego passed a resolution recognizing "community planning groups" (City Council Policy 600-05), and by 1976 it had established further legal guidelines regarding community planning groups (CPGs, in Policy 600-24).[21]

But, since then, community planning groups have had limited access to political power, and to changing the quality of life in their own communities. Their only recourse has been informal, spontaneous citizen movements to confront policies that negatively impact their community. One of the most important examples emerged in the Latino community of Barrio Logan, an enclave that suffered a number of negative land use decisions, including the twin disasters of construction of a major freeway (the Interstate 5) and a regional bridge (the Coronado Bridge), both of which sliced through the heart of the community. By the late 1970s, faced with the prospect of a proposed California Highway Patrol station being built under the Coronado Bridge in the epicenter of the barrio, the community mobilized and fought a pitched battle against the city and state. This campaign ultimately was successful in displacing the police station project, replacing it with a local gathering space called Chicano Park. It marked the beginning of three decades of community activism, and the growth of a sense of community and ethnic identity in defending the neighborhood space.

The battle for slow neighborhoods will be built around creating and defending a better quality of life at the neighborhood scale. Slow neighborhoods will incorporate the values of smart urban design, including walkable public spaces, affordable housing, social justice, diversity, and sustainability. But these values must find their way into the circles of political power, most likely via grassroots social movements and better informed citizens. Slow neighborhoods can find inspiration from several ongoing movements both within the U.S. and across the planet.

They include: livable streets, community-based economic development, and the local food movement. The "livable streets" movement is a broad-based coalition operating across numerous cities in the U.S., which defines itself as being "organized around the principles of public health through active living, economic vitality and quality of life. It's an innovative approach that encompasses all modes of transportation and seeks a balanced system."[22]

The number of community-based movements emphasizing the street as a community resource has been growing over the last decade across the U.S. These include, for example, the New York City Street Renaissance movement, the San Francisco Great Streets project, Streets for People in Seattle, Livable Streets in Boston, and Placemaking Chicago.[23] They all have in common the goal of recuperating neighborhood streets as civic spaces for people and not merely corridors for cars. Projects advocate grassroots activism to convert streets and open spaces into pedestrian-friendly neighborhood spaces, such as local markets, public plazas, and bike-friendly pathways. In New York City, this movement has helped turn Times Square into a more pedestrian-friendly space; similar outcomes are occurring in Chicago, San Francisco, Seattle, Portland, and other major cities in the U.S.

Citizens can also become engaged in their communities by advocating remapping efforts where local ecological preservation, walkability, and compactness become the priorities. "Ecocity zoning" would focus on fortifying primary and secondary centers, gathering spaces, and activity nodes. Innovative zoning and transfer of development rights could then be used to retrofit existing neighborhoods or plan new ones that are more compact and pedestrian in scale.[24] Further, community groups could begin to restore local ecology by, for example, placing signage around their neighborhood that identifies local natural elements (creeks, streams, and canyons) or even local wildlife nesting areas. In Berkeley, California, a group called Urban Ecology did precisely that.[25] In San Diego, California, there is a movement to restore the vast canyonlands that meander through and around urban neighborhoods, including creating signage and improving or maintaining trails that connect the canyons to the neighborhoods.[26]

Examples of community-based economic development and local food represent two other features of a slow neighborhood approach. A slow neighborhood is seen as more than a residential destination for people in their cars; it is a place with multiple functions—a village that people walk to for work, shopping, or leisure activities. It has shops, businesses, offices, pedestrian scale activities, and a variety of modes of transportation— walking, biking, BRT (bus rapid transit), light rail transit, jitney or taxi services. It is a community that is more sustainable, since some of its residents actually live and work in it, and others produce food that is used in local restaurants or sold locally in farmer's markets. The local community economic development platform is built around using such tools as neighborhood-based banks and credit unions, promoting culture and the arts, and local investment.[27]

Some experts argue that community economies should be built around a community-based food system, where local food is connected to the bioregion, and where the unique ecosystem of a community is tapped in a sustainable way. A community-based food system has been defined as being socially embedded, economically invested, and integrated across food production, processing, distribution, consumption, and waste disposal to build health, wealth, connection, and capacity in a particular place. The advantages of a community-based food system include: improving the health and well-being of the population; enhancing the local community's economic wealth and vitality; increasing connections and opportunities to improve food access and meet demand; and expanding the capacity to produce, process, distribute, and consume food locally and regionally.[28] The value of community-based food systems is enormous— millions of dollars can be recuperated within communities through local food production, distribution, marketing, and consumption. Growing and consuming local food provides local jobs, helps people eat healthier foods, cuts down on the cost of transporting produce, protects local communities from national and international crises that might threaten their food supply, and helps promote local environmental awareness. This will inherently lead to slower and more sustainable neighborhoods.

Citizen-based coalitions are taking back streets and revitalizing neighborhoods through the creation of formal community associations or non-governmental organizations in the United States. Locally driven political movements are also trying to alter the traditional tools of urban planning (zoning, permits, building codes) to revitalize and slow down life at the neighborhood scale. In cities across the United States, General Plans or master plans are being updated to address the loss of community suffered during the half century of suburban development.[29] In Latin America, one finds similar concerns emerging over the last three or four decades, though their expression has been different. In Brazil and Mexico, dissatisfaction with the failures of modernist planning led to spontaneous, organic citizen responses. Rather than push for formal political or institutional changes, organic, citizen-based movements simply evolved, though they later encouraged elected officials to support them. Examples from Brazil and Mexico are noteworthy.

Slower Urbanism in Rio de Janeiro, Brazil

Link to a map of Rio de Janeiro showing traditional neighborhoods, http://www.lonelyplanet.com/maps/south-america/brazil/rio-de-janeiro/.

Neighborhood-based slow urbanism has thrived in older parts of Rio de Janeiro, even though, as noted in Chapter 5, many residents have moved to wealthy suburbs. Rio's high density development is built into the largest urban rain forest on the planet, a tropical wilderness that drains down into Rio across very mountainous terrain. This rain forest, called the *Mata Atlantica*, has been designated a World Biosphere Reserve by the United Nations Education, Scientific and Cultural Organization (UNESCO).[30] In Rio, this ecological presence has the potential to engage citizens in slower behaviors. Austrian writer Stefan Zweig, who visited and eventually lived in Rio, once observed this about its ecological setting: "The city and the sea and the green and the mountains, all these flow into each other like music."[31]

Rio's neighborhood-based public spaces—parks, gardens, patios, promenades, plazas—draw attention to local ecology. The Brazilian landscape designer Roberto Burle Marx based much of his design on Rio's ecosystem. His work inspired a generation of Brazilian architects, designers, and city

Figure 6.2 The Ecosystem of Rio de Janeiro—Its Rain Forest, Mountains, Bays—Create the Ingredients for a Slower Urbanism
Source: Photo by Lawrence A. Herzog

planners to better utilize public spaces in Rio and other cities. As one critic notes: "By organizing native plants in accordance with the aesthetic principles of the artistic vanguard, especially Cubism and abstractionism, he created a new and modern grammar for international landscape design."[32]

Burle Marx produced an extensive portfolio of major design works in the city, many of which gained international prominence and focused attention on the links between nature and the built city. Rio's largest park, the bayside *Aterro do Flamengo* built on reclaimed seafront just southwest of downtown, was a Burle Marx design. He also was responsible for colorful abstract stone mosaics along the Copacabana beachfront promenade, and for crafting or inspiring numerous other parks, gardens, museum patios, and other spaces around the city, not to mention the proliferation of small nurseries that sell plants, and the push to preserve open spaces and jungle in and around the city. These

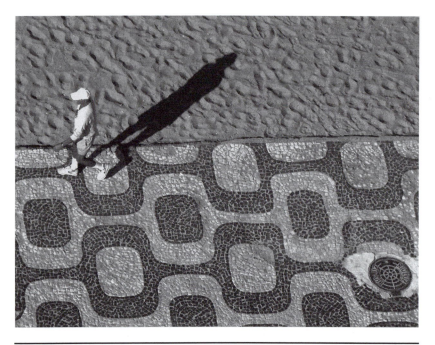

Figure 6.3 Roberto Burle Marx Inspired Mosaic Tile Eco-designs along Rio Beachfront
Source: Photo by Lawrence A. Herzog

neighborhood-based design traditions represent a uniquely Brazilian form of slow urbanism, grounded in local ecology and design, and stimulating a stronger neighborhood sense of place and walkability.[33]

One example of Rio's organic attachment to street life and to neighborhoods is the case of the revitalization of the "bloco" or neighborhood block party parade tradition, as part of Rio's annual Carnaval celebration. The formal mega-"samba parades" in the samba stadium became central to February "Holy Week" (*Semana Santa*) celebrations in Rio as the Carnaval became a global event after the 1960s. Giant "sambadromes" were built to house soccer stadium sized crowds who paid over $100 to see these six or eight hour shows. Meanwhile, the older tradition of Carnaval neighborhood block parties had begun to die out in the 1970s and 1980s.

But in the 1990s, the blocos began to reappear. They have surged as alternatives to the more expensive, overcommercialized and media-hyped sambadrome parades. Blocos are celebrations of traditional

Figure 6.4 Parque Lage Epitomizes Slow Design Approach in Older Rio Neighborhoods
Source: Photo by Lawrence A. Herzog

neighborhoods as unique places. They usually begin as small gatherings of musicians and dressed up marchers on a plaza or park, typically local community groups or clubs. There is no charge to march in these parades. People paint their faces, don wild outfits (clowns, Asian dancers, men dressed in drag, or people who look like celebrities) and march and play music. The crowds build as they wend their way through a community. More local musicians, residents, store owners, visitors, tourists join in, and soon thousands are wildly parading on a route through the area. The "bloco" ends in a giant neighborhood party on an open plaza or street, where the music can go on late into the night, with eating, drinking, neighbors mingling, everyone enjoying and sharing a real place in a moment of openness.

The Slow Movement in Downtown Querétaro, Mexico

Link to a map of Querétaro, Mexico's historic downtown, showing traditional neighborhoods, https://maps.google.com/maps?q=down town+map,+santiago+de+queretaro,+mexico&hl=en&ie=UTF-8&ei=9vCGUcyEH4GuigKimoGwDA&ved=0CAgQ_AUoAjgK

Figure 6.5 "Bloco" Celebration in Santa Teresa Neighborhood of Old Rio
Source: Photo by Lawrence A. Herzog

In Mexico, citizens have started to reassert control over their own history and over cultural spaces that are part of their daily, lived experience. This happened in the city of Querétaro, Mexico, a metropolitan region of one million population about 130 miles north of Mexico City. One of the fastest growing cities in Mexico, Querétaro's downtown was economically distressed only two decades ago.

During the 1950s and 1960s, the industrial boom in Querétaro led to a period of dramatic urban growth; the city's population expanded from 60,000 to nearly one million in the next four decades. This massive growth, the exodus of capital and people to the suburbs, and the emergence of automobiles posed challenging questions about the future of downtown. Before the 1980s, Mexico did not have any kind of national planning legislation that gave cities the power to engage in large scale

Figure 6.6 Main Square, Querétaro, Mexico
Source: Photo by Lawrence A. Herzog

redevelopment or historic preservation.[34] As a result, valuable heritage was often removed or left to deteriorate. But across Mexico many historic cities like Querétaro had the advantage of a regional tradition of pride in local history, and respect for the past.[35]

With strong local leadership and citizen support, a revitalization effort in Querétaro's historic quarter began in the 1980s and picked up steam after that. One project focused on removing traffic and creating pedestrian *andadores* (promenades) downtown. The revitalization programs brought diverse interest groups together—the governor, the municipality, the federal agency in charge of historic monuments, INAH (National Institute of Anthropology and History), as well as families who owned land, houses, and businesses in downtown.[36]

Central to the downtown redevelopment model employed in Querétaro was an emphasis on protecting the center of the city from automobile traffic by reinventing protected pedestrian scale public spaces. A system of interconnected walking spaces—plazas linked by closed off pedestrian promenades—was created. The two anchoring plazas in this system were the main square, or Plaza de Armas, and an adjacent square called the Jardín Zenea. The Plaza de Armas is a rectangular, Renaissance-style square first laid out in the sixteenth century. It continues to preserve its original form today—two-story colonial buildings, with covered portals on two sides. A three-sided "u-shaped" hedge of laurel trees runs along the interior edge of the plaza, creating a parallel edge to the buildings. Zenea Garden sits upon the former atrium of the San Francisco convent. To the west, following a one block interruption, a string of pedestrian promenades leads to the third major anchor in the downtown public space system: Hidalgo Garden. This public plaza also lies on a former religious space—the Santa Clara convent. Plaza Hidalgo is another rectangular space in the French romantic landscape tradition—it is also surrounded by a wall of green, one-story high laurel bushes, impeccably pruned to proportionately match the buildings.

Figure 6.7 Tree Covered Plaza in Downtown Querétaro
Source: Photo by Lawrence A. Herzog

Downtown Querétaro is an example of grassroots mobilization that produced a slow urbanist community that also became economically viable. Local leaders and citizens built a policy that combined historic preservation, properly scaled commercial development, traffic management, and urban design programs oriented toward pedestrianized streets and public plazas.[37] The number of residents living downtown increased, along with the inventory of local "slow" businesses (boutiques, restaurants, hotels, cafes, bookstores, and art galleries).[38] Mexico's enclosed historic plazas, which were the centers of urban life in the colonial period, can still play a role in modern urban life. By linking the enclosed historic squares through a series of pedestrianized streets, and then using street markets and other commerce to attract business, the city has been able to invigorate the public life of downtown, create safe pedestrian environments, and attract residents and businesses back to the center of the city. Further, the city was able to achieve this by building a coalition of business interests, local politicians, and residents of surrounding neighborhoods, all of whom supported closing off downtown streets and protecting pedestrian scale life in public spaces.

The Slow Self

The process of slowing down, in the end, must begin with city dwellers themselves. We need to find a balance between our "eco-centric" (caring about the environment) and "ego-centric" (being concerned with oneself above all else) selves. An eco-centric life, or a life anchored by "deep ecology," speaks to a shift in consciousness, where each person sees him or herself as an engaged ecological being, whose behaviors may impact the earth. This challenges some basic values of our culture. Western religion has been termed "anthropocentric," where the earth is viewed as a sphere that humans can shape to their whim. But, as Carl Sagan, the respected astro-physicist, once pointed out, it is also the case that "efforts to safeguard the environment must be infused with a vision of the sacred."[39]

Despite the growth of a new "green" consciousness, there is a difference between what might be termed "scientific ecology" and "deep ecology." Scientific ecology rests on the notion of humans as detached observers who study nature using the principles of modern science. By collecting data about the natural environment, analyzing it, and producing scientific theory, it is assumed that scientists generate information and knowledge that will ultimately filter back to everyone else. But this "scientific ecology" approach positions nature as something distant—a subject to be studied and understood mainly by experts (scientists). The everyday citizen ends up being let off the hook too easily, while scientists and engineers are expected to solve the world's environmental problems.

In the epilogue to a compendium of his life works, planning scholar John Friedmann offered six strategies for the future of city planning. One of those six that he highlights is the "convivial city that nourishes the spirit," where "social and cultural dimensions trump consumerism."[40] From a different point of view, former Vice President Al Gore argues that too many citizens place environmental issues outside their everyday mindset and, with all the distractions of busy modern life, end up not engaging in any meaningful advocacy.[41]

Men and women in Western cultures suffer from "an alienation of spirit." This alienation comes from placing too much emphasis on the individual. Modern education, it is argued, focuses on individuals, while giving less attention to human connections to family, clan, or the land. Material "things" (houses, cars, flat screen TVs, laptops, guns) are posed as measures of self-worth or personal meaning. The idea of separate citizens can be traced back to Greek and Roman philosophers, and to early modern thinkers like René Descartes, who famously coined the phrase "I think, therefore I am." Some believe, ultimately, that over time this philosophy may have contributed to a society that places too much focus on the self, and not enough on being engaged with visceral experiences beyond the self, such as being in nature. The idea is to find ways to balance the personal against more collective priorities.[42]

Since the 1970s, when Earth Day and the environmental movement began in the U.S., the "deep ecology" view began to surface. This view argues that since all humans are inherently connected to earth, they are participants in the making or destruction of their ecosystem. Deep ecology challenges traditional Western religious notions of the "conquest" of nature. It is rooted in a more Eastern philosophical approach, where the driving narrative is the interconnectedness of all beings.[43] Deep ecology has its origins, in part, in the "Gaia hypothesis," an idea developed by a former NASA chemist James Lovelock in the 1960s. It espoused the reciprocity between humans and all plant and animal life, individual responsibility to protect the future survival of humanity, and the primacy of values (life) over technology.[44]

Deep ecology also draws inspiration from Eastern religion. The origins of Taoism lie in the observation of nature, from monasteries in the hills of China dating back to at least five centuries B.C. Many Taoist principles are based on the use of lessons from the natural world to understand the human one. This is illustrated in a passage from the *Daode Jing*, one translation of which reads:

> Humanity follows the earth.
> Earth follows nature.
> Nature follows Tao.
> Tao follows what is so.[45]

Taoism emphasizes the wisdom of organic order. The Chinese alphabet is based on ideograms (pictures) derived from nature, creating a more visual aesthetic than Western alphabetic writing, which is based on sound. The Chinese alphabetic symbols for many words—sun, moon, earth, rain, or birth—are all constructed around visual references to nature. As one author writes: "Alphabetic writing is a representation of sound, whereas the ideogram represents vision, and furthermore represents the world directly."[46] Thus the word "bird" in English has nothing in it that reminds us of a bird, while in Chinese the written word for bird makes visual reference to it. Traditional Chinese writing—calligraphy, or "dancing with a brush"—contrasts sharply with the utilitarian Western alphabet, which is so much less natural and expressive. Calligraphy emphasizes "going with the flow"; the artist paints words that become "the same beauty which we recognize in moving water."[47]

Taoists argue that "the way of nature," though asymmetrical and unregimented at times, has its own logic. The respected Taoist writer and philosopher Alan Watts points out that when you look at a landscape painting in China, "as soon as this beauty is pointed out, it is immediately recognized, though we cannot say just why it appeals to us."[48] The essence or truth inherent in nature, and the inevitability of natural cycles, are captured in this Taoist written verse: "As I sit quietly, doing nothing, Spring comes, and grass grows of itself."[49]

Water is an extremely important natural element in Taoism. It epitomizes the axiom of "effortlessness" ("going with the flow") central to Taoist belief. In the natural world, when water meets resistance, it simply flows around the obstacle. The principle of "harmonious action" is built on the idea that, rather than fight natural cycles or even life situations, it is better to act in concert with observed patterns and cycles.[50] Interestingly, the Chinese character for nature is, in fact, the character for a person, with two horizontal lines added—one for the earth below and another for the sky above. Individuals who live in harmony with nature and with others are more likely to be part of the sustainable community movements mentioned earlier in this chapter.

Figure 6.8 Water and Nature Are Critical to Buddhist and Taoist Ideas about Slowing Down
Source: Photo by Lawrence A. Herzog

A central idea borrowed from Buddhism can also be applied to slowing down in cities. It is the concept of "mindfulness" or "mindful awareness," which emphasizes being engaged in each of life's moments. Being attuned to one's immediate surroundings is a form of mindfulness. To strengthen one's awareness, one of the better known tools in Buddhism is meditation. The act of meditation might be considered a kind of training technique for slowness, although that is not its stated purpose for Buddhists.[51] Meditation involves relaxing the mind and sitting for a period of time each day, awake, but in a calm, detached state. Meditation instructors will point out that, in Western culture, there is a tendency to live the waking life in constant thought, with ideas racing through one's head. Further, they argue that, without quiet moments to reflect and allow one's intuition to flourish, creativity may be stifled. Buddhists believe that by meditating, by slowing down our minds (and our bodies), we achieve a more restful and healthy state, which then allows us to plug back into our ordinary lives in a more meaningful and healthy way. For example, Buddhists speak of mindful walking, "not in order to arrive, but just to watch."[52]

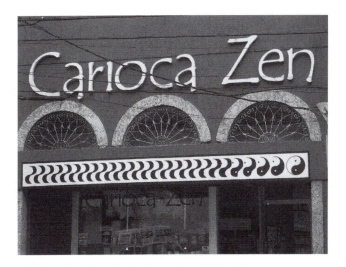

Figure 6.9 A Health Food Store Called "Carioca Zen" in Rio de Janeiro's South Zone
Source: Photo by Lawrence A. Herzog

Mindfulness is now understood to contribute to public health. For example, the practice of meditation has evolved within mainstream culture as a source of stress reduction, not only for popular use but also in the health profession, where the concept of Mindfulness Based Stress Reduction is entering medical practice.[53] Indeed, meditation is even being recognized as legitimate by Health Maintenance Organizations in the U.S. and other health insurance carriers around the world, and is being added as an employee benefit by some large companies in cities in the West.[54] One might also mention the growing popularity of yoga, which is now being incorporated into the fitness education curriculum for public schools from New York to California.[55]

How would Taoism or Zen Buddhism apply directly to slow urban design? For one, by shifting consciousness away from the self, urban citizens would begin to change their lifestyles, and become more compassionate toward neighbors.[56] Another impact would be to slow down city dwellers' lives, causing them to spend more time mindfully experiencing their neighborhoods as social places. Mindful living would very likely translate to more people using slower forms of transportation, from bicycling to walking. Nationally, there is already a growing trend for people to move to pedestrian scale places where they can more slowly engage in everyday urban living—from less stressful travel to work or shop, to visits with friends and neighbors. And, as mentioned, slowing down tends to rekindle our connection to nature.[57] In a slower world, urban residents will want to preserve their neighborhood quality of life and the surrounding ecosystem.

Slowness as a Virtue

I have argued in this book that various forms of "slowness" will help make cities more sustainable. But our Western sense of time can be summarized in one word: impatience. We are so accustomed to convenience, instant gratification, and immediacy that we often have trouble being patient. This also can make us short-sighted, as we tend to view the world in small blocks of time—semesters at the university, the length of a work project, or the four-year term of a politician. Our political and cultural clock, however, matches up very poorly with nature—since the earth's systems move deliberately and slowly. River basins are carved over thousands or even millions of years. Geology, climate, and topography all shift slowly. Thus, any transformation in our way of life that can slow us down will have the side effect of making us more sensitive to the rhythm of land we must live in harmony with.

Fast urbanism has a tendency to neutralize place. Places are created by people who share a common connection to the land, the larger bioregion, or to their community. Places can literally be created by a single unique physical attribute—a river, canyon, mountain, mesa, or valley. Yet twenty-first century technologies that speed up our lives tend to dislodge us from appreciating the places we occupy. We have created technologies that encourage this disconnection between people and place. The well known "clothesline paradox," often cited in sustainable development narratives, is a good example of how "higher" technology can compromise place. The "paradox" lies in the simple fact that, in many regions of the world, sunny weather makes it possible to employ a place-based clothes drying technology—hanging laundered clothes to dry in the sun on an outdoor clothesline—rather than using an electric drier! Drying laundry on an outdoor line is a good metaphor, too, because it is truly a slow city activity and also one well suited to the climate of southern latitudes of the Americas (the southwest U.S., Mexico, and Brazil) that I have written about in this book.[58]

A practical example of mindful urbanism could come in the form of high tech companies working with local governments to invent a technical way for individuals to monitor their ecological footprint in their city and community. For example, why not construct applications ("apps") for smart phones, or local government websites where citizens could create "personal ecological audit" forms? A reward system might then be set up to recognize individual behaviors that are more sustainable. Such an ecological audit could ask simple questions such as: what speed (fast or slow) does the daily experience consist of? How much time is spent walking within the community? What are some behaviors that would connect people to neighborhoods or to the natural environment? How much of a person's daily or weekly time falls in the "fast world" (driving a car, on the internet, on a cell phone, or using one's computer) vs. the "slow world" (walking, hiking, riding a bicycle, talking with neighbors or with people in a cafe, or working in a garden)?

Slow cities work best when there is citizen-based community engagement, and more public life. In an increasingly privatized world, with fewer public places where residents regularly meet, and everyone moving quickly and separately, there is a diminishing sense of community political will. City dwellers are beginning to realize that it's time to take back a more public way of life, and the civic spaces to experience that life either in reinvented suburbs or in more compact traditional neighborhoods. To move to a new paradigm of urban living, citizens need to be inspired to get out of their cars, off their computers, and out into public places or nature. We need citizens engaged in the idea of sustainable environments and communities. The next wave of innovation and change should be built around a paradigm that modifies fast cities with slower design policies. Suburbs and cars are not about to disappear, but we should be headed toward a new era with more diverse community prototypes and lifestyles across our urban peripheries, as we begin to respond to the ecological challenges of our planet.

Notes

1   Website for the new urbanism movement, http://www.newurbanism.org/.
2   They included Radburn, New Jersey, Sunnyside Gardens in Queens, NYC, and Greenbelt, Maryland.
3   See Stephen Wheeler, *Planning for Sustainability*. New York: Routledge, 2004, 135.
4   These developments are reviewed in Peter Calthorpe and William Fulton, *The Regional City*. Washington, D.C.: Island Press, 2001.
5   Keith Pezzoli, "Bioregionalism," the Global ARC, Global Action Research Center, 2013. Unpublished essay.
6   John Friedmann, *Insurgencies: Essays in Planning Theory*. New York: Routledge, 2011.
7   For example, state, regional, and local government in the United States uses the designation of "flood plains" in low-lying urbanized regions. Since the 1960s, flood plains have been mapped and managed by state and federal agencies; see James M. Wright, *The Nation's Response to Flood Disasters*. Madison, WI: Association of State Floodplain Managers, 2000.
8   The State of California Department of Forestry and Fire Protection—CALFIRE—developed a "Fire Hazard Severity Zone" in 2005, where the state is responsible for protecting development against wildfires. See CALFIRE website, http://www.fire.ca.gov/fire_prevention/fire_prevention_wildland.php.
9   CALFIRE Fact Sheet: California's Fire Hazard Severity Zones, www.fire.ca.gov/wildland_zones.php (my emphasis).

10 In San Diego County, rural estate zoning (twenty or forty acre lots) was the norm at the edge of wilderness areas in the eastern backcountry zone. Yet, beginning in the 1990s, the building industry began lobbying to allow landowners to rezone their land for suburban subdivision. In 1998, a citizen group opposing this move for its overuse of water, and fire hazard dangers, sponsored an initiative called the Rural Heritage Watershed Act. It was defeated after the building lobby spent tens of millions of dollars to defend suburban lot zoning.

11 Tony Perry, "San Diego Must Boost Fire Spending, Feinstein Says," *Los Angeles Times*, November 28, 2007, http://articles.latimes.com/2007/nov/28/local/me-hearing28.

12 www.citymayors.com/environment/slow_cities.html.

13 See the Slow Food website at http://www.slowfood.com/.

14 See the *Cittaslow* charter at http://www.cittaslow.net/download/ DocumentiUfficiali/2009/newcharter%5B1%5D.pdf.

15 Heike Mayer and Paul Knox, "Slow Cities: Sustainable Places in a Fast World," *Journal of Urban Affairs*, 28 (4), 2006, 321–34.

16 http://www.cittaslow.org/section/association, consulted April, 2013.

17 Paul L. Knox, "Creating Ordinary Places: Slow Cities in a Fast World," *Journal of Urban Design*, 10 (1), February, 2005, 1–11.

18 James Howard Kunstler, "How Bad Architecture Wrecked Cities," TED, May, 2007, http://www.ted.com/talks/james_howard_kunstler_dissects_suburbia.html.

19 John Friedmann makes this point in his 2011 book, when he speaks of six strategies for urban futures. One of those strategies is to restore civic life and local citizenship. See Friedmann, 2011. Robert Putnam's book *Bowling Alone* (New York: Touchstone, 2001), as discussed in Chapter 2, documents the decline of community during the suburban era in the late twentieth century.

20 Claire Crane, *Citizens Coordinate and the Battle for City Planning in San Diego*. San Diego, CA: Citizens Coordinate for Century 3, 2010.

21 City of San Diego, website on Community Planning Groups, http://www.sandiego. gov/planning/community/cpg/index.shtml.

22 Livable Streets website, http://www.livablestreets.info/mission.

23 Fred Kent, Project for Public Spaces, http://www.pps.org/projects/new-york-city-streets-renaissance/.

24 Richard Register, *Ecocities*. Gabriola Island, B.C.: New Society Publishers, 2006.

25 Sym Van der Ryn and Stuart Cohen, *Ecological Design*. Washington, D.C.: Island Press, 1996.

26 See San Diego Canyonlands, *Strategic Plan*, March, 2013, http://www.sdcanyonlands. org/images/pdfs/sdcl_strategic_plan_2013march.pdf.

27 San Francisco Community Congress, *A People's Economic Vision for San Francisco*, June 9, 2011, http://sfcommunitycongress.wordpress.com/.

28 See Eric S. Bendfeldt, Martha Walker, Travis Bunn, Lisa Martin, and Melanie Barrow, *A Community-Based Food System: Building Health, Wealth, Connection, and Capacity as the Foundation of Our Economic Future*. Blacksburgh: Virginia Tech Extension, May, 2011, http://pubs.ext.vt.edu/3306/3306–9029/3306–9029-PDF.pdf.

29 For example, the city of San Diego, California, created an updated General Plan called the "City of Villages," which is entirely built around formal recognition of the goal of creating walkable, pedestrian scale, "smart" communities in the future. See City of Villages plan at http://www.sandiego.gov/planning/genplan/pdf/generalplan/ adoptedtoc.pdf. See also http://www.sandiego.gov/planning/genplan/pdf/generalplan/ adoptedsfelem.pdf, retrieved 1/14/14.

30 See UNESCO website at http://www.unesco.org/new/en/natural-sciences/
    environment/ecological-sciences/man-and-biosphere-programme/.
31 Stefan Zweig, *Brazil: Land of the Future*. Stockholm: Bermann Fisher, 1941, 173.
32 Larry Rohter, "A New Look at the Multitalented Man Who Made Tropical
    Landscaping an Art," *New York Times*, January 20, 2009, http://www.nytimes.
    com/2009/01/21/arts/design/21burl.html.
33 There is also a local cultural affinity for "tropical organic infrastructure"—which
    pervades parks, plazas, street markets, flower stands, kiosks, and food vendors. The life
    of the street is inherently tied to nature, in the form of literally selling both products
    derived from local ecology (fruits, vegetables, herbs, fish) and handicrafts that also
    derive from nature (necklaces, jewelry, musical instruments). The well known "Feira
    Hippie" (Hippie Market) in Ipanema is a place where craftspeople who live in nearby
    favelas sell organically made products.
34 The Law of Human Settlements was passed in 1983.
35 Carlos Arvizu, field interview, Querétaro, 2001.
36 Alejandro Cabrera, field interview, Querétaro, 2001.
37 Querétaro's downtown, as in other Mexican cities, was overrun by street vendors by the
    1980s and 1990s. Street vendors in downtown zones have been a growing problem for
    urban planners throughout Mexico. On the one hand, vendors represent a tradition of
    commerce in public space dating back to the Aztecs. On the other hand, the density
    of vendors in some Mexican cities has threatened to paralyze public places and drive
    everyday citizens away. In Querétaro, both the state and local governments were quick
    to impose restrictions on street vendors and not allow them to build a political power
    base in the historic center. State government used police and other officials to clear
    vendors out of the historic center's parks, gardens, plazas, and promenades. Formal street
    vendor policies and regulations were put in place—these included a photo-credential
    program, identification cards, a negotiating commission, a public fund to finance vendor
    management projects, and a plan to create alternate sites for vendors, in public markets
    for example. This dual approach—enforcement and planning—allowed Querétaro to
    avoid the confrontational politics that occurred between local officials and street vendors
    in places like Mexico City and Morelia, cities where it has been much more difficult to
    remove vendors from the historic center. See, for example, Cabrera, 2001.
38 Municipalidad de Querétaro, *Plan parcial de desarrollo urbano—delegación centro historico*.
    Querétaro: Municipalidad de Querétaro, 2000.
39 Alan Hunt Badiner, *Dharma Gaia: A Harvest of Essays in Buddhism and Ecology*.
    Berkeley, CA: Parallax Press, 1990.
40 Friedmann, 2011, 235.
41 Al Gore, *Earth in the Balance*. New York: Rodale, 2006.
42 David Suzuki, *The Sacred Balance*. Toronto: Greystone Books, 1997.
43 See also the earlier work of Aldo Leopold and his concept of the "land ethic" in Aldo
    Leopold, *A Sand County Almanac*. New York: Oxford University Press, 1949.
44 See Badiner, 1990.
45 *Daode Jing*, chapter 25. A full text (and slightly different translation) can be found in
    Ralph Alan Dale, *Tao Te Ching*. New York: Barnes and Noble, 2002.
46 Alan Watts, *Tao: The Watercourse Way*. New York: Pantheon, 1975, 14.
47 Ibid., 15.
48 Watts, 1975, 46.
49 Ibid., 43.
50 A more contemporary version of this argument, with practical examples for everyday
    life, is offered in the excellent book by Carl Honore, *In Praise of Slowness*. New York:
    HarperOne, 2005.

51 In Buddhism, meditation is considered a tool to free the mind from distraction, to become clear headed and lucid, to continue on a path of awakening and enlightenment. See Thicht Nhat Hanh, *Zen Keys*. New York: Doubleday, 1974.

52 Thich Nhat Hanh, *Peace in Every Step*. New York, Bantam Books, 1991.

53 See Jon Kabat Zinn, *Full Catastrophe Living*. New York: Delta, 2005.

54 Meditation has even been recommended as a strategy for persuading gang members and members of terrorist groups to renounce violence, http://m.theatlanticcities.com/politics/2013/02/what-ex-gang-members-and-former-political-extremists-have-common/4681/.

55 See Mary Billard, "In Schools: Yoga without the Spiritual," *New York Times*, October 7, 2011, http://www.nytimes.com/2011/10/09/nyregion/in-yoga-classes-at-schools-teachers-avoid-the-spiritual.html?_r = 0; see also Jodi Mardesich, "Yoga in Schools," *Yoga Journal*, http://www.yogajournal.com/for_teachers/2189, retrieved 1/14/14.

56 One of the central tenets of the teaching of the Dalai Lama is the importance of compassion. See http://www.dalailama.com/messages, retrieved 10/26/13.

57 There are numerous references to nature in the teaching of Buddhism. See the Dalai Lama's references to the environment at http://www.dalailama.com/messages/environment, retrieved 11/11/13.

58 Ironically, it has been pointed out that many gated communities and other residential zones in the U.S. have their own rules and regulations for land and property alterations. In many of those communities, hanging clothing out to dry on an outdoor line is expressly forbidden. See Ian Urbina, "Debate Follows Bills to Remove Clotheslines Bans," *New York Times*, October 10, 2009.

BIBLIOGRAPHY

American Lung Association. 2009. State of the Air. Washington, D.C.: American Lung Association. http://www.stateoftheair.org.

Arreola, Daniel and James Curtis. 1993. *The Mexican Border Cities*. Tucson: University of Arizona Press.

Arvizu, Carlos. 2001. Field Interview. Querétaro.

A.T. & T. Television ad, "Faster or Slower," at http://www.ispot.tv/ad/7AVh/at-and-t-faster-or-slower-featuring-beck-bennett, retrieved 3/7/13

Badiner, Alan Hunt. 1990. *Dharma Gaia: A Harvest of Essays in Buddhism and Ecology*. Berkeley: Parallax Press.

Ballard, Richard and Gareth A. Jones. 2011. "Natural Neighbors: Indigenous Landscapes and Eco-estates in Durban, South Africa." *Annals, Association of American Geographers,* 101 (1): 131–148.

Barbassa, Juliana. 2012. "At Fifty, 'The Girl from Ipanema' Still Making Heads Turn." *San Diego Union Tribune*, Associated Press, July 29: E-3.

Barringer, Felicity and Pat Mulroy. 2010. Quoted in "Water Use in the Southwest Heads for a Day of Reckoning." *New York Times* September 27. http://www.nytimes.com/2010/09/28/us/28mead.html?_r=2.

Baruch, Joshua. 2011. "The Reddit phenomenon," http://psupopculture.wordpress.com/2011/02/01/the-reddit-phenomenon-how-social-news-reveals-what-we-really-care-about/.

Beauregard, Robert. 2006. *When America Became Suburban*. Minneapolis: University of Minnesota Press.

Bendfeldt, Eric S., Martha Walker, Travis Bunn, Lisa Martin, and Melanie Barrow. 2011. *A Community-Based Food System: Building Health, Wealth, Connection, and Capacity as the Foundation of Our Economic Future*. Blacksburgh: Virginia Tech Extension, May. http://pubs.ext.vt.edu/3306/3306-9029/3306-9029-PDF.pdf

Berman, Marshall. 1988. *All That is Solid Melts into Air: The Experience of Modernity*. New York: Penguin.

Bertolucci, Jeff. 2010. "Cell Phone-Related Driving Deaths on the Rise," *PC World*, September 20. http://www.pcworld.com/article/205795/cell_phone_related_deaths_on_the_rise_govt_study.html, retrieved 3/1/13.

Blakely, Edward J. and Mary Gail Snyder. 1997. *Fortress America: Gated Communities in the the United States*. Washington, D.C.: Brookings Institution.

Borsdorf, Alex, Rodrigo Hidalgo and Rafael Sanchez. 2007. "A New Model of Urban Development in Latin America: the Gated Communities and Fenced Cities in the Metropolitan Areas of Santiago and Valparaiso, Chile." *Cities,* 24 (5): 365–378.

Bredenoord, Jan and Otto Verkoren. 2010. "Between Self-help and Institutional Housing: A Bird's Eye View of Mexico's Housing Production for Low and Lower Middle Income Groups." *Habitat International,* 34: 359–365.

Breen, Henry. 2011. "Southern Nevada Water Conservation Efforts Heralded," *Las Vegas Review Journal,* June 3.

Brookings Mountain West program, University of Nevada, Las Vegas at http://brookingsmtnwest.unlv.edu/publications/

Brooks, Sarah. 2000. "Innovative Waste Utilization and the Concerned Residents of South Phoenix." http://www.umich.edu/~snre492/Jones/Sarahbrooks.htm

Bruegmann, Robert. 2005. *Sprawl: A Compact History.* Chicago: University of Chicago Press.

Cabrera, Alejandro. 2001. Field Interview. Querétaro.

Caldeira, Teresa. 2000. *City of Walls: Crime, Segregation and Citizenship in Sao Paulo.* Berkeley: University of California Press.

Caldeira, Teresa. 1996. "Fortified Enclaves: the New Urban Separation." *Public Culture,* 8: 303–328.

California Department of Forestry and Fire Protection (CALFIRE), CALFIRE Fact Sheet: California's Fire Hazard Severity Zones. http://www.fire.ca.gov/wildland_zones.php.

CALFIRE Website. http://www.fire.ca.gov/fire_prevention/fire_prevention_wildland.php.

Calthorpe, Peter and William Fulton. 2001. *The Regional City.* Washington, D.C.: Island Press.

Capron, Guernola and Martha de Alba. 2010. "Creating the Middle Class Suburban Dream in Mexico City." *Culturales (UABC)* Enero-Junio: 161.

Cara, Jose F. 1999. "Type 2 Diabetes in Children—A Concern About a Growing Threat." *American Academy of Pediatrics.* Cited at www.medscape.com.

Cardoso, Adauto Lucio. 1990. *O Espaço do Capital: A Barra da Tijuca e a Grande Promoção Imobilaria.* Rio de Janeiro: Instituto de Pesquisa e Planejamento Urbano e Regional. IPURR/UFRJ.

Carr, Stephen, et al. 1992. *Public Space.* Cambridge: Cambridge University Press.

Carrasco Gallegos, Brisa Violeta. 2009. "Tijuana: Border, Migration and Gated Communities." *Journal of the Southwest,* Winter, 51 (4): 457–475.

Cervero, R. 1996. "Mixed Land Use and Commuting: Evidence from the American Housing Survey." *Transportation Research Part A,* 30 (5): 361–77.

Cervero, R. and R. Graham. 1995. "Commuting in Transit versus Automobile Neighborhoods." *Journal of the American Planning Association,* 61: 210–225.

Cittaslow. Consulted July 2012. <http://www.cittaslow.org/section/association>.

Cittaslow Charter. <http://www.cittaslow.net/download/DocumentiUfficiali/2009/newcharter%5B1%5D.pdf>.

City Mayors. <http://www.citymayors.com/environment/slow_cities.html>.

Cohen, Marcos, and Jorge Ferreira da Silva. 2010. "Evaluation of Collaborative Strategies for Ecotourism and Recreation Activities in Natural Parks of Rio de Janeiro." *Revista de Administracão Publica,* 44 (5), Sept/Oct.

Collet Bruna, Gilda and Heliane Comin Vargas. 2009. "The Shopping Centers Shaping the Brazilian City." In *Beyond Brasilia,* ed. V. Del Rio and W. Siembieda. Gainesville: University of Florida Press. 104–119.

Comisión Estatal de Vivienda, Querétaro. 1994. *Volver a Nuestras Calles.* (Queretaro).

CONAVI (National Housing Confederation). 2012. *Sustainable Housing in Mexico.* Mexico, D.F.: SEMARNAT (Secretaria de Medio Ambiente y Recursos Naturales)/

INFONAVIT/SHP/. <http://www.conavi.gob.mx/documentos/publicaciones/2a_
   Sustainable_Housing_in_Mexico.pdf>.
Costa, Lucio. 1969. *Plan Piloto Para Urbanizacão da Baixada Compreendida Entre a Barra
   da Tijuca, O Pontal de Sernambetiba e Jacarepagúa.* Rio de Janeiro: Agencia Jornalistica
   Image.
Costa, Gabriela da. 2004. "Environmental Impacts on Lagoon Tijuca and Lagoon
   Camorim: Barra da Tijuca, Rio De Janeiro, Brazil." International Planning History
   Society Conference, Barcelona, Spain.
Costa Silva, Gabriela da. 2008. "Urban Watershed Management Decision-making in
   Jacarepagua Lowland Watershed, Rio de Janeiro, Brazil." International Planning
   History Society Conference, Chicago, U.S..
County of Maricopa. 2001. Eye to the Future: Maricopa County Comprehensive Plan.
   Phoenix, Arizona: Maricopa County Board of Supervisors.
Coventry, Martha. 2004. "Super-sizing America: Obesity Becomes an Epidemic."
   University of Minnesota, *UM News,* Winter.
Cox, Wendell. 1999. "The Crusade Against Urban Sprawl: Assaulting the American
   Dream." *Demographia,* February. <www.demographia.com>.
Coy, Martin. 2006. "Gated Communities and Urban Fragmentation in Latin America: the
   Brazilian Experience." *Geojournal,* 66: 121–132.
Coy, Martin and Martin Pohler. 2002. "Gated Communities in the Latin American
   Megacities." *Environment and Planning B: Planning and Design,* 29: 355–370.
Crane, Claire. 2010. *Citizens Coordinate and the Battle for City Planning in San Diego.* San
   Diego: Citizens Coordinate for Century 3.
Critser, Greg. 2003. *Fat Land.* New York: Houghton Mifflin.
Cruz, Teddy. 2002. In City Projects, *Mixed Feelings: San Diego/Tijuana.* Documentary film,
   Produced and directed by Phillip Rodriguez.
Daode Jing, Chapter 25. 2002 In *Tao Te Ching,* by Ralph Alan Dale. New York: Barnes and
   Noble.
Dailey, Keli. 2013. "Eight Great Wine Bars." *San Diego Union Tribune,* February 26. http://
   www.utsandiego.com/news/2013/feb/26/best-wine-bars/?print&page=all retrieved
   4/10/13.
Davila, Arlene. 2012. *Culture Works.* New York: NYU Press.
Davis, Mike. 2007. "Diary: California Burns." *London Review of Books,* November 15.
Davis, Mike. 2006. *Planet of Slums.* New York: Verso.
Davis, Mike. 2002. "Las Vegas Versus Nature." In *Dead Cities: And Other Tales,* by Mike
   Davis. New York: New Press. 85–105.
Davis, Mike. 1999. *The Ecology of Fear.* New York: Vintage.
Davis, Mike. 1990. *City of Quartz.* New York: Verso.
Davis, Mike, and Daniel B. Monk, eds. 2007. *Evil Paradises.* New York: The New Press.
De Moraes, Vinícius, et al. "Garota de Ipanema," lyrics by Vinícius De Moraes, Norman
   Gimbel, Antonio Carlos "Tom" Jobim.
Dear, Michael. 2000. *The Postmodern Urban Condition.* Oxford: Blackwell.
Dear, Michael and Gustavo Leclerc. 2003. *Postborder City: Cultural Spaces of Bajalta
   California.* New York: Routledge.
Del Rio, Vicente and Denise de Alcantara. 2009. "The Cultural Corridor Project:
   Revitalization and Preservation in Downtown Rio de Janeiro." In *Beyond Brasilia,* ed.
   V. del Rio and W. Siembieda. Gainesville: University of Florida Press. 125–143.
Della Cava, Marco R. 2008. "Time Flies. Having Fun? They Can Help." *USA Today,*
   January 28: D-1-D-2.
Dillon, Sam. 1989. "Mexico City Spawns Distant Suburbs." *New York Times,* December 18.
Dos Passos, John. 1925. *Manhattan Transfer.* New York: Houghton Mifflin.

Duany, Andres, Elizabeth Plater-Zyberk and Jeff Speck. 2000. *Suburban Nation.* New York: North Point Press.

DeBuys, William. 2013. "The Least Sustainable City: Phoenix as a Harbinger for our Hot Future," March 17. http://grist.org/author/william-debuys/

Duerr, Maia. 2010. "The Future of Contemplative Practice in America: Buddhism in the West." *Patheos,* July 5. <http://www.patheos.com/Resources/Additional-Resources/Future-of-Contemplative-Practice-in-America-Buddhism-in-the-West.html>.

Durco, Mel. Quoted in Rothman, *Neon Metropolis: How Las Vegas Started the 21st Century.* New York: Routledge: 278–79.

The Economist. 2013. "Protests in Brazil: Taking to the Streets," June 22. http://www.economist.com/news/americas/21579857-bubbling-anger-about-high-prices-corruption-and-poor-public-services-boils-over

Edwards, Andrew. 2007. "I.E. Sees Heavy Growth—in Fatness." *San Bernardino County Sun,* November 29. <http://www.sbsun.com/search/ci_7585339>.

Eppinghaus, Annie G., Marcia Poppe and Vera Tangari. 2007. "A Barra de Tijuca e a Apropriacão dos Espacios Publicos e Semi-Publicos, Quatros Estudios de Caso." Unpublished essay.

Ewing, Reid, Tom Schmid, Richard Killingsworth, Amy Zlot and Stephen Raudenbush. 2003. "Relationship between Urban Sprawl and Physical Activity, Obesity and Morbidity." *American Journal of Health Promotion,* September-October, 8 (1): 47–57.

Ewing, Reid, R.A. Scheiber, and C.V. Zegeer. 2003. "Urban Sprawl as a Risk Factor in Motor Vehicle Occupant and Pedestrian Fatalities." *American Journal of Public Health,* 93 (9): 1541–45.

Excelsior. January 15, 1961, cited in Capron, Guernola and Martha de Alba. 2010. "Creating the Middle Class Suburban Dream in Mexico City." *Culturales (UABC)* Enero-Junio: 171.

Farabee, Mindy. 2007. "It's Afternoon in America." *San Diego City Beat,* April 25: 9.

Fast Cities. 2007. <http://www.fastcompany.com/magazine/117/features-fast-cities-intro.html>.

Fast Company. <www.fastcompany.com/magazine/117>.

Fernandez Galiano, Luis. 2005. "Spectacle and Its Discontents, or the Elusive Joys of Architainment." In *Commodification and Spectacle in Architecture,* Edited by Williams Saunders. Minneapolis: University of Minnesota Press. 1–7.

Ferriss, Tim. *The 4-hour Workweek.* Cited in "Time Flies. Having Fun? They Can Help," by Marco R. Della Cava. *USA Today* January 28, 2008: D-2.

Fineberg, Jonathan. 2003. *Art Since 1940.* New York: Prentice Hall.

Fire Prevention and Protection. Fire Safe Council Background Document for Senate Bill 838. <www.firesafecouncil.org>.

Flexner, Stuart and Doris Flexner. 1993. *Wise Words and Wives' Tales: The Origins, Meanings and Time-Honored Wisdom of Proverbs and Folk Sayings Olde and New.* New York: Avon Books.

Flint, Anthony. 2006. *This Land: The Battle Over Sprawl and the Future of America.* Baltimore: Johns Hopkins University Press.

Flores Peña, Sergio. 2010. "Are First Generation Suburbs of Mexico City Shrinking? The Case of Naucalpan." In *Shrinking Cities South/North,* Edited by I. Audirac and J. Arroyo Alejandre. Mexico, D.F.: Juan Pablos Editorial. 113–147.

Florida, Richard. 2002. *The Rise of the Creative Class.* New York: Basic Books.

Ford, Larry R. 2003. *America's New Downtowns.* Baltimore: Johns Hopkins University Press.

Franck, Frederick. 1993. *Zen Seeing, Zen Drawing.* New York: Bantam.

Frank, Lawrence and Peter Engelke. 2005. "Multiple Impacts of the Built Environment on Public Health," *International Regional Science Review,* 28 (2): 193–216.

Friedman, Naomi and Ray Minjares. 2005. "The Public Health Effects of Sprawl." *Congressional Briefing Summary*. Washington, D.C.: Environmental and Energy Study Institute.

Friedmann, John. 2011. *Insurgencies: Essays in Planning Theory*. New York: Routledge.

Frunk, Howard, Lawrence Frank and Richard Jackson. 2004. *Urban Sprawl and Public Health*. Washington, D.C.: Island Press.

Fulton, William. 1997. *The Reluctant Metropolis: The Politics of Growth in L.A.* Point Arena: Solano Books Press.

Gaffney, Christopher. 2012. "The BRT's of Rio de Janeiro." Presentation at the Congress of Latin American Studies Association (LASA), May, San Francisco.

Garcia Peralta, Beatriz and Andreas Hofer. 2006. "Housing for the Working Class: A New Version of Gated Communities in Mexico." *Social Justice*, 33 (3): 129–141.

Garfinkel, Perry. 2006. *Buddha or Bust*. New York: Three Rivers Press.

Garfinkel, Perry. 2005. "Buddha Rising." *National Geographic*, Special Issue, December. http://ngm.nationalgeographic.com/ngm/0512/feature4/index.html

Gauderman, W.J., Melonnel, R., et al., 2000. "Association between air pollution and lung function growth in southern California children." *American Journal of Respiratory and Critical Care Medicine*, 162 (4): 1383–90.

Geist, Johann F. 1982. *Arcades: The History of a Building Type*. Cambridge: MIT Press.

Geller, Martine. 2012. "Coke, McDonalds Slam NY City Bid to Ban Big Soda Cups." *Reuters* May 31. <http://www.reuters.com/article/2012/05/31/us-usa-sugarban-reaction-idUSBRE84U1BN20120531>.

George, Liane. 2006. "North Americans and Their Cars." *MacLeans Magazine*, February 27.

Girouard, Mark. 1985. *Cities and People*. New Haven: Yale University Press.

Global Footprint Network. <http://www.footprintnetwork.org>.

Gober, Patricia. 2006. *Metropolitan Phoenix: Place Making and Community Building in the Desert*. Philadelphia: University of Pennsylvania Press.

Godfrey, Brian J. 1991. "Modernizing the Brazilian City." *Geographical Review*, January, 81 (1): 18–34.

Godfrey, Brian J. 1999. "Revisiting Rio de Janeiro and Sao Paulo." *Geographical Review*, January, 89 (1): 94–121.

Gomes, Ana Cristina and Vicente del Rio. 1998. "A Outra Urbanidade: A Construção da Cidade Pos Moderna e o Caso da Barra da Tijuca." In *Arquiteitura: Pesquisa e Projeto*, ed. by Vicente del Rio. Rio de Janeiro: Universidade Federal do Rio de Janeiro.

Gore, Al. 2006. *Earth in the Balance*. New York: Rodale.

Goss, Jon. 1993. "The Magic of the Mall: An Analysis of Form, Function, and Meaning in the Contemporary Retail Built Environment." *Annals of the Association of American Geographers*, March, 83 (1): 18.

Gotsch, Peter. 2009. *NeoTowns—Prototypes of Corporate Urbanism*, Ph.D. dissertation, Karlsruhe Institute of Technology, Germany.

Gottdiener, M., et al. 1999. *Las Vegas: The Social Production of an All American City*. Oxford: Blackwell.

Griffin, Ernst and Larry Ford. 1980. "A Model of Latin American City Structure." *Geographical Review*, 70: 397–422.

Grynbaum, Michael. 2012. "New York Plans to Ban Sale of Big Sizes of Sugary Drinks." *New York Times*, May 30. <http://www.nytimes.com/2012/05/31/nyregion/bloomberg-plans-a-ban-on-large-sugared-drinks.html?pagewanted=all>.

Halsey, Richard. 2008. *Fire, Chaparral and Survival in Southern California*. San Diego: Sunbelt Publications.

Hamilton, William. 1999. "How Suburban Design is Failing Teenagers." www.nytimes.com May 6.

Hanh, Thich Nhat. 1974. *Zen Keys.* New York: Doubleday.

Hanh, Thich Nhat. 1991. *Peace in Every Step.* New York: Bantam Books.

Hansen, Kyle B. 2010. "Las Vegas Gets Failing Grade in Air Quality Report."
Las Vegas Sun, April 28. http://www.lasvegassun.com/news/2010/apr/28/
las-vegas-gets-failing-grade-air-quality-report.

Hargreaves, Steve. 2011. "Nuclear Waster Back to Yucca Mountain?" *CNN Money* July 11. <
http://money.cnn.com/2011/07/06/news/economy/nuclear_waste/index.htm>.

Harris, Arthur. 1972. *Sport in Greece and Rome.* Ithaca, New York: Cornell University Press.

Hawken, Christopher. 2007. "Ignoring Nature, We Build Our Way Into Fire's Path." *Los
Angeles Times,* October 20: A-1.

Hayden, Dolores. 2004. *A Field Guide to Sprawl.* New York: WW. Norton.

Hazlehurst, John. 2007. "Arizona Would Bear Brunt of Water Restrictions." *Colorado
Springs Business Journal,* October 5.

Heim, Carol. 2001. "Leapfrogging, Urban Sprawl and Growth Management: Phoenix,
1950–2000." *American Journal of Economics and Sociology,* January: 3.

Herzog, Cecilia, and Ricardo Finotti. 2013. "Local Assessment of Rio de Janeiro: Two Case
Studies of Urbanization Trends and Ecological Impacts," in T. Elmqvist, et al., eds.
Urbanization, Biodiversity and Ecosystem Services: A Global Assessment. Springer.

Herzog, Lawrence A. 2010. "Crisis in the Periphery: Ecological Decline and 'Sunbelt
Suburbs' in the U.S." *Cadernos ProArq (Brazilian Journal of Professional Architects),* 2010,
14: 7–17.

Herzog, Lawrence A. 2007. "Living Large." *San Diego Union Tribune.* Op-Ed Essay, March
16: B-7.

Herzog, Lawrence A. 2006. *Return to the Center: Culture, Public Space and City Building in a
Global Era.* Austin: University of Texas Press.

Herzog, Lawrence A. 2003. "Rebuilding San Diego: Fires, Suburbs and the Public Interest."
San Diego Union Tribune Op-Ed. Essay, November 14: B-7.

Herzog, Lawrence A. 1999. *From Aztec to High Tech.* Baltimore: Johns Hopkins University
Press.

Herzog, Lawrence A. 1990. *Where North Meets South: Cities, Space and Politics on the U.S.-
Mexico Border.* Austin: University of Texas Press/CMAS.

Hess, Alan. 1995. *Viva Las Vegas.* San Francisco: Chronicle Books.

Hiernaux, Daniel and Alicia Lindon. 2002. "Modos de Vida y Utopias Urbanas." *Ciudades,*
53 enero-marzo: 26–32.

Hirschberg, Lynn. 2006. "Sofia Coppola's Paris." *New York Times,* September 24: travel section.

Hiss, Tony. 1991. *The Experience of Place.* New York: Vintage Books.

Holston, James. 1989. *The Modernist City.* Chicago: University of Chicago Press.

Honore, Carl. Author webpage <http://www.carlhonore.com>.

Honore, Carl. 2004. *In Praise of Slowness.* New York: HarperOne.

Hughes, Robert. 1992. *Barcelona.* New York: Random House.

Hughes, Robert. 1991. *The Shock of the New.* New York: McGraw Hill.

Instituto Brasileiro de Geografia e Estadistica. <http://www.ibge.gov.br>.

Instituto Brasileiro de Geografia e Estadistica. 2007. Metropolitan area population data.
<http://www.ibge.gov.br>.

Instituto Municipal de Planeación de Tijuana (IMPLAN). 2003. *Plan de Desarrollo Urban
Centro de Población Tijuana.* B.C., 2002–2005. Periódico Official, Sept 13.

International Workers of the World. "More Time for Life" in Industrial Worker
Supplement. www.iww.org.

"It's a Larger World After All." <www.miceage.micechat.com/allutz/al100907c.htm>.

Jablonski, Silvio and Martinus Filet. 2008. "Coastal management in Brazil: a political
riddle." *Ocean and Coastal Management,* 51: 541.

Jewel, Mark. 2007. "Revamped Retailer Steps into Niche for Plus-sized Items." *Washington Post*, August 25: F-13.

John Jay College of Criminal Justice/CUNY. 1997. "Gated Enclaves Are Not Just for the Well-Heeled." *Law Enforcement News*, May 15.

Johnson, K. and J. McKinley. 2007. "Rethinking Fire Policy in the Tinderbox Zone." *New York Times*, October 28.

Jones, Gareth and Maria Moreno-Carranco. 2007. "Mega-projects: Beneath the Pavement, Excess." *City*, July, 11 (2): 144–164.

Kabat-Zinn, Jon. 2005. *Full Catastrophe Living*. New York: Delta

Kandell, Jonathan. 1988. *La Capital: The Biography of Mexico City*. New York: Henry Holt.

Kasser, Tim. 2002. *The High Price of Materialism*. Cambridge: MIT Press.

Kent, Fred. 2012. "The New York City Streets Renaissance." Project for Public Spaces, http://www.pps.org/projects/new-york-city-streets-renaissance/

King, Anthony. 2004. *Spaces of Global Cultures*. New York: Routledge.

Klein, Norman. 2002. "Scripting Las Vegas: Noir Naifs, Junking Up and the New Strip." In Rothman, Hal and Mike Davis, eds. 2002. *The Grit Beneath the Glitter: Tales from the Real Las Vegas*. Berkeley: University of California Press. 17–29.

Klein, Norman. 1993. "A Glittery Bit of Urban Make Believe." *Los Angeles Times,* July 18. http://articles.latimes.com/1993-07-18/local/me-14440_1_movie-set, retrieved 3/27/13.

Knox, Paul K. 2005. "Creating Ordinary Places: Slow Cities in a Fast World." *Journal of Urban Design,* 10 (1), February: 1–11.

Kotkin, Joel. 2005. "Phoenix Rising: A City of Aspiration." *Goldwater Institute Policy Report*, April.

Kotkin, Joel. 2005. "Rule Suburbia: The Verdict In, We Love It There." *Washington Post*, February 6.

Krieger, Alex. 2006/2007. "Review of Sprawl, A Compact History," *Harvard Design Magazine*. Fall/Winter.

Krieger, Alex. 2005. "The Costs and Benefits of Sprawl." In *Sprawl and Suburbia*, ed. William Saunders. Minneapolis: University of Minnesota Press, 44–56.

Kruse, Kevin and Thomas Sugrue. 2006. *The New Suburban History*. Chicago: University of Chicago Press.

Kumar Sen, Ashish. 2005. "The Malling of America," *Span*, March/April, 3–7. http://span.state.gov/wwwfspmarapr7.pdf

Kunstler, James Howard. 2008. "Driving Toward Disaster." *San Diego Union Tribune*, May 28: Opinion B-7.

Kunstler, James Howard. 2007. "How Bad Architecture Wrecked Cities." TED, May. http://www.ted.com/talks/james_howard_kunstler_dissects_suburbia.html

Kunstler, James Howard. 2007. Blog commentary, June 25. <http://www.kunstler.com/mags_diary21.html>.

Kunstler, James Howard. 2006. "Review of Sprawl: A Compact History." *Salamagundi*. Skidmore College, Vol. 152, Fall

Kunstler, James Howard. 1993. *The Geography of Nowhere*. New York: Free Press.

Kunstler, James Howard. nd. "Las Vegas: Utopia of Clowns." Unpublished Essay. <http://www.kunstler.com>.

Landes, David S. 1983. *Revolution in Time: Clocks and the Making of the Modern World*. Cambridge: Harvard University Press.

Lang, Robert and Arthur Nelson. 2011. "Megapolitan America." *Places: Forum of Design for the Public Realm*, November 14. <http://places.designobserver.com/feature/megapolitan-america/30648/>.

Lang, Robert, and Patrick Simmons. 2003. "Edge Counties: Metropolitan Growth Engines." *Census Note 11*. Fannie Mae Foundation, June.

Las Vegas, Nevada. City of. "Sustainable Las Vegas" document at: http://lasvegasnevada.
    gov/files/Sustainable_Las_Vegas.pdf
Las Vegas, Nevada. City of. Sustaining Las Vegas program. http://www.lasvegasnevada.gov/
    sustaininglasvegas/.
Lasch, Christopher. 1979. *The Culture of Narcissism.* New York: W.W. Norton.
Lassiter, Matt. 2004. "Apathy, Alienation, and Activism: American Culture and the
    Depoliticization of Youth." Golden Apple Lecture, January 28. http://www-personal.
    umich.edu/~mlassite/applelecture.html
Lee, Mike. 2007. "Building Patterns to Blame." *San Diego Union Tribune*, October 25: A-7.
Leinberger, Christopher. 2011. "The Death of the Fringe Suburb." *New York Times*,
    December 2.
Leitão, Geronimo. 2000. *A Construcão do Eldorado Urbano: O Plano Piloto da Barra da
    Tijuca e Baixada de Jacarepaguá 1970/1988.* Niteroi: Editorial da Universidade Federal
    Fluminense.
Leitão, Geronimo. 2008. Field interview. May.
Leopold, Aldo. 1949. *A Sand County Almanac.* New York: Oxford University Press.
Levin, Doron. 2011. "Why Small Cars are Actually Selling Now." *CNN Money* August 4.
    <http://tech.fortune.cnn.com/2011/08/04/why-small-cars-are-actually-selling-now/>.
Lida, David. 2008. *First Stop in the New World.* New York: Riverhead Books.
Livable Streets. 2012. website, http://www.livablestreets.info/mission
Louv, Richard. 2005. *Last Child in the Woods.* New York: Algonquin Books.
Low, Setha. 2003. *Behind the Gates: Life, Security and the Pursuit of Happiness in Fortress
    America.* NY: Routledge.
Low, Setha and Neil Smith, eds. 2005. *The Politics of Public Space.* New York: Routledge.
Lucy, W.H. 2003. "Mortality Risk Associated with Leaving Home: Recognizing the
    Relevance of the Built Environment," *American Journal of Public Health,* 93 (9):
    1564–69.
Mackenzie, James T., Roger Dower and Donald DT Chen. 1992. "The Going Rate:
    What It Really Costs to Drive." *World Resources Institute Report.* New York: WRI.
    http://pdf.wri.org/goingrate_bw.pdf
Mahler, Jonathan. 2005. "The Soul of the New Exurb." *New York Times Magazine*, March 27:
    30–37.
Malloy, Richard. 2013. "Dialogue on Development." In Richard Malloy et al., eds. *Design
    with the Desert.* CRC Press. http://books.google.com/books, retrieved October 9, 2013.
Manilow, Barry, et al. "Copacabana (At the Copa)." Words and Music by Barry Manilow,
    Bruce Sussman, and J. Feldman.
Marco, Meg. 2007. "Obesity: We're Too big for Disneyland's It's a Small World."
    Consumerist. October 29. http://consumerist.com/2007/10/29/obesity-were-too-big-
    for-disneylands-its-a-small-world/. Retrieved on 4/8/13.
Maricopa, Arizona, County of. 2013. Green Government Program. http://www.maricopa.
    gov/greengovernment/
Marques, Marcelo. 2008. Interview. São Paulo, Brazil. March.
Mayagoitia, David. 2012. "New Community Developments in Tijuana." Presentation to
    Urban Land Institute, San Diego, June 7.
Mayagoitia, David. 2012. President of DEITAC, a private economic development agency in
    Tijuana. Interview. June 27.
Mayer, Heike, and Paul Knox. 2006. "Slow Cities: Sustainable Places in a Fast World."
    Journal of Urban Affairs, 28 (4): 321–34.
McLuhan, Marshall. 1964. *Understanding Media.* New York: McGraw Hill.
Melby, Caleb. 2012. *The Zen of Steve Jobs.* New York: Wiley.

Mendiburu, Diego. 2011. "Vivir en un Gueto." *Emeequis,* July 11: 29–36. <http://www.m-x. com.mx/2011-07-10/vivir-en-un-gueto/>.

McKinnon, Shaun. 2012. "The Air We Breathe: Surrounded by Pollution." *Arizona Republic,* January 29. http://www.azcentral.com/news/air-quality/?content=1-overview

MGM City Center. http://www.citycenter.com.

Miller, G.Wayne. 2007. "No Place Like Home." *San Diego Union Tribune,* June 11. D-3.

Miller, G.E. 2010. "U.S. is Most Overworked Developed Nation in the World." 20 Something Finance, October 12. http://20somethingfinance.com/ american-hours-worked-productivity-vacation/

Mitchell, John. 2001. "Urban Sprawl." *National Geographic Magazine (online)* July. http://ngm.nationalgeographic.com/ngm/data/2001/07/01/html/ft_20010701.3.html

Mitchell, Stacy. 2011. "Can You Say 'Sprawl'? Walmart's Biggest Climate Impact Goes Ignored." *Grist,* November 29. <http://grist.org/business-technology/2011-11-29-can-you-say-sprawl-walmarts-biggest-climate-impact-goes-ignored/>.

Monkkonen, Paavo. 2011. "Do Mexican Cities Sprawl?" *Urban Geography,* 32 (3): 406–423.

Monkkonen, Paavo. 2009. "The Housing Transition in Mexico: Local Impacts on National Policy." *Working Paper* D09–001. University of California, Berkeley.

Monnet, Jerome. 1995. *Usos e Imagenes del Centro Historico de La Ciudad de Mexico.* D.F.: Departamento del Distrito Federal.

Moody's Analytics. 2010. *Envisioning Nevada's Future: Goals and Strategies for Advancing Our Quality of Life.* Nevada Vision Stakeholder Group.

Morris, Douglas. 2005. *It's A Sprawl World After All.* Canada: New Society Publishers.

Morris, Meaghan. 1993. "Things to Do with Shopping Centers." In *The Cultural Studies Reader,* Edited by Simon During. New York: Routledge. 391–409.

Muehe, Dieter. 2010. "Brazilian coastal vulnerability to climate change." *Pan-American Journal of Aquatic Sciences,* 5 (2): 173–183.

Municipalidad de Querétaro. 2000. *Plan Parcial de Desarrollo Urbano—Delegación Centro Historico.* Querétaro: Municipalidad de Querétaro.

National Safety Council website. 2010. "National Safety Council Estimates that At Least 1.6 Million Crashes Each Year Involve Drivers Using Cell Phones and Texting." See http://www.nsc.org/Pages/NSCestimates16millioncrashescausedbydriversusing cellphonesandtexting.aspx. Retrieved 3/21.13.

National Highway Traffic Safety Administration. 2002. *Traffic Safety Facts 2001. A Compilation of Motor Vehicle Crash Data,* Washington, D.C.

Neuwirth, Robert. 2004. *Shadow Cities.* New York: Routledge.

Nevada State Demographer's Office. 2010. Population Projections for Nevada's Counties 2010 to 2030. Reno, NV: Nevada Small Business Development Center. http:// nvdemography.org. Nevada Vision Stakeholder Group, 2010. *Envisioning Nevada's Future: Goals and Strategies for Advancing Our Quality of Life.*

New Urbanism Website Bibliography. <http://www.newurbanism.org/newurbanism/ featuredbooks.html>.

Nobre, Ana Luisa. 2008. Interview. May.

Offer, Avner. 2006. *The Challenge of Affluence.* New York: Oxford.

Office of the U.S. Trade Representative. <http://www.ustr.gov/countries-regions/americas/ mexico>.

Oldenburg, Ray. 1999. *The Great Good Place.* New York: Marlowe and Co.

Ordoñez, Franco. 2008. "Mexico is Second-fattest Nation After U.S." *San Diego Union Tribune,* March 24.

Organization for Economic Cooperation and Development (OECD). 2005. *Handbook of Economic Globalisation Indicators.* Paris: OECD.

Pacione, Michael. 2009. *Urban Geography: A Global Perspective.* 3rd ed. New York: Routledge.

Paz, Octavio. 1961. *The Labyrinth of Solitude.* New York: Grove Press.

Perlman, Janice. 1980. *The Myth of Marginality.* Berkeley: University of California Press.

Perry, Tony. 2007. "San Diego Must Boost Fire Spending, Feinstein Says." *Los Angeles Times,* November 28. <http://articles.latimes.com/2007/nov/28/local/me-hearing28>.

Peters, Tom and Robert Waterman. 1992. *In Search of Excellence.* New York: Harpers Business.

Pezzoli, Keith. 2013. "Bioregionalism." The Global ARC, Global Action Research Center, Unpublished essay.

Phillips, Dom. 2013. "Thousands on Streets in Brazil Protests." *The Guardian,* July 11. http://www.theguardian.com/world/2013/jul/12/thousands-streets-brazil-protests

Phoenix, Arizona, City of. 2013. Green Phoenix program. See the link at: http://phoenix.gov/greenphoenix/sustainability/index.html.

Plantinga, Andrew J. and Stephanie Bernell. 2005. "A Spatial Economic Analysis of Urban Land Use and Obesity." *Journal of Regional Science,* 45 (3): 473–492. August.

Plantinga, Andrew J. and Stephanie Bernell. 2007. "The Association between Urban Sprawl and Obesity." *Journal of Regional Science,* 47 (5): 857–879. December.

Piperato, Susan. 2012. "American Cities Are Revitalizing Their Downtowns and Recreating Their Profiles." *National Real Estate Investor,* March 28. <http://nreionline.com/city-reviews/new-jersey/american_cities_revitalizing_downtowns_03282012/>.

Porter Benson, Susan. 1979. "Palace of Consumption and Machine for Selling: The American Department Store, 1880–1940." *Radical History Review,* 21, Fall: 199–221.

Project for Public Spaces. <http://www.pps.org/>.

Project for Public Spaces. <http://www.pps.org/great_public_spaces/one?public_place_id=997>.

Project for Public Spaces. "Launching the Place-making Movement," December 20, 2013. http://www.pps.org/blog/launching-the-placemaking-movement/.

Project for Public Spaces. "What Makes a Successful Place?" <http://www.pps.org/info/placemakingtools/casesforplaces/gr_place_feat>.

Putnam, Robert. 2001. *Bowling Alone.* New York: Touchstone.

Quinn, Bill. 2005. *How Walmart is Destroying America.* Berkeley: Ten Speed Press.

Rapino, Melanie A. and Alison K. Fields. 2012. "Mega Commuting in the U.S." U.S. Census, Social and Economic Housing Division, Washington, D.C., 2012. http://www.census.gov/hhes/commuting/files/2012/Paper-Poster_Megacommuting%20in%20the%20US.pdf

Register, Richard. 2006. *Ecocities.* Gabriola Island, B.C.: New Society Publishers.

Relph, Edward. 1976. *Place and Placelessness.* London: Pion.

Rezende, Vera, and Geronimo Leitão. 2004. *O Plan Piloto para a Barra de Tijuca e Biaxada de Jacarepagua.* Rio de Janeiro: CREA-RJ.

Rheingart, Gabriel. 2008. Field interview. Rio de Janeiro, May.

Rice, Carol L. and James B. Davis. 1991. "Land Use Planning May Reduce Fire Damage in the Urban Wildland Intermix." General Technical Report, U.S. Department of Agriculture, Forest Service, Pacific Southwest Research Station.

Ritzer, George. 1996. *The McDonaldization of Society.* London: Pine Forge Press.

Roberts, John. 1999. "Do Suburbs Create Teen Rage?" *CBS News Reports,* www.cbsnews.com June 7.

Robinson, Sara. 2012. "Bring Back the 40 Hour Work Week." Salon.com, March 14. http://www.salon.com/2012/03/14/bring_back_the_40_hour_work_week/

Rohter, Larry. 2009. "A New Look at the Multitalented Man Who Made Tropical Landscaping an Art." *New York Times,* January 20. <http://www.nytimes.com/2009/01/21/arts/design/21burl.html>.

Rosen, Christine. 2005. "The Overpraised American." *Hoover Institution Policy Review,* October/November.

Ross, Andrew. 2011. *Bird on Fire.* New York: Oxford University Press.

Ross, Andrew. 2011. "The Dark Side of the 'Green' city." *The New York Times,* November 6. http://www.nytimes.com/2011/11/07/opinion/in-phoenix-the-dark-side-of-green. html?_r=0

Rothman, Hal. 2002. *Neon Metropolis: How Las Vegas Started the 21st Century.* New York: Routledge.

Rothman, Hal and Mike Davis, eds. 2002. *The Grit Beneath the Glitter: Tales from the Real Las Vegas.* Berkeley: University of California Press.

Ruiz, Rebecca. 2007. "America's Most Sedentary Cities." *Forbes Magazine* October 29. http://www.forbes.com/2007/10/28/health-sedentary-cities-forbeslife-cx_rr_ 1029health.html

Russell, James S. 2005. "Privatized Lives: On the Embattled Burbs." In *Sprawl and Suburbia,* ed. William Saunders, Minneapolis: University of Minnesota Press, 91–109.

Sabatini, Francisco, Gonzalo Caceres, and Jorge Cerda. 2001. "Residential Segregation in Major Cities in Chile," *EURE,* 27 (82), December: 21–42.

Salcedo, Rodrigo and Alvaro Torres. 2004. "Gated Communities in Santiago: Wall or Frontier," *International Journal of Urban and Regional Research,* 28 (1): 27–44.

Salvaggio, Marko, and Robert Futtrell. 2012. "Environment and Sustainability in Nevada." In Dmitri N. Shalin, ed. *Social Health of Nevada.* Las Vegas: UNLV Center for Democratic Culture. http://cdclv.unlv.edu/healthnv_2012/environment.pdf, retrieved 10/30/13.

San Diego, City of. 2012. Website on Community Planning Groups, http://www.sandiego. gov/planning/community/cpg/index.shtml.

San Diego Association of Governments (SANDAG). 2009. Regional *Comprehensive Plan for 2030,* SANDAG. <http://www.sandag.org>.

San Diego Association of Governments (SANDAG). 2010. Populations Projections. <http://www.sandag.org>.

San Diego Canyonlands. 2013. *Strategic Plan,* March. http://www.sdcanyonlands.org/ images/pdfs/sdcl_strategic_plan_2013march.pdf

San Francisco Community Congress. 2011. *A People's Economic Vision for San Francisco,* June 9. http://sfcommunitycongress.wordpress.com/.

Saunders, William, ed. 2005. *Commodification and Spectacle in Architecture.* Minneapolis: University of Minnesota Press.

Scarpaci, Joseph. 2005. *Plazas and Barrios.* Tucson: University of Arizona Press.

Schlosser, Eric. 2005. *Fast Food Nation.* New York: Harper.

Schneider, Annamarie and Curtis Woodcock. 2008. "Compact, Dispersed, Fragmented, Extensive? A Comparison of Urban Growth in Twenty-five Global Cities using Remotely Sensed Data, Pattern Metrics and Census Information." *Urban Studies,* March, 45 (3): 659–692.

Schor, Juliet. 1992. *The Overworked American.* New York: Basic Books.

Schwab, J. and S. Meek. 2005. "Planning for Wildfires." American Planning Association, Planning Advisory Service, Report No. 529/530.

Schwartzer, Mitchell. "The Spectacle of Ordinary Building." In William Saunders, ed. *Sprawl and Suburbia.* Minneapolis: University of Minnesota Press, 2000, 74–90.

Sengupta, Somini. 2011. "FTC Settles Privacy Issue at Facebook." *New York Times* November 29: B-1. <http://www.nytimes.com/2011/11/30/technology/facebook-agrees-to-ftc-settlement-on-privacy.html>.

Sennett, Richard. 1976. *The Fall of Public Man.* New York: Alfred Knopf.

Short, John Rennie and Yeong-Hyun Kim. 1999. *Globalization and the City.* New York: Prentice Hall.

Sibaja, Marca, Jenny Barchfield and Bradley Brooks. 2013. "One Million Brazilians Hit the Streets." *Huffington Post,* June 21, 2013. http://www.huffingtonpost.com/2013/06/21/brazil-protests-2013_n_3478101.html.

Sirkis, Alfredo. 2008. Field interview. Rio de Janeiro. May.

Sklair, Leslie. 2006. "Iconic Architecture and Capitalist Globalization." *City,* 10 (1): 21–47.

Sklair, Leslie. 2008. "Iconic Architecture and Capitalist Globalization." In P. Herrie and E. Wegerhoff eds. *Architecture and Identity.* Berlin: Lit Verlag/Habitat International, 2008. 207–19

Sklair, Leslie. 1991. *Sociology of the Global System.* Baltimore: Johns Hopkins University Press.

Slow Food Website. <http://www.slowfood.com/>.

Soares Macedo, Silvio. 2009. "The Vertical Cityscape in Sao Paulo." In *Beyond Brasilia,* ed. V. Del Rio and W. Siembieda. Gainesville: University of Florida Press. 82–103.

Sorkin, Michael, ed. 1992. *Variations on a Theme Park.* New York: Hill and Wang.

Spotts, Gregg. 2005. *Walmart: The High Cost of Low Price.* New York: Disinformation Books.

Stamberg, Susan. 2009. "Landmark at the Louvre: The Pyramid Turns Twenty." *National Public Radio,* December 7. <http://www.npr.org/templates/story/story.php?storyId=121097261>.

Stone, Brian. 2008. "Urban Sprawl and Air Quality in Large U.S. Cities." *Journal of Environmental Management,* 86: 688–698.

Suarez, John. 2008. "Building Better in Latin America." *Urban Land,* September: 173.

Sucher, David. 2003. *City Comforts.* Seattle: City Comforts.

Surface Transportation Policy Project. 2002. *American Attitudes Toward Walking and Creating More Walkable Communities.*

Suzuki, David. 1997. *The Sacred Balance.* Toronto: Greystone Books.

Talen, Emily. 2011. "Sprawl Retrofit: Sustainable Urban Form in Unsustainable Places." *Environment and Planning B: Planning and Design,* 38: 952–978.

Trust for America's Health. 2005. *F as in Fat.* Washington D.C.

U.S. Bureau of the Census. 2006. *Metropolitan Growth Statistics: 2000–2006.* Washington, D.C.: U.S. Department of Commerce.

U.S. Bureau of Transportation Statistics. 2006. U.S. Department of Transportation.

U.S. Census of Population and Housing. 2000. *Demographic Trends of the Twentieth Century.* Washington, D.C.: U.S. Department of Commerce.

U.S. House of Representatives Hearing. 1997. "Road Rage: Causes and Dangers of Aggressive Driving." July 17. Washington, D.C.

U.S. News and World Report. 2008. "General Motors, Others Decide the SUV is Dead." June 4. http://usnews.rankingsandreviews.com/cars-trucks/daily-news/080604-General-Motors-Others-Decide-the-SUV-is-Dead/

U.S. Surgeon General. 2006. *Physical Activity and Health.* Washington, D.C.: U.S. Department of Health and Human Services.

UNESCO Website. <http://www.unesco.org/new/en/natural-sciences/environment/ecological-sciences/man-and-biosphere-programme/>.

Urbina, Ian. 2009. "Debate Follows Bills to Remove Clotheslines Bans." *New York Times,* October 10.

Valenzuela, Alfonso. 2007. "Santa Fe: Megaproyectos Para Una Ciudad Dividida." *Cuadernos Geograficos,* 40: 53–66.

Valladares, Licia. "Social Science Representations of Favelas in Rio de Janeiro, An Historical Perspective." Lanic Resource Papers, University of Texas, Austin, nd. <http://www1.lanic.utexas.edu/project/etext/llilas/vrp/valladares.pdf>.

Van der Ryn, Sym and Stuart Cohen. 1996. *Ecological Design.* Washington, D.C.: Island Press.

Venturi, Robert, Steven Izenour and Denise Scott Brown. 1997. *Learning From Las Vegas*. Cambridge: MIT Press.

Vincent, James. 2014. "Yahoo brands Nick D'Aloisio's Summly app for mobile-news focus" http://www.independent.co.uk/life-style/gadgets-and-tech/ces-2014-yahoo-rebrands-nick-daloisios-summly-app-for-mobilenews-focus-9045993.html. January 8.

Violanti, J.M. 1997. "Cellular phones and traffic accidents." *Public Health*, 111 (6): 423–28.

Walker, Margath, David Walker and Yanga Villagómez Velásquez. 2006. "The Wal-Martification of Teotihuacan: Issues of Resistance and Cultural Heritage." In Stanley D. Brunn, ed. *Wal-Mart World*. New York: Routledge. 213–224.

Wall, Alex. 2006. *Victor Gruen: From Urban Shop to New City*. Barcelona: Actar.

Walshe, Sadhbh. 2013. "Las Vegas: the Reinvention of Sin City as a Sustainable City." *The Guardian*. Thursday April 25.

Ward, Peter. 1998. *Mexico City*. 2nd ed. New York: John Wiley.

Watts, Alan. 1975. *Tao. The Watercourse Way*. New York: Pantheon.

Whybrow, Peter C. 2005. *American Mania: When More Is Not Enough*. New York: W.W. Norton.

Whyte, William H. 1980. *The Social Life of Small Urban Spaces*. Washington, D.C.: The Conservation Foundation.

Wilson, Alex, and Jessica Boehland. 2005. "Small is Beautiful: U.S. House Size, Resource Use and the Environment. "*Journal of Industrial Ecology*, Winter/Spring. <http://www.greenbiz.com/news/2005/07/12/small-beautiful-us-house-size-resource-use-and-environment>.

World Bank. 2011. *Creating More Livable Cities: The Case of Rio de Janeiro*. Washington, D.C.: World Bank/Latin American and Caribbean region (LAC), No. 172. December.

World Bank. 2011. World Development Indicators database, July. Gross domestic product (2010). http://data.worldbank.org/indicator/NY.GDP.MKTP.CD/countries

Wright, James M. 2000. *The Nation's Response to Flood Disasters*. Madison: Association of State Floodplain Managers.

Yee, Daniel. 2005. "Big Bottoms Crushing Airlines Bottom Lines." *Tucson Citizen*, November 5.

Young, L.R. and M. Nestle. 2002. "The Contribution of Expanding Portion Sizes to the U.S. Obesity Epidemic." *American Journal of Public Health*, 92: 246–249.

Zee, D.M. and C.M. Sabio. 2006. "Temporal Evaluation of the Contaminated Plume Dispersion at Barra da Tijuca Beach, Rio de Janeiro, Brazil." *Journal of Coastal Research*, 39: 531–536.

Zukin, Sharon. 2003. *Point of Purchase: How Shopping Changed American Culture*. New York: Routledge.

Zukin, Sharon, et al. 1998. "From Coney Island to Las Vegas in the Urban Imaginary." *Urban Affairs Review*, 33 (5): 625–653.

Zukin, Sharon. 1996. *The Cultures of Cities*. New York: Wiley/Blackwell.

Zweig, Stephan. 1941. *Brazil: Land of the Future*. Stockholm: Bermann Fisher.

INDEX

Custom Materials
DELIVER A MORE REWARDING EDUCATIONAL EXPERIENCE.

University Readers® — Custom Publishing Evolved.

Routledge — Taylor & Francis Group

The Social Issues Collection

This unique collection features 250 readings plus 45 recently added readings for undergraduate teaching in sociology and other social science courses. The social issues collection includes selections from Joe Nevins, Sheldon Elkand-Olson, Val Jenness, Sarah Fenstermaker, Nikki Jones, France Winddance Twine, Scott McNall, Ananya Roy, Joel Best, Michael Apple, and more.

1 Go to the website at routledge.customgateway.com

2 Choose from almost 300 readings from Routledge & other publishers

3 Create your complete custom anthology

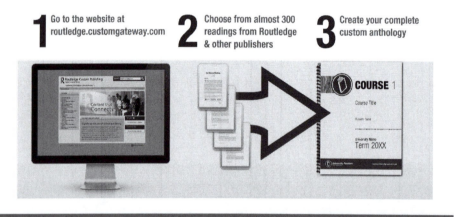

Learn more:
routledge.customgateway.com | 800.200.3908 x 501 | info@cognella.com

University Readers is an imprint of Cognella, Inc. ©1997-2013

33757886R00160

Printed in Great Britain
by Amazon